**AN INSPIRATIONAL FABLE OF PROFOUND
AND ETERNAL WISDOM**

Look Ma,
Life's Easy

*How Ordinary People Attain Extraordinary
Success and Remarkable Prosperity*

Ernie J. Zelinski

VISIONS INTERNATIONAL PUBLISHING

ISBN: 978-0-9813118-2-1 (Print)
ISBN: 978-0-9813118-6-9 (eBook)

Published in French by Stanké International, Montreal, Canada
Published in Spanish by Amat Editorial, Barcelona, Spain
Published in Chinese by CITIC Publishing House, Beijing, China
Published in Korean by Mulpure Publishing, Seoul, South Korea
Published in Russian by Prime-Evroznak Ltd. Co., St. Petersburg, Russia

Direct any inquiries about foreign rights and quantity purchases to:
Ernie Zelinski
Visions International Publishing
P.O. Box 4072
Edmonton, Alberta, Canada, T6E 4S8
Phone (780) 434-9202
E-mail: vip-books@telus.net

Printed in Canada

Dedicated to all the truly creative, adventurous souls throughout the ages who have been willing to risk, be different, challenge the status quo, ruffle a few feathers, and in the process, truly make a big difference in this world.

Other Life -Changing Books by Ernie J. Zelinski

The Joy of Not Working: A Book for the Retired, Unemployed, and Overworked (over 290,000 copies sold and published in 17 languages)

How to Retire Happy, Wild, zand Free: Retirement Wisdom That You Won't Get from Your Financial Advisor (over 275,000 copies sold and published in 9 languages)

Career Success Without a Real Job: The Career Book for People Too Smart to Work in Corporations

101 Really Important Things You Already Know, But Keep Forgetting (Over 50,000 copies sold and published in 10 languages)

Introduction

Look Ma, Life's Easy is a delightfully insightful guide for making your wildest dreams come true. It is filled with gems of wisdom that, if used as directed, will not only help you make a big difference in this world, but will also result in your attaining extraordinary success and remarkable prosperity.

Let's face it. Life is too short to achieve only the ordinary. Everyone would like to live an extraordinary life — to have their life matter and to make a big difference in this world. Whoever accomplishes this is deemed to be exceptionally successful.

Successful individuals continually attain extraordinary results by realizing that their personal limitations are self-imposed and work to exceed them. In doing so, they experience financial independence, true happiness, and personal freedom. But how does one become inspired to do this too?

That's where this inspirational fable comes into the picture. It presents a story of transformation that will inspire ordinary individuals to feel like they too can truly achieve extraordinary results and make a big difference in this world. Sheldon, a young adult, meets Brock, a successful middle-aged man who has attained extraordinary success and remarkable prosperity in his life, and the story unfolds.

As an intriguing part of the story, Sheldon finds a mysterious book of thought-provoking proverbs called *Life's Secret Handbook* by a pay phone. The proverbs from this handbook appear liberally throughout the story from then on. These eternal proverbs will delight and inspire every reader.

More important, you will be amazed by the simplicity of the main message in *Look Ma, Life's Easy*. It's so simple yet so powerful. The message is based on The Easy Rule of Life.

This moving parable emphasizes the importance of following The Easy Rule of Life so that we all can experience satisfaction, financial independence, true happiness, and personal freedom in our lives. The Easy Rule of Life simply states that when we take the easy and comfortable way, life ends up being difficult and uncomfortable. When we take the difficult and uncomfortable route, however, life ends up easy and comfortable.

Look Ma, Life's Easy will help you follow this important principle so that you achieve more success in all aspects of modern living. Superbly blending important success principles with eternal spiritual wisdom, this inspirational fable teaches as it delights. It can enrich and enhance the life of every person who would like to accomplish more in this world.

Look Ma, Life's Easy is one of those inspirational books that is both a page-turner and a life-changer. The book's rich story along with the profound proverbs from its companion *Life's Secret Handbook* will compel you to question your own life story and assess whether it is time for you to change.

You will be driven to ask, "Am I going to let my past or my potential determine my destiny? Am I going to live life by chance or by choice? Am I going to live someone else's story or am I finally going to use my God-given talent to claim a life that is truly my own?"

All told, there are only a few inspirational fables that in some way, to some degree, inspire people to much greater heights and even greatness. *Look Ma, Life's Easy* is one of them.

1

*Imagine that you are in control of
your life.*

Now, the question is:

Why do you have to imagine this?

As Sheldon walked west along Robson Street, the black 1959 Mercedes-Benz 190 SL convertible caught his eye. The two-seater, which had its top down, was a sight to behold — there wasn't one scratch anywhere on its shiny paint. It looked as new as it might have looked sitting in the dealer's showroom in 1959. The cockpit had the original red leather seats and upholstery.

Sheldon had often dreamed about owning an older touring sports car like this beauty. He had seen five, maybe six, of these when he visited Beverly Hills but none quite as pristine as this one. From what he had learned in car magazines, this model had only a four-cylinder engine. It had twin Solex carburetors, however, and so had decent acceleration for an older automobile. What he liked about this antique sports car

1

was that it normally came with a soft fold-down top as well as a hard top.

As Sheldon walked past the Mercedes, a middle-aged man stepped out of a men's fashion boutique, right in front of him, on his way to the driver's door. He wasn't a large man, about five foot 11 and 160 pounds. Trim and with just a hint of gray in his blonde hair, he looked in his early forties.

Without much thought, Sheldon blurted, "That's sure a nice car. I've always liked the Mercedes 190 SL more than most other older sports cars. I sure wish I could be lucky enough to own one, like you."

"Thanks for the nice words about the car," the man said cheerfully. "Like you, I always wanted to own one; so I finally bought one two years ago. By the way, my name is Brock."

"Nice to meet you. I'm Sheldon."

"Incidentally, what makes you think that you have to be lucky to own a 190 SL?" asked Brock. "If I can do it, so can you."

"Yeah, right," uttered Sheldon. "A young black guy doesn't have a chance of buying a car worth $30,000 or more, especially here in Vancouver. It's hard enough to pay for food and shelter here. Besides, I'm going to college right now. I have a part-time job at Starbucks, but it doesn't pay much. Even if I had a full-time job, I don't think I could make enough money to buy a car like that."

"Why not?" countered Brock. "It's amazing what you can create in your life when you are willing to make it happen. Black, white, or purple — a man can always do and get more out of life than he thinks possible. The question you have to ask yourself is: are you prepared to make it happen, no matter what it takes?"

"That's easy for you to say," came the swift reply from Sheldon. "I bet you had 100 times more opportunity than I do, when you were younger. I'm always facing disadvantages and being discriminated against because of my race. I'll have to face this for the rest of my life, and that means I'll probably never be as successful as people like you, who end up owning fancy cars."

"Maybe. Maybe not," stated Brock. "First, don't assume that I had things handed to me. As a kid, I was far from being privileged. I was raised on a farm. My parents' total income was always below the poverty line, so I never received a lot of material things or financial support from them."

He paused for a moment, remembering, then continued, "Later, in my twenties, I got a university degree in Engineering by financing it with student loans. I hated being an engineer though, and quit after only five years. In my thirties, I went back to the university and obtained an MBA. For the next few years, I worked only part-time. When I was forty-five, I was totally broke. I felt I was a failure, considering most people my age had good jobs, drove new cars, and owned nice houses."

"You were broke at forty-five? How old are you anyway?" asked Sheldon. "I would have guessed you were in your early forties now."

"You figure it out," Brock suggested. "That was only seven years ago. In fact, I was worse than broke at that time. I had a beat-up old car that doubled in value every time I filled it up with gas. My income was negligible, and I had over

$40,000 in debts. My apartment was only halfway furnished. I felt like the starving artist in Paris. But I took responsibility for my life, and I decided to change things. Now I have three cars. I also managed to buy and totally pay off a nice house. The most important thing is that I truly enjoy how I earn my living."

"You must have gotten yourself a high-paying job with a lot of overtime to have bought a house and three cars in just seven years."

"On the contrary. I don't have a job in the normal sense of the word. I am self-employed and work far fewer hours than most people. In fact, I work an average of four hours a day and make a comfortable living at it."

"Nice work if you can get it," pronounced Sheldon.

"Not get it," Brock insisted. "I didn't get my type of work. I created it by doing what had to be done. I achieved my prosperity through purpose and making a difference in this world."

"Sounds like you have an easy life. What do you do for a living?"

"I'm an author and professional speaker. It's a joyful and satisfying life that I wouldn't trade for anything. Be clear, however, that it's both easy and it isn't."

"What do you mean by that?" asked Sheldon.

"What I mean is that if it was totally easy, everyone would be doing it. The fact is, millions of people with far greater talent and opportunity than I have would like to be doing the same thing I am. But they won't do it — even though they can — because there's a price to pay."

Sheldon was puzzled. "A price to pay for having an easy life?" he asked.

"Definitely," answered Brock. "Everything worthwhile in life has a price. Getting to where I am today didn't take a lot of hard physical work — no long hours at a workplace — but it did take emotional work and creativity. It also takes effort to maintain a meaningful life when you already have an easy lifestyle."

"I'm not sure I understand why you have to work at maintaining a meaningful life if you have an easy life!" replied Sheldon, somewhat bewildered.

"I have to motivate myself to keep my life interesting and purpose-driven, instead of coasting along and having an easy and comfortable time."

"Whatever the case," frowned Sheldon, "I sure would like to be in your shoes financially."

"As I already emphasized, within a few years you can get to be as well-off as I am. If you put your mind to it."

"I hardly think so," Sheldon protested. "I moved here from L.A. to work on a Marketing degree at City College. Even if I finish the program, I could never get a high-paying job and earn enough money to get to your position. Black people don't get the best-paying jobs, you know, even if they have an education. I'm seriously thinking about quitting my third term so that I can get a full-time job now."

"What? The City College program has only four terms and it's March already. Why would you want to quit halfway through a term? It would be only another six months from now until you finished and got your degree."

Sheldon shook his head. "It's harder than you think. Right now I'm walking to college and my part-time job. Walking takes up a lot of my time. I would have to walk to school and work for another six months, and maybe a year after finishing college. Having a car would make it so much easier, but I can't do that on a part-time job."

"It may be difficult, but there is a big difference between something that is difficult and something that is impossible," responded Brock. "And just because something is difficult is no reason for not doing it. In fact, the idea that something is difficult is a good reason for doing it. This all relates to The Easy Rule of Life."

"What the heck is The Easy Rule of Life?" Sheldon asked.

"A basic principle of the universe, but a very powerful one. In fact, I'm writing a book on it right now. Here's how The Easy Rule of Life works," announced Brock. He pulled a curled-up paper napkin out of his pocket and quickly made a sketch on it.

"This is the essence of The Easy Rule of Life," he resumed. "If you always do the easy and comfortable thing, life ends up being difficult and uncomfortable. If you do the difficult and uncomfortable thing, however, life ends up being easy and comfortable.

"The Easy Rule of Life applies to virtually all areas of our lives. How well you follow The Easy Rule of Life determines how much satisfaction, prosperity, and happiness you achieve throughout your whole life."

"How does The Easy Rule of Life apply to me?" asked Sheldon. "I'm already doing the difficult and uncomfortable by living the unpleasant and deprived life that I live."

"I am not so sure that your present life is as unpleasant and deprived as you make it out to be. It's all relative. It's also a matter of perception," Brock responded. "I can see one thing, though – you're destined to have a difficult and uncomfortable life in the long term because you are taking the easy and comfortable way in important areas of your life."

"Hardly. Name one."

"The most important one is that you suffer from a case of victim mentality, because of what you erroneously perceive as your disadvantages. You are taking the easy and comfortable way by declaring yourself a victim just because you are a young black man. First, I must warn you that there is a real danger with this. Once you become seriously addicted to feeling like a victim, you will play the game of victim consciousness to no end. You will lie down in front of a car, let it run over you, and then blame the car's driver."

Brock added, "Being a victim is the easy way out, because you have someone or something else to blame for your position in the world. Sadly, this will end up being the difficult and uncomfortable road in the long term. By choosing victim consciousness, you are giving up your power as a human being. Accomplishment, satisfaction, and happiness are hard, if not impossible, to achieve in this state."

"But as a twenty-three-year-old black guy, I'm at a disadvantage compared to many people in this world."

"No doubt you are, but so what? As a young adult, I was also disadvantaged compared to most people my age. Yet I have accomplished a lot more, including writing a best-selling book, than millions of the people who were more privileged than I was. And I know that many people in this world, who have fewer advantages than you do, will accomplish more than I have."

"I find that hard to believe."

"You should be careful with what you believe. False beliefs about your limitations will hold you back in life. To make my point, let me ask you this: How far do you think a young black woman, from a poor family, with a weight problem, and who was sexually molested as a kid can go in life?"

"Not very far," responded Sheldon. "She has everything going against her, especially being poor and black."

"I wouldn't downplay the weight and sexual molestation problems just because you never had them," smiled Brock. "Now, if someone told you that this young black, overweight woman from a poor family, who was molested as a kid, would become the most powerful woman in television, what would you say?"

"No way," uttered Sheldon defiantly.

"Just what I thought you would say," Brock nodded. "Well, in fact, the woman I described is none other than Oprah Winfrey. Look where she is today! She is arguably the most powerful woman in television. She is unarguably also the highest paid. Her income is continually in the tens of millions of dollars per year. How do you think she arrived at her present position?"

"She must have had a lot of good luck and big breaks along the way. Things that other black people don't get," asserted Sheldon.

"At your age, I probably would have thought the same — that her success was due to great luck and big breaks," admitted Brock. "Over the years, however, I've come to the conclusion that most of us experience some great opportunities throughout our lives. The problem is that most of us don't take advantage of them. Oprah was able to get to where she is because she didn't waste her time being fascinated by her disadvantages. She also chose not to be a victim of her past circumstances for the rest of her life. She took advantage of her opportunities instead. Indeed, she was successful because her actions corresponded with The Easy Rule of Life."

Sheldon, still very skeptical, replied, "It would be extremely difficult for someone like me to achieve even a tenth of what Oprah has achieved."

"As I stated before, there's a big difference between the difficult and the impossible," Brock stressed. "The fact is that extraordinary things are accomplished by ordinary people every day. Oprah is just one of many examples. We can all accomplish many significant things in life. It just takes going beyond the excuses. In your case, the fact that you are a young black man may make it more challenging for you than for many privileged people, but it doesn't make it impossible."

Brock continued, "The difficult and uncomfortable thing you have to do is give up your act of being disadvantaged. You are doing yourself a great disservice and placing limitations on what you can accomplish in your lifetime. You are stealing from yourself by not giving yourself the positive space to attain your dreams. The healthiest, happiest, and most successful people in this world are following their dreams, and making a good portion of them come true. They forget about their shortcomings and circumstances, and use their creativity to attain these dreams."

"But I'm not creative," objected Sheldon.

"That's utter nonsense. Everyone has the ability to be creative. Ordinary people who use their creative ability accomplish extraordinary things. In fact, this is the topic of my first book. It's called *Thinking Big in a Small World*. It shows you how to be more creative. You can apply it to all areas of life, including getting a great job, even when jobs are hard to get. I can give you a copy of the book. There's one in my car."

"No, that's okay. To tell you the truth, I don't like reading much, aside from car magazines and the odd science fiction novel. I have to force myself to read my college books."

Brock smiled at Sheldon. "Perhaps reading some inspirational books would get you on track to getting some of the things you want out of life. You could certainly get yourself a Mercedes 190 SL a lot quicker with a little inspiration."

"From what other people tell me, self-help books don't work. They just make authors like you rich," Sheldon replied negatively.

"No doubt these books make some authors rich," agreed Brock, "but they also are highly beneficial. Self-help and inspirational books have helped many people attain success, happiness, and personal freedom. This includes Oprah. She read many books during her rise to fame and fortune. To this day, she still reads many books, and some of them are inspirational. And I can unequivocally say that books have helped me greatly over the years. I wouldn't have the vocational and financial success that I have today without the help of other authors' inspirational books."

"Then why don't more people benefit from these books?" asked Sheldon.

"The problem with most people is that they read these books, but never put the knowledge into practice. So nothing ever changes in their lives. This gets back to The Easy Rule of Life. People take the easy and comfortable way by neglecting to apply the important things they've learned. They don't take the time to change anything. No wonder their lives turn out difficult and uncomfortable."

"Well," Brock added, "there's no point in discussing this any further if you aren't even going to read my book, or any others for that matter, let alone apply what's in them. In any event, it was nice meeting you, Sheldon. I only work four or five hours a day, but there's still a limit to how much of my day I can spend on leisure activities. I want to get home to put in some time on my new book."

"I also have to get going, or I'll be late for work," Sheldon remarked. "Nice meeting you too."

"Don't forget The Easy Rule of Life," insisted Brock. "It's a truly life-changing principle, and you should give it some serious thought. Think about whether you want to take the easy and comfortable way out and quit college right now. It will just make your life difficult and uncomfortable in the long term. Trust me, do the difficult and uncomfortable by finishing your degree, and you'll have a much easier and more comfortable life in the near future."

"I'll do my best," shrugged Sheldon. "I sure didn't expect to get a sermon on my way to work."

"You should pay much more attention to the synchronicity in your life. Maybe you needed a sermon, and that's why you got one. But that's another story. Have a good evening at work," Brock replied amiably. He got into the Mercedes 190 SL.

As Sheldon continued on his way to work, he thought about the word synchronicity. His pastor in Los Angeles had used the word interchangeably with Divine intervention, to denote meaningful coincidences that happen in people's lives. Reverend Thomas had stated that these chance encounters often change people's lives dramatically for the better, but only if they're open to them. Sheldon also remembered Reverend Thomas saying, "When the student is ready, the master will appear."

"Could this guy Brock be a wise person who could teach me something important?" wondered Sheldon. *"No,"* he decided, *"this man can't be a master of anything significant. This is just a strange coincidence."*

As he entered Starbucks for his shift, he tried to dismiss the event as nothing more than just any other coincidence — just an accidental event that he should forget. Deep down, he admitted that there was some truth to what Brock had said, but he tried to convince himself that the only thing he liked about this eccentric lay preacher was his pristine Mercedes 190 SL.

****

When Sheldon left work later that night, it was cool and raining. He had to walk to his Aunt Lena's house, where he lived, because the transit workers were on strike and no city buses or rapid transit trains were operating. *"Boy, it sure would be nice to have a car,"* he mused as he walked.

His thoughts came back to the sleek black Mercedes 190 SL, and what it would be like to own one like it. He also recalled his conversation with the car's owner. It all seemed so strange, that this man's formula — The Easy Rule of Life — was supposed to help him become more successful and get him a 190 SL. Even stranger, Brock had claimed that this philosophy would also help him attain satisfaction and happiness throughout his life.

As Sheldon strode by a telephone booth, he noticed a small gift-sized book by the phone. It looked like someone had left the book there inadvertently. He stopped to look at it, and saw that it was an expensive hardbound volume in what looked like suede — something he had never seen before. *Life's Secret Handbook (Reminders for Adventurous Souls Who Want to Make a Big Difference in This World)* said the cover.

He picked it up the book and quickly leafed through it. The pages contained a collection of proverbs and short passages. He turned back to the inside front cover and read the handwritten words, almost too small for normal eyesight to see.

> To whoever winds up with this handbook: You are privileged to own one copy of only 500 printed; billions on this planet do not own one. It is no accident that this handbook has found its way to you. Your duty is to put it to good use. Open this handbook at random and reflect on the content. Perhaps the words on the page you arrive at will be of life-changing significance to you. Please share what you learn with others. — Traveling Monk from the Himalayas

"What a weird day," Sheldon mused. *"First that Brock dude, and now this strange little book. Why did I find it? Who is this traveling monk from the Himalayas? It's pretty dumb for someone to print only five hundred copies of a book — an expensive looking one at that — and leave a copy for someone — anyone — to find."*

He shifted his eyes to the first page and read the proverb there. It was typeset in an elegant old-world font, much different from what is normally used in the modern book trade.

Every great accomplishment in the history of humanity started with one small thought.

We all have these thoughts.

𝒻ew people do anything with theirs, however.

𝒲hat do you intend to do with yours?

Sheldon closed the book and put it in his jacket pocket to keep it from getting wet. *"This must be a cosmic joke,"* he thought. *"I don't much like reading, and yet I end up finding an inspirational book, what the monk calls a spiritual guide. Too bad I don't have the phone number of that Brock dude. He likes inspirational books and would probably give me $50 for an expensive hardbound book written by some gypsy monk."*

As he continued on his way home, Sheldon recollected the first passage in the handbook. With his amazing memory, he remembered it word for word. He recited it to himself, whispering, *"Every great accomplishment in the history of humanity started with one small thought. We all have those thoughts. Few people do anything with theirs, however. What do you intend to do with yours?"*

This passage made Sheldon think even more seriously about what was in the handbook. He pulled it out of his pocket, shielded it from the rain, and read the second passage.

𝒮earch, above all, for dreams worth pursuing.

Having found these dreams, dare to pursue them with all your heart and soul.

It is a mistake not to.

The regret of unfulfilled dreams is the most sorrow you will ever experience.

In an instant Sheldon remembered some of the dreams he had when he was a teenager. Back then, he had wanted to become well known, highly successful, and respected by others. He had especially wanted to become a person for members of his community to look up to. Jesse Jackson was one of his heroes, because he had accomplished this.

Even now, there was no way that Sheldon wanted to end up living day to day, carving out a grindstone existence from a job that led nowhere. He certainly didn't want to become a drug dealer, like two of his former acquaintances, making a lot of money but always living on the edge with the possibility of going to jail for many years.

To be open to the great rewards that the Universe wants to bestow on you, you must have an idea or a dream or a passion.

And you must act on it.

You must turn the inspiration within
into powerful, purposeful action.

You must resonate in body, mind, and
spirit – and vibrate with the kind
of imagination, frequency, and
creativity that transcends ordinary
human behavior.

"Maybe there is something to what that Brock guy said," Sheldon concluded. *"I can consider finishing my college marketing program before I look for a job. Oprah would never have gotten to where she is if she hadn't persisted in getting an education and following her dreams. She also wouldn't be where she is if she settled for just any ordinary job so that she could make a meager living and buy a car."*

Being successful and happy in this
world is not as hard as you believe.

Keep these two generally unknown
truths in mind:

What appear to be the easiest things
in life are often the most difficult;

And what appear to be the most
difficult are much easier than most
people ever imagine.

Sheldon didn't fully understand how the fourth proverb could apply to him. It was now pouring rain, though, so he put the handbook back in his pocket to protect it, and ran for the house.

When he arrived at his aunt's house that night, he placed the handbook on the coffee table in the living room. He contemplated reading more of the book, but decided that he'd had enough inspiration for one day. Instead, he started working on an assignment for his college sales course. After an hour, he was too tired to continue. He had completed less than three-quarters of the assignment, but he was sure he would get a passing grade anyway. He had always been able to put less time into his studies than most students, while still winding up in the top 25 percent of the class. He had taken full advantage of that in high school and college.

He concluded that he was too tired even to watch TV, a favorite activity that consumed the majority of his free time. Shortly after he climbed into bed, he fell into a deep sleep. In his most prominent dream that night, he found a high-paying job and met a wonderful young woman. Whenever he took her out on the town, he was proudly driving his own silver Mercedes 190 SL.

****

The next morning, the sun was shining again. Sheldon walked to City College, still wanting a car just as much as the day before. It was an uneventful day. He spent the morning, and the better part of the afternoon, attending classes. He forced himself to go to the library for an hour after school, to work on an Organizational Behavior term paper. After an hour of intensive work, he decided that he'd had enough of college studies for the day.

Late in the afternoon, he arrived back home. His aunt was a nurse who worked late night shifts, and he rarely saw her. As usual, she was already gone for work. He made himself something to eat and ate alone, reading a magazine about exotic cars. The cover story was about the Porsche 924 Carrera. He wanted this modern-day sports car just as much as he wanted the older Mercedes 190 SL.

This was one of his evenings off from his job at Starbucks, where he worked four nights a week. His conscience told him that he should be taking advantage of a night off and working on his college courses. He didn't want to work on them, though, as he felt that it could be a waste of time to do assignments and term papers if he was quitting college in mid-term.

He sat around instead, and soon grew quite bored. He had no money to go out to the Purple Elephant for a few drinks with the regulars, and concluded that the most enjoyable thing he could do was watch a baseball game on TV. Later, he could watch a movie. As he reached for the remote control on the coffee table, he accidentally knocked the copy of *Life's Secret Handbook* on the floor. He picked it up and read from the pages where it had fallen open. Sheldon didn't know quite why, but the passage seemed to be written specifically for him.

When you are experiencing boredom, no doubt you have chosen it.

The question you have to answer is:

Why?

The passage on the opposite page was just as serendipitous.

Be careful with your negative
thoughts.

They are a thousand times more
powerful in contributing to failure
and unhappiness than the worst of
adversity can ever be.

He turned the page, thinking. The two sentences that stood alone on the new page provided more food for thought.

Adventure may have its risks.

Security and routine, however, can
be much more injurious to the soul.

He reminisced about the dreams that he used to have when he was a teenager. He admitted to himself that he could do more than just watch TV and spend time on the Internet on his day off. Instead, he could be doing something important to pursue his dreams of having a better life than his father and mother had. Eventually he shifted his sight to the next page.

Alter your thoughts and behavior,
and you will not only change
yourself, but change the world
around you.

Whatever psychic energy you put
into the Universe will be reflected
back at you.

The more positive energy you put
into imagining and creating a
happy and successful life, the more
it will manifest itself in the real
world.

Sheldon thought, *"Nice way to emphasize the importance of a positive attitude."* For a few moments, he pondered what he had just read. Then he remembered what Reverend Thomas had said in church one Sunday. *"No matter how you look at it, negative, cynical, or pessimistic thinking emanating in the mind is destructive to the human spirit. Creative, positive thought will liberate the potential of your mind, body, and soul."*

Over the years, Reverend Thomas had been Sheldon's main inspiration, giving him emotional support to go to college and pursue a meaningful life. Since moving to Vancouver, Sheldon missed the insights that his pastor used to share with him. The passages in *Life's Secret Handbook* were good reminders of some of the valuable advice he used to receive from the man.

Taking full advantage of the present
to live the moment and at the same
time make a big difference in this
world is undeniable proof of your
agreement to live your life now –
while you have it – and be dead
later – when you are.

~

Be sure of one thing:

Success will elude you as long as
you are doing what's wrong for
you;

And needless to say, success will
come easily when you are doing
what's right for you.

These six proverbs, especially the last one, encouraged Sheldon to think a little more carefully about his direction in life. In time, his thoughts came around to The Easy Rule of Life. He imagined it just as Brock had previously drawn it. *"Perhaps I should do the difficult and uncomfortable, and at least finish my third term before I quit college,"* he pondered. *"That way I won't have to go through the trouble of repeating it later if I want to come back and finish my degree."*

At this point Sheldon decided to devote two hours to studying that evening. Because he had often gone stir-crazy studying at home alone, he headed for the Bread Garden, a coffee bar and deli in trendy Kitsilano. He occasionally studied here, while drinking coffee and watching women. He brought along *Life's Secret Handbook*, in case he needed inspiration while he was studying.

No one can compel you to become
    prosperous and free.

You will become prosperous and free
    when you want to.

Be prepared for surprises.

For instance, there will be some
    delightful work involved.

****

When Sheldon entered the Bread Garden, he went right to the service counter and purchased a regular coffee. He would have preferred a latte, but couldn't afford one. He sat at his favorite spot for studying – a small table in the corner by the front window, where he could watch the service counter and still look out the window.

As usual, he found it difficult and uncomfortable to study diligently, so he spent a portion of his time watching the customers come and go. He even picked up a newspaper and read the sports page for about twenty minutes. After about an hour and a half, he became bored and decided that he'd had enough of studying for the night. He hadn't put in as much time as he had planned, but he felt proud of himself for having studied at all, instead of watching TV all evening.

Sheldon began to pack his books and other stuff into his knapsack, and then was surprised to see Brock, the Mercedes 190 SL owner, walking out of the adjoining room of the Bread Garden, where customers sat if the front room was too full. Brock noticed Sheldon at the same time, and smiled at him.

"Hello Sheldon," came the greeting from Brock. "Imagine running into you again so soon."

"Hi," Sheldon responded. "It is strange to run into you two days in a row, isn't it?"

"The universe works in strange ways," smiled Brock. "It's also interesting to see you studying."

"Oh, I just put an hour and a half into my economics course, but I was about to leave."

"I was doing some work myself; in fact, I've been working on my new book for the last three hours. But how come you're still studying? Have you changed your mind about quitting your college program?"

"Not entirely, but I've been thinking of at least finishing the third term before I quit, then taking a year off. You know, another strange thing happened to me after I met you yesterday. It made me consider finishing the third term," replied Sheldon.

Sheldon told Brock about finding *Life's Secret Handbook*. He brought out the handbook, showed Brock the opening note by the traveling monk, and handed it to him.

"Very interesting," Brock commented after reading the first passage. He opened the handbook near the middle.

It's futile to dream about what could
have been.

Your past is always going to be the
way it was, so stop trying to
change it.

Live never to be embarrassed by your
failures and your past, even if
other people are.

Whatever you have done, love
yourself for having done it.

Brock took the time to read another proverb.

Be careful with taking action on
those crazy creative ideas your
inner Spirit says that you should
take action on.

There will be major consequences in
your life.

There will be achievement,
satisfaction, and prosperity.

And you will sleep happily at night.

Brock passed the handbook, still open, back to Sheldon, and smiled. "This little book seems like a real treasure of spiritual and inspirational wisdom. You should feel fortunate to have found it."

"Actually, it still boggles me," admitted Sheldon, glancing at a proverb on another page. "It's weird that I found this little book on the same day as I told you I didn't want a copy of your creativity book, because I didn't like reading books very much."

"That goes back to what I told you yesterday. Pay more attention to the synchronicity in your life," Brock reminded Sheldon. "Trust me, taking advantage of synchronistic events like this one can change your life."

"My pastor back in L.A. used to tell me the same thing. Do you see a lot of synchronicity yourself?" asked Sheldon.

"Of course," Brock insisted. "While writing my first book, there were many times when I required some information or an example for a particular topic. Then, from out of nowhere, in totally unexpected ways, the information or examples appeared.

"It finally dawned on me that these occurrences were more than accidental. People who write about synchronicity say that we create these events through our energy flow. I don't claim to fully understand synchronicity, though. Remember, I'm just an expert on The Easy Rule of Life."

"Yeah, right," protested Sheldon. "Now that you mention it, I've been thinking about how you don't practice what you preach. You continually violate your own rule of life, but expect others to follow it."

Sheldon hesitated, then continued, "To be honest with you, it irks me that you only work four or five hours a day and make a good living. You're taking the easy and comfortable route while others are doing the difficult and uncomfortable by working a lot more and making less money than you."

"Sheldon, your point is well made, and it appears to be a very good observation on the surface," said Brock. "Look closer, though, and you'll see that it isn't the case. First of all, I took the difficult and uncomfortable route to get where I am today. I paid my dues. Most people wouldn't be willing to risk going without a regular paycheck, even for a week. They also wouldn't risk losing their savings by self-publishing and promoting a book, which I did.

"Secondly, I am highly efficient during the hours I work. Most people are too lazy to learn the techniques that I use religiously. I pay attention to the important things and disregard the trivial. The mass of humanity takes the easy way by not paying much attention to what they do. People spend most of their time on insignificant matters, and very little time on important ones.

"Thirdly, I work for myself. This means I have to create my own work projects and motivate myself to complete them. Generally speaking, people who work for organizations can't figure out what to do on their own. Their work is clearly all laid out for them. Truth be known, it doesn't take even a quarter as much motivation, intelligence, and creativity to go to work for someone else as it is does to work for yourself, and make a comfortable living at it."

"Okay, you've made your point," Sheldon relented. "It may not be easy getting to where you are, but I hope I have the same opportunity someday."

"As I told you yesterday, you can accomplish a lot more than you think you can. Pay attention to the opening maxim in your little handbook, the one that challenges you to do something with your thoughts. Oprah accomplished something significant because she did something with her ideas. So can you."

Brock paused, and then added, "Incidentally, what are you doing on Wednesday evening?"

"It's my night off work. Aside from studying for an hour or two, which I can do during the day, I don't have much planned. Why do you ask?"

"I'm the instructor in three personal development seminars for adult underachievers, sponsored by the Government's Career and Personal Development Department. The foundation of the seminar is The Easy Rule of Life, and teaching people how to take responsibility for their lives to achieve success.

"I need an assistant for all three seminars, to help me with registrations and operating the laptop for overhead projections. I'll pay you $25 an hour for four hours if you'll help. I only speak for three hours. Just operate the laptop while I'm making my presentation, and get it ready for the next one. This way you can get the impact of the whole seminar and make yourself $100 at the same time."

"Twenty-five smackers an hour! I only make $10 at Starbucks. Sure I will do it. I could sure use the money."

"Don't do it just for the money, do it for the learning as well. This is how you should choose all work, including your career. My hope is that the seminars will inspire you to do great things in the future, and the $100 you earn just ends up being an insignificant bonus for helping me."

Brock paused and looked out the window. "I have to leave now for an appointment downtown. I can give you a ride if you're heading that way."

"As a matter of fact, I am. It would be great to get a ride in your car."

They walked out of the Bread Garden, Sheldon looking forward to a ride in the Mercedes 190 SL. "Where's your car?" he asked.

"Right here," Brock smiled. He walked to the driver's side of a silver Porsche Carrera 924 convertible, with its top down, parked right in front.

"This Porsche 924 is yours too!" Sheldon shouted out. "This is another of my dream cars. And silver is my favorite color."

"The 924 and the 190 SL are my toy cars for summer driving. I have a Lexus for the colder months."

"A Lexus too? How did you get three great cars and a house – fully paid off – in just seven years?"

"Stick around, kid. I'll learn you a lot," quipped Brock, intentionally making the grammatical error. "Pay close attention to what I have to say about The Easy Rule of Life in my seminars. Start following the principles associated with it, and you can also buy your own 190 SL and 924 as your toy cars in a few years. If that's what you really want out of life."

*A dream without a plan kindled by
your inspired action is just a wish
that the Universe has little interest
in supporting.*

*Inspired action leads to transcendent
wonder and smiles of good fortune.*

*That is to say, supreme blessings of
prosperity from the Universe are
the result of supreme impassioned
inputs from you.*

In a way that he couldn't fully explain, Sheldon actually looked forward to attending Brock's first seminar. Sure, the $100 was important to him, but he also relished the thought of doing something different from attending his mundane college classes. He was still a little leery about Brock's advice relating to The Easy Rule of Life, though the handbook suggested that he shouldn't have been.

*Open your mind to opinions other
than your own.*

*The people whose opinions you most
fear may be the wise ones from
whom you can learn most.*

****

2

Be a LEARNER first.

Become a MASTER second.

And remain a STUDENT forever.

At 6 o'clock on Wednesday evening Sheldon arrived at the Landmark Hotel on Robson, where Brock's seminar was scheduled to begin an hour later. Brock was already there, dressed in pressed black slacks and an expensive blue dress shirt. He greeted Sheldon amiably. Sheldon helped set up the audio-visual equipment in the auditorium, then Brock gave him a crash course on operating the laptop for projecting seminar visuals onto the overhead screen.

As the participants arrived, Sheldon registered everyone and gave them their nametags. The female attendees seemed to outnumber the men but not by much. Many of the attendees were in their twenties, while many were older, including a man who appeared to be in his late fifties.

After all of the seventy-three attendees were registered, Sheldon sat down by Brock's laptop. As he waited for Brock to begin the presentation, he brought out *Life's Secret Handbook*, which he had brought along in case he got bored. He opened it randomly to see what passage would appear.

> Making a big difference in this world
>   is not dependent on the conditions
>   in your life.
>
> This is solely dependent on the
>   temperament of your soul.

He also read the passage on the opposite page.

> Much of the difference you make
>   tomorrow will start with what you
>   do today.
>
> The question is:
>
> What seeds of accomplishment do
>   you intend to plant before the end
>   of the day?

At precisely 7 o'clock Brock stepped onto the platform and walked to a lectern. He placed a notebook, several sheets of paper, and a glass of water on top of the lectern, and then put on a microphone headset. He turned his head slowly from left to right, his laser-focused brown eyes scanning the audience. Within a few seconds the crowd fell silent.

It was an odd but exciting feeling for Sheldon to watch a professional speaker work his trade. From the moment Brock started speaking, Sheldon found him fascinating. There was a pronounced personality change from the public Brock to the seminar instructor Brock. He was much more energetic, dynamic, and animated in front of an audience. There was something about his confidence and ease in front of seventy-three people that sent a shiver through Sheldon. *"How could he be so intense in such a relaxed way?"* he mused.

Over the next three hours of speaking to the audience, Brock's voice varied widely. At times he shouted for effect, at times he whispered, and the rest of the time he talked in a loud and authoritative manner. The expression on his face went from warmth to total indifference, and then back again.

Occasionally a smile accompanied the humorous parts of his presentation. Although Brock was charismatic and fascinating during the presentation, he could also be arrogant and downright irritating. He certainly wasn't boring, though, like most of the school teachers and college instructors that Sheldon had witnessed over the years.

Brock started the presentation in a loud, authoritative voice that, when amplified through the PA system, made it sound as if he was shouting.

"HELLO. MY NAME IS BROCK MELLOR. I'M YOUR SEMINAR INSTRUCTOR. I'VE BEEN HIRED BY THE CAREER AND PERSONAL DEVELOPMENT DEPARTMENT TO HELP YOU ACHIEVE MORE IN LIFE. YOU HAVE ALREADY PARTICIPATED IN A SERIES OF CAREER DEVELOPMENT SESSIONS ON THE IMPORTANCE OF PURSUING AN IMPORTANT

CAREER. MY DUTY IS TO HELP YOU ACHIEVE SUCCESS AND SATISFACTION, NOT ONLY IN YOUR WORK LIVES, BUT ALSO IN YOUR PERSONAL LIVES.

"THE PRINCIPLES THAT I'M GOING TO SHARE WITH YOU IN THE NEXT THREE SEMINARS ARE PRINCIPLES THAT CAN CHANGE YOUR LIVES IMMENSELY. THESE PRINCIPLES ARE HIGHLY EFFECTIVE, BUT SOME OF YOU WILL DOUBT THEM, SOME OF YOU WILL RESIST THEM, SOME OF YOU MAY EVEN END UP HATING THEM. THAT'S YOUR CHOICE. JUST BE CLEAR THAT IGNORING THESE PRINCIPLES CAN DRASTICALLY LIMIT YOUR VOCATIONAL, FINANCIAL, AND PERSONAL SUCCESS.

"I am advocating these principles simply because they work. I have applied these principles rigorously, and with great success, for the last ten years. I went from being unemployed, having no major purpose in life, and possessing $40,000 in debt, to creating a career that I love and a lifestyle that I wouldn't trade for anything in this world. Today I work only four to five hours a day. Yet I make twice as much money as most people, even those who work two to three times as much as I do.

"You can achieve as much as I have — even more — if you want it badly enough. The counselors at the Career and Personal Development Department have told me that their assessments of all of you indicate impressive talent and great potential. Yet, for some unknown reason, you have chosen to be underachievers. My duty is to give you direction on how to make your lives work, by being more successful in the things that are important to you.

"One last note before we get started: I would like to stress that I don't intend to lecture in the purest sense of the word. I was greatly influenced by the words of Stephen Leacock: 'Most people can tire of a lecture in fifteen minutes, clever people can do it in five, and sensible people don't go to lectures at all.' "

A gentle wave of nervous laughter broke out across the room at this stage. Brock didn't change his stoic facial expression as he continued.

"Since I know that all of you are sensible people, I also know that it would be futile for me to conduct a lecture. Therefore, I encourage everyone to fully participate in the seminar by questioning what I have to say, as well as sharing any experiences that are related to what I have to say. We'll also have several exercises and I expect everyone to get totally involved in those."

Brock's voice dropped down a few decibels as he continued. "We'll start with the most important principle for experiencing more success, more satisfaction, and more happiness in your lives. It's what I call The Easy Rule of Life. This rule or principle will be the foundation for the subject matter we're going to discuss in the next three sessions."

Brock walked away from the lectern to stand near where Sheldon was sitting, and then asked him to project a PowerPoint slide of The Easy Rule of Life onto the overhead screen. The diagram on the screen was similar to the one Brock had previously hand drawn for Sheldon, only it was much neater and easier to read.

Ernie J. Zelinski

THE EASY RULE OF LIFE

Brock pointed to the left side of the diagram and spoke. "The Easy Rule of Life tells us that when we take the easy and comfortable route, life turns out to be difficult and uncomfortable. Ninety percent of us continually choose this route because short-term comfort is more appealing. We choose to ignore the impending long-term negative consequences in favor of the instant gratification we hope to attain."

Brock then pointed to the right side of the diagram and continued. "The other option is to take the difficult and uncomfortable route. When we do this, life ends up being easy and comfortable. People who take this route know that they must experience occasional short-term discomfort for long-term gains.

"Let me warn you that The Easy Rule of Life is something like the law of gravity. Mess around with the law of gravity by walking off the top of a building, and see what happens to you. It will knock you on your ass.

"The same thing applies with The Easy Rule of Life. Mess around with it by taking the easy way, and you'll also wind up on your ass. It gets you every time. By the time this session is over, you may get frustrated with this idea, and even want to blame me for The Easy Rule of Life. But remember — I have nothing to do with it. I didn't create it. I just observed that this is the way life works, and now I am telling you that we have to make the best of the situation."

Brock faced the audience directly now, and walked several feet to the right of the lectern.

"Be clear that The Easy Rule of Life influences every area of our lives, including satisfaction at work, financial gain, friendship, marriage, parenting, love, health, and leisure. The degree to which you apply The Easy Rule of Life will determine how much success, satisfaction, and happiness you achieve throughout your whole life," he declared.

"For example, let's assume that you are about to start work as a stockbroker. If the average stockbroker makes fifteen cold calls a day on the telephone, you can take the easy and comfortable route and make only five calls. This way you won't have to face as much failure and rejection. Clearly, your life is going to end up difficult and uncomfortable, because you won't make much money with this philosophy. As a matter of fact, you'll probably wind up being fired sooner or later.

"On the other hand, if you take the difficult and uncomfortable route by making thirty-five sales calls a day compared to the average fifteen, you will undoubtedly experience a great deal of failure and rejection. Your life will end up being easy and comfortable in the future, however, because you will make a lot of new contacts. You will also make more sales and eventually wind up being the top salesperson in the company.

"This is just one example of many that I can give you about how The Easy Rule of Live applies to our lives. The problem with always choosing the comfortable way is that, in the long run, it will turn out to be very uncomfortable. The biggest obstacle to success is the discomfort of doing the necessary things we must do to *attain* that success. We impulsively gravitate toward less pain and more pleasure. We opt for the easy way, because we are seeking total comfort at all costs."

Brock continued, raising his voice considerably at this point. "THERE'S ONE BIG PROBLEM WITH ALWAYS CHOOSING THE EASY WAY IN LIFE. IT ENSURES THAT YOU WILL WIND UP IN ONE OR MORE OF LIFE'S RUTS. AND THE ONLY DIFFERENCE BETWEEN A RUT AND A GRAVE ARE THE DIMENSIONS."

A wave of laughter erupted across the room before Brock was able to continue.

"IN THE RUT, YOU GET TO JOIN THE LIVING DEAD, AND IN THE GRAVE YOU GET TO JOIN THE DEAD DEAD."

More laughter.

Brock paused for a few seconds before he continued in a firm but more subdued voice.

"If you want to be truly alive and experience a sense of achievement and satisfaction, you have to concentrate on doing many difficult and uncomfortable things. It's difficult and uncomfortable to be highly organized; it's difficult and uncomfortable to pay attention to the important things in life; it's difficult and uncomfortable to save money; and it's difficult and uncomfortable to keep agreements. Regardless of how difficult and uncomfortable these things are, though, I suggest that you give up your comfort zones and start doing them. There are probably one hundred different areas in your lives where you are taking the easy and comfortable way at this time."

At this point Erica, a slender, attractive woman in her mid-twenties, seated in the middle of the fourth row, called out, trying to get Brock's attention. "Mr. Mellor . . ."

Brock glanced at the woman's nametag and acknowledged her. "Erica, just call me Brock instead of Mr. Mellor, and then I won't have to feel like my dad is in the room when you address me."

This comment brought a few chuckles before Erica was able to say cheerfully, "Brock, pardon me for stating this but to me you're coming across as a sadist! You're advocating nothing but a whole lot of suffering in this world with The Easy Rule of Life."

Brock moved off the stage and closer to where Erica was seated.

After a short pause, he started off with a whisper. "I beg to differ. I am not a sadist and I am not advocating a life full of SUFFERING. I'm certainly not advocating long-term SUFFERING, if that's what you are implying. I am in favor of short-term SUFFERING so that you don't have to experience long-term SUFFERING.

"No doubt, Erica, if you want to avoid SUFFERING today, it's easier and more comfortable to be messy than to be organized; it's easier and more comfortable to spend money than to save it; it's easier and more comfortable to be oblivious to the important things in life than to pay attention to them; and it's easier and more comfortable to break agreements than to keep agreements. Unfortunately, all these actions will make life difficult and uncomfortable in the long term because they will rob you of accomplishment, satisfaction, success, and happiness. With The Easy Rule of Life I am a proponent of a moderate amount of discomfort now, as that all adds up to a big payoff of satisfaction and happiness in the long term.

"So Erica, to repeat, I am not a sadist and I am not advocating a life of nothing except for SUFFERING. Keep in mind that I don't work more than four or five hours a day. I have a more balanced lifestyle than 95 percent of North Americans. This is not SUFFERING. Unlike many people, I enjoy both my work life and personal life immensely."

"It sounds to me like you enjoy your life so much because you have an easy life," smiled Erica.

"Not quite," Brock announced, "I built this life because one day I realized how right the wise people of this world are. These people know that true happiness can't be found by idlers who spend all their time sleeping, relaxing, and partying. I may work fewer hours a day than most people, but I do many more difficult and uncomfortable things in four hours than they do in eight or twelve hours. I work harder in those four hours than most people do during their entire twelve-hour shift."

Brock continued, "I would like to sum up my response to your initial question, Erica. Don't look at taking the difficult and uncomfortable way as suffering. Look at it as a form of price paying. You can actually feel satisfied and content when you know that you are paying the price today for something that will bring you great rewards in the future."

"Okay, put in those words, I agree with you," said Erica. "To a large degree, maybe not as much as you, I already live my life this way."

"Great, I am glad I have at least one person on my side this early in the session. It's always easier to preach to the converted," smiled Brock.

Brock walked back onto the podium. "It shouldn't be that hard to see that The Easy Rule of Life has applications in all areas of our lives. But for some reason many adults violate The Easy Rule of Life throughout their whole lives. On the other hand, highly successful people follow The Easy Rule of Life all their lives. They realize that they must abide by it for the rest of their lives if they want continued success and happiness. Since you are no longer juveniles, all of you should have learned by now that nothing of major consequence comes easily. You must pay the price of a little discomfort for anything that adds to your long-term happiness.

"As an aside, I would like to point out that even children over ten years old will see many applications of The Easy Rule of Life. My girlfriend Silvina teaches at a school for delinquent kids. She shared The Easy Rule of Life with thirteen- and fourteen-year-old kids in her class. Much to her surprise, the kids were extremely receptive to it and came up with parallels when applying it to their own lives. Here are some of the kids' comments. Silvina recorded them for me."

Brock motioned to Sheldon to project a new frame onto the overhead screen, then starting reading aloud from the frame.

How Junior High Students Relate to The Easy Rule of Life

• Student #1 stated, "Taking the easy way out by not brushing my teeth means that I will have to deal with cavities, pain, and my dad having to pay dentist's bills. Taking the difficult way by brushing every day means I will have nice teeth without any fillings when I grow up."

• Student #2 stated, "Watching TV instead of studying for exams is the easy way out but it will lead to failure, having to repeat a grade, and having my parents mad at me. Studying, which is difficult and uncomfortable, will help me pass the grades and go to university for a good career."

• Student #3 stated, "Taking the easy way out by eating junk food would make me fat and ashamed of myself. I would have to do the difficult and uncomfortable and eat healthy food if I wanted to lose weight."

• Student #4 stated, "Easy money selling drugs leads to family pain, danger, death, and jail."

After Brock finished reading, he remarked, "It's noteworthy that even young teenagers will acknowledge the benefits of paying a price today for rewards to be reaped sometime in the future. If students in their early teens can see the value of applying The Easy Rule of Life to their lives, adults should be able to see the value in applying it to theirs as well. Clearly, if all of us applied The Easy Rule of Life more often, we would have far fewer lingering problems and attain much more success."

Brock paused and went back to the lectern, where he glanced at his notes.

"Let's address where most of our life's trials and tribulations originate. Our problems — especially the whoppers — begin with our belief systems. For some strange reason human beings find it easy to hang onto belief systems that don't work, instead of adopting new ones that do. Indeed, this is the first area where you should apply The Easy Rule of Life.

"It's important that you take the time to challenge all your beliefs — especially your most cherished ones. As difficult and uncomfortable as this may be to accept, your most cherished beliefs are potentially the most dangerous to your mental health. In fact, practically every hard-core belief ends up being a form of disease, interfering with psychological well-being."

Suddenly a bushy-haired, bearded man in his mid-thirties put up his hand, and without waiting for Brock's acknowledgment, blurted, "Brock, what's wrong with having beliefs? We need beliefs to function in life. Without beliefs, we would have no mental framework from which to operate."

"Brent, we all need a mental framework consisting of points of view and values to function as human beings," countered Brock. "Nonetheless, we should continually question these values and points of view, especially when they become hard-core beliefs. Most people's beliefs — especially those related to what brings satisfaction and happiness in life — are erroneous assumptions, myths, and pure fiction.

"For example, one cherished belief is that life ought to be easy. Yet no human being has a truly easy life. We must all

43

face problems and difficulties, regardless of our position in society. To the surprise of many, rich and famous people have just as many problems as we do — and in most cases, even more. Just read the newspapers and you'll see how many serious problems the rich and famous have.

"Associated with this life-ought-to-be-easy belief is the one-big-deal-in-life belief. We all like to think that there is some big deal — a chance event such as a lottery win or a perfect relationship or some savior — that is going to make our lives easy and comfortable. Trust me, there is no "one big deal" that will bail you out of your problems and your despair. You'll always have problems, and regardless of how much money you have, your happiness will be dependent upon a myriad of other things that money can't buy. We'll handle the money and happiness angles later, though."

Brock continued, "So, to repeat, it's in your best interest to do the difficult and uncomfortable thing and admit that your beliefs may be suspect. Indeed, your beliefs are probably the biggest reason you haven't attained as much satisfaction and happiness as you would like. Beliefs run your life and rob you of satisfaction and happiness. And when you become fanatical about your beliefs — whether religious, political, environmental, or economic — you are as close as you can get to being certifiably crazy.

"The problem with the human mind is that it can trick itself into believing what it wants to believe. It will believe what has no relationship to reality, what isn't good for the world, and even what isn't good for the mind itself. The main reason is that every human mind wants to be right about its beliefs at all costs. It doesn't want to admit that it might have started believing something that was false. Unfortunately, being right at all costs, whether it's about beliefs or anything else, is much like being a dead hero — there is no payoff.

"Instead of having to be right about all your beliefs, and hanging onto them, challenge your most cherished ones regularly. At the same time, encourage your mind to encounter thoughts that it might not otherwise encounter. This will keep your mind fresh and open to the way the world is, instead of the way it ought to be. Failure to constantly challenge your most cherished beliefs will lead to a false perception of reality. And if there is anything that will keep you from success, contentment, and achievement, it's perceiving reality in a way that has absolutely no relationship to the way it actually is."

As Brock looked toward the back of the room, he noticed a raised hand. It belonged to Ben, the oldest of all the seminar participants. The man had thinning hair, glasses, and a slightly stooped posture.

"Yes, Ben?" Brock asked.

"Brock, each of us has a different perception of reality. This doesn't make anybody's perception right or wrong," observed Ben. "How can you claim that your interpretation of reality is better than mine or any other person's in this room?"

Sheldon, intently watching seminar proceedings, momentarily reflected on a maxim he had read earlier in *Life's Secret Handbook*:

> **H**ave you ever considered that your
> perception of reality could be
> wrong?

If you haven't, this is a sure sign that
it is!

Sheldon also recalled the accompanying maxim.

Be extremely careful with what you
perceive as reality.

Any misperception of it is a lie.

This will cause you all sorts of big
problems in life.

You are liable to wind up a bystander
in an exciting and happening
world.

Brock responded to the trainee's question. "Ben, it's true that we all interpret reality differently, to some degree. But your perception of reality better be close to what reality is and not what it ought to be. There's only one reality, as sure as the sun does shine. It's the same for everyone, regardless of the fact that everyone perceives it differently. Trying to create your own reality can be futile, and even highly dangerous to the point of being deadly."

"How can having a unique perception of reality be deadly?" demanded Ben.

"Here's one example: believe in a reality where gravity doesn't exist and you'll have major problems. Gravity won't go away, regardless of how much you stop believing in it. If you walk off the end of a tall building, your perception of reality will prove to be a lot less valid — and a lot more deadly — than mine, where I accept and highly respect gravity."

Subdued laughter sounded around the room at this statement.

"Ben, let me give you another example. If you walk out on the street and suddenly see a Greyhound bus bearing down at you at 50 miles per hour, your perception of reality is only valid to the degree that you understand you better move fast, or you're a dead duck. You may have a belief that the bus ought to stop. Whether it will is another matter altogether. Your perception of the bus and all other aspects of reality better be right on the money, because reality doesn't care how you perceive it. It will just go on being the way it is.

"These are two examples of how your erroneous perception of reality can be detrimental to living a full and satisfying life. We'll cover other examples, like erroneously perceiving yourself as a victim in life, perceiving yourself as a lot less creative and talented than you are, perceiving that you can avoid a lot of failure in life, and perceiving that the way to happiness is through a totally comfortable life, in other seminars.

"The fact is this — people who are out of touch with these aspects of reality aren't going to get very far in life. On the other hand, people who live life according to what reality is, rather than the way it ought to be, reap great rewards."

While Brock paused briefly to look at his notebook, Sheldon stole a peek in *Life's Secret Handbook*.

$\mathcal{D}$o you matter?

$\mathcal{B}$eing cool and hip may be the best
racket that you can come up with.

$\mathcal{H}$ow profound and beneficial is it to
you, however, if you are cool and
hip – but your life has little
meaning?

"One of the most important disparities between people's perception of reality and the way reality actually is," Brock continued, "involves how much they believe that they are victims in this world. Indeed, claiming that one is a victim is one of the most popular activities in Western society today. The truth is that most people who perceive themselves as victims are actually trying to take the easy way out, by passing blame for their problems onto someone else. Blame invariably allows self-affirmed victims to shun responsibility for their lives.

"Society and governments are two common entities that people like to target for their problems. I think the favorite target is one's parents, however. Many people with the victim mentality blame their parents for their own problems in adulthood, such as alcoholism, drug addiction, financial difficulties, and incompatible relationships. Unfortunately, this is a self-destructive practice that does absolutely nothing to create a better life."

"What's wrong with blaming your parents for the way you are?" protested Ursula, a blonde woman in her mid-thirties with a Dutch accent. "My parents caused me a whole lot of grief in my life. I had a rotten childhood. My father and mother abused me by depriving me of love and a lot of other things that they could have given me, but didn't. If they had been better parents, my life wouldn't be so messed up."

"Look, Ursula," interjected Brock. "Do you think that your life has to *continue* being messed up just because you didn't have perfect parents? Why would you think that? You have to accept that your parents aren't messing up your life *today*."

"I totally disagree with you," argued Ursula. "If my parents had been like other people's parents, my life wouldn't be so difficult today."

"What makes you think that your parents were so bad? Whose standards are you using?"

"Mine," snapped Ursula.

"Well, let's use my standards, just for argument's sake," he suggested.

Brock directed his gaze away from Ursula, toward the audience in general to ask a question. "Who here in this room has parents who were perfect, or parents who were close to being perfect?"

Everyone in the auditorium looked around and noticed that not one hand went up.

Brock addressed Ursula again, "As you can see Ursula, no one here has parents who were even close to being perfect."

Again, Brock directed his gaze at the audience. "Now, who here in this room feels that their parents could have done a much better job at parenting than they actually did?"

All the other people in the room, including Sheldon, raised their hands this time.

Brock continued. "Ursula, I can assure you that if I was to ask the same two questions in a room full of the most successful people in the world, the responses would be no different from what we have in this room. My point is, no one in this world has or ever had parents who were close to being perfect. Virtually everyone feels that their parents could have done a better job."

Ursula, red faced by now, blurted in a tremulous voice, "The fact that no one ever has perfect parents doesn't hide the fact that some parents do much better than others."

"So what?" Brock shot back. "People who have great parents end up screwing their lives up beyond belief, and people who have lousy parents use this as motivation to attain their dreams. If you want to screw up your life, there's no shortage of excuses. Regardless of the job your parents did, the best thing for you is to quit blaming them and start taking responsibility for your life.

"Ursula, I can also assure you that many of the most successful people in this world had parents with worse parenting skills than your parents had. These people didn't blame their parents for their own shortcomings. They took what they learned from their parents and made the best of it. The thing you have to accept is that your parents probably did the best that they could under the circumstances they had to face. Their shortcomings and their abuse — if you label it as such — were a result of their own upbringing, their values, their beliefs, and their fears. If they didn't have any better parenting skills, how could they have been better parents?"

Ursula shrugged and didn't say anything.

Brock then stated, intensely and dramatically, "To be a highly effective person, and a better parent yourself, it's in your long-term interests to develop a case of amnesia for what your parents did wrong. Instead of focusing on what your parents did wrong, focus on what they did right. In most cases, people who do this realize that their parents did at least five times as many right things as they did wrong ones. The problem with blaming your parents is that it stops you from moving forward in your life. If you want to have a better life tomorrow, the time to stop being a victim is today."

Ursula was obviously resisting everything that Brock was saying. Again in a tremulous voice, she pronounced, "People have a right to blame their parents. Parental abuse is a well-known fact. There's even a support group formed in the United States for people who have been abused by their parents."

Showing a great deal of patience, Brock responded, "Undoubtedly, there are many people who blame their parents for why they're experiencing a miserable life. In my opinion, joining a support group will just perpetuate one's suffering. The longer people believe that blaming their parents is justified, the longer their own lives will remain miserable. I once knew a grouchy man in his late fifties who blamed his misery on his parents, even though they had died many years earlier. He was one of the least happy people I've ever met. As this man proved, remaining a victim because of your upbringing for the rest of your life is no way to create a happy life.

"In fact, any excuse that you use to be a victim will deter you from making positive changes in your life. You can be too poor, too female, too underprivileged, too short, too tall, too black, too white, too undereducated, or not funny enough — the list is endless. The list is also totally irrelevant if you want to become successful and make a difference in this world."

Again, Ursula interrupted. "How can you say that all these factors are irrelevant? Some of them may be, but being female is a great disadvantage! Women face insurmountable discrimination that holds them back from success and happiness. Women are victims because of the oppression they face from men. This has happened for centuries, and it's still happening today. I can even tell that there are many male chauvinists here today, who want to suppress women and oppose their liberation."

Brock paused, and then responded wryly, "Look Ursula, perhaps you can point out the chauvinistic guys in this room at the end of the session. After I have a little talk with them, they'll all be liberated males, and every one of them will be happy to have you — or any other female in this room — change the oil in their muscle cars."

Laughter erupted across the room from both sexes, but Ursula didn't seem to see any humor in the comment.

Brock continued, "In case you didn't get it, Ursula, my last comment was intended partly for humor's sake and partly to get you thinking a little more precisely about what it takes to be truly liberated. Don't get me wrong, I accept that there has been unwarranted discrimination against women, and that there still is. I also recognize the incredible injustices and inequities that exist in the world. I know that hundreds of millions of people have limited or very little opportunity.

Generally speaking, this is far from being the case in the Western world, however. Here, even people with serious disadvantages have great opportunities for being successful and making a real difference.

"Overcoming any disadvantages is a case of mind over matter. Clearly, whether individuals seriously think that they are victims of the government, their parents, society, or the opposite sex, the end result is the same. There is no payoff in the way of success and happiness. People can never be liberated if their biggest game in life is being a victim. How can they? To satisfy their perverted belief system, they will always — consciously or subconsciously — set it up so that they are victims. In this way, they can always find some reason to blame someone else for their problems."

"Then who are we *supposed* to blame for our problems?" asked an oriental man named Ting. He used a joking tone of voice to let Brock know that he didn't believe in the victim mentality.

Brock smiled. "I believe that you know the answer to your question, Ting. Allow me to ask another question in answer to yours. How many times have you heard highly successful people say that one of the keys to their success has been their ability to blame someone else for their problems?"

Ting smiled in agreement, "Obviously, the answer is none. But don't some people experience satisfaction from being a victim?"

"Clearly, Ting, debating whether being a victim is really satisfying is tantamount to debating whether zero is a real number. Obviously, in either case, the answer is NO, and further debate is a total waste of time. Sure, I concede that some people get a perverse sense of satisfaction from being a victim, but this isn't the type of satisfaction that contributes to peace of mind and personal well-being.

"People suffering from victim consciousness whine a lot about what's wrong with the world. And there are two major problems with focusing on all this wrongness. The first is that it simply doesn't do you any good. You can complain about the government or the unscrupulous corporations or all the alleged conspiracies or the super-rich people who control most of the money in this world. Nothing will happen, however, except that you will waste a lot of time and energy with your complaining.

"More important — much, much more important — is that complaining is an addiction. Once you get really good at complaining, you become a true professional, and you start looking for anything and everything to complain about. You get so immersed in complaining that it becomes a lifestyle, one devoid of creative accomplishment, success, and prosperity. In the end, your life doesn't work and you are the sole reason — not the things that you complained about.

"The final score on playing the victim game is that it offers no meaningful payoffs. Dwelling on inequities and injustices can seriously hinder your chances for achieving success in all areas of your life. The truth is, everyone has some sort of handicap or shortcoming when compared to someone else."

Patrick, a big man close to 250 pounds, with long black hair and dressed like a member of the Hells Angels, now spoke up.

"Brock, all people may individually have some shortcomings compared to someone else in this world, but most people, even in Western society, are greatly disadvantaged compared to the rich and privileged."

"No doubt our handicaps and shortcomings are of varying degrees," remarked Brock. "It's not the degree of handicap or disadvantage, however, that holds people back. It's how much they dwell on these handicaps and disadvantages."

"Are you suggesting that people should ignore their disadvantages?" asked Patrick.

"Absolutely," answered Brock. "There are millions of people who lead worthwhile and highly successful lives, even though they are physically handicapped, have been raised in the ghettos, had limited formal education, or had cruel parents. Some of these individuals didn't even have any parents. The one thing that these highly effective people don't do or didn't do is play the victim game."

Brock continued, "If you ask greatly disadvantaged people who became highly successful how they were able to accomplish so much, they'll say that ignoring these disadvantages was precisely the reason that they became successful. They were too busy setting goals, determining which activities they had to partake in to achieve these goals, and actually achieving their goals, to think about their disadvantages.

"Because they were so busy accomplishing things, they had no time to pay attention to their shortcomings. I would advise that every one of you in this room do the same if you want to achieve something significant sometime in your life."

****

Whatever is important and life-changing to the human soul has to start with difficulty and discomfort.

Make today the day you started the difficult and uncomfortable process that transformed your life.

For Sheldon, time passed quickly during the seminar. Occasionally one or two trainees dozed off momentarily. He had to assist Brock with the overhead projections, so Sheldon didn't have the luxury of cat napping during the session. As it turned out, though, he didn't want this luxury, because he was seeing much value in the seminar. He paid close attention to every word Brock said, and even wished he'd brought a notebook to take notes.

Several trainees seemed annoyed with the overemphasis on why it was so important that they give up being a victim and take responsibility for their lives. Sheldon himself found this part of the seminar useful. He realized how much Ursula, the woman with a Dutch accent, suffered from the victim mentality, and how it would hold her back in life if she didn't overcome this affliction. He also realized how people could create their own victim act, regardless of whether they were male or female, slender or fat, rich or poor, talented or handicapped, and black or white. More and more Sheldon began to see the importance of giving up any victim mentality of his own, and taking full responsibility for his life.

The only time that Sheldon's mind momentarily drifted away from the room was when he was glancing at *Life's Secret Handbook*.

The mark of your unhappiness is the depth of your belief in how much you are a victim.

Argue for why you are a victim of circumstances, and guess what?

You are one.

You get to be right about it.

The important question is:

Do you want to be right about it or do you want to be happy?

Sheldon felt privileged to have what could be the only copy of *Life's Secret Handbook* in Vancouver, possibly even in Canada or North America. Although the handbook's short, gentle, and poetic passages sharply contrasted Brock's brash and authoritative style, there was an incredible philosophical relationship between the passages and the principles that Brock emphasized. For Sheldon, the passages provided additional impact to the applications of The Easy Rule of Life.

The world is much easier to live in when you take 100 percent responsibility for your life.

Taking 100 percent responsibility for your life is your willingness to be the author of all your experiences — including those that you are embarrassed about and that don't make you proud.

****

With half an hour left before the scheduled break in the seminar, Sheldon noticed two young men with know-it-all sneers in the back row of the auditorium. They continued to talk loudly and laugh freely throughout the speech. Obviously, the two men were also irritating many of the other seminar attendees.

Brock had shown a great deal of patience for these two men throughout the seminar. When it was apparent that the two agitators had no intentions of stopping on their own, though, Brock paused to stare at them. The men fell silent. As soon as he resumed his presentation, however, they continued their conversation. This time Brock decided that he'd had enough and responded by bellowing at them.

"LOOK, YOU TWO IN THE BACK OF THE ROOM. IF YOU WANT TO SOCIALIZE, STARBUCKS IS JUST DOWN THE STREET. AND IF YOU WANT TO RUN A SEMINAR, YOU MUST GO TO SCHOOL FOR EIGHTEEN YEARS LIKE I DID. IT'S ALSO

IMPERATIVE THAT YOU GET SOME SPEAKING EXPERIENCE AND A MOTIVATIONAL TOPIC TO SPEAK ABOUT. EVEN IF YOU ATTAIN THESE QUALIFICATIONS, YOU AREN'T GOING TO RUN YOUR SEMINAR IN THIS ROOM. YOU STILL HAVE TO GET YOUR OWN GIG WITH YOUR OWN AUDIENCE AND YOUR OWN ROOM."

There was an uncomfortable silence as Brock walked back to the lectern to look at his notes. As he glanced up, he noticed one of the two men leaving toward the back exit.

"HEY, WHERE ARE YOU GOING?" snapped Brock.

"I'm leaving," shot back the stocky native man, who carried his buckskin jacket. "I'm heading over to the Career Development Department to make a complaint about you and your seminar material. I don't have to put up with all this garbage. I also resent your personality. You're a total jerk — a fascist pig is more like it."

"No problem with the complaint," replied Brock confidently. "I take full responsibility for being a fascist pig. I am a fascist pig simply because this is what works best in getting a bunch of underachievers to get their lives to work a whole lot better.

"And just for your sake: I have presented my seminars at least fifty different times. The powers that be at the Career and Personal Development Department have asked me back again and again. They even doubled my fees this time because of the results that underachievers like you attain with The Easy Rule of Life. Results don't lie, in other words."

By this time Brock had walked to the back of the room. He glanced quickly at the man's name tag before he asked, "So, Joe, what's actually driving you out of this room?"

"You are, with your arrogance," Joe shot back.

"No, I'm not," scoffed Brock. "Your fragile ego is driving you out. Think about it. Everything I just said was heard by your friend as well as you."

Brock quickly took a side glance at the other man's name tag and then continued. "Yet Terry's not leaving. And all the other things that I said about The Easy Rule of Life were directed at everyone else in the auditorium, as well as you. Guess what? No one else is leaving. Unless I'm God, how can I be driving you out of this room, and forcing everyone else to stay at the same time?"

Joe shrugged but didn't answer.

"Look Joe. It's your choice — and not God's or mine — whether you stay or leave. You are totally responsible for your own actions here. Sure, you can take the easy way out by being a quitter, as you've probably done for most of your life. No doubt you can leave here and go down to the local bar, which is the home of dull people and the center of trivial conversation.

"I can assure you that hanging around with a bunch of losers will give you an important lesson in how NOT to be successful in life. Sure, you'll get to tell them about this seminar and how bad I was at presenting it. You'll get to tell them your version of the story. You can also make The Easy Rule of Life wrong, and everyone else in this room wrong for staying here. But not one thing in your life will change. You will continue to be an underachiever who doesn't live up to his full potential. The saddest part is that there will be little satisfaction and joy in your life.

"On the other hand, Joe," Brock added, "I guarantee that if you do the difficult and uncomfortable thing, and stay for the rest of this seminar and the next two, you'll be glad that you did. Your life will be turned around 180 degrees. It will be on the plus side like never before. All you have to do is adopt The Easy Rule of Life and start applying it in a few areas of your life. And if you still want to file a grievance against me with the Career Development Department, just think how many more serious complaints you will have after the end of the third session."

Laughter and applause erupted across the room in welcome relief after the heavier moments.

Brock continued, amiably now, "Joe, I know that you — like everyone else in this room — are a creative, talented human being who deep down wants to make a real difference in this world. If you stay and support all the other people in this room in making their lives better, they will support you in making your life better."

He then turned his attention back toward the audience and asked, "Who here wants to support Joe in staying and making a major contribution, not only to this group, but to his own life?"

All the other participants, including Sheldon, put up their hands.

"So what's it going to be, Joe? Are you going to sell out on your fellow students by leaving, or are you going to display a good deal of valor and class by staying?"

A few moments of silence elapsed before Joe, in an almost inaudible voice, stated, "Okay, I can agree to stay until the end of this seminar but I'll decide later whether I want to go to the next two."

Everyone in the room applauded as Joe walked back to his chair and sat down.

"Thank you, Joe," responded Brock. "I want to personally acknowledge you for showing courage in making the difficult decision to stay. Trust me, if you make more of these types of decisions in your life, you are going to make a big difference in this world. You may even be destined for incredible fame and fortune."

Brock walked back to the podium, where he stood for about thirty seconds before he continued. "Look, I don't want anyone thinking that Joe is any different from anyone else in this room. This includes me. We all have the tendency to bail out of important projects when the going gets tough. In fact, we often quit important projects because of minor irritations instead of major ones."

Sheldon, still highly attentive to the seminar proceedings, was surprised to hear Brock's next words.

"Let me share a personal example about the price we pay when we give up in the face of a bit of discomfort. I quit my university undergraduate program in engineering twice before I finally finished it. One time I stayed out an extra year. This cost three years total. If I had completed the program in four years, instead of seven, I would have discovered what I wanted to do with my life a lot sooner.

"The important point here is that giving up — whether for a minor or a major reason — is the easy way out, and normally creates a lot of regret, frustration, and dejection in our lives. Clearly, quitting important projects when the going gets tough isn't going to bring any of us accomplishment, achievement, or satisfaction. So Joe, thanks again for making an important contribution by showing us all that it takes courage to continue important assignments in the face of the temptation to quit."

This exchange between Brock and Joe would prove to have a measurable impact on Sheldon, particularly in regard to whether he should quit college.

> Trust not what inspires other
> members of society to choose a
> career.
>
> Trust what inspires you.
>
> From this decision alone will come
> over a third of your satisfaction or
> misery in life.

****

Next there was a short coffee break, during which Sheldon overheard three of the trainees amiably talking with great admiration about Brock's ability to keep them off-balance with his verbal karate. Other trainees discussed the episode between Joe and Brock, acknowledging Brock's remarkable skill in getting Joe to stay until the end of the seminar.

For a few seconds Sheldon fantasized about what it would be like to conduct personal development seminars and handle the seminar participants with the same psychological dexterity as Brock. He dismissed this as nothing more than a fantasy, though, because he didn't think he could ever develop the knowledge and skills required to become a seminar presenter.

> Thank God that life isn't always easy.
>
> Where would your satisfaction come from?
>
> And the boredom would be unbearable.

The second half of the seminar centered on The Easy Rule of Life as it pertained to getting more satisfaction in life, avoiding most of life's problems, and the importance of keeping agreements. Brock began by emphasizing the folly of striving for total comfort in one's life.

"This statement always surprises many people in my sessions: Living in total physical comfort doesn't mean personal fulfillment, nor does it mean personal joy or a feeling of success. In fact, the lust for total comfort is a hindrance to success."

"What's wrong with wanting to be comfortable in life?" asked Ron, a lanky, bearded man with brown shoulder-length hair tied back in a ponytail.

"The choice of comfort is a paradox," replied Brock. "Most of us need to tackle and conquer challenging tasks before we can experience a sense of accomplishment and satisfaction. It's so easy to forget what brings us true satisfaction in our lives."

Brock paused, directed his glance from Ron to the general audience, and then stated, "To make my point, allow me to ask if anyone in this room has ever experienced an incredible high after you accomplished something that you initially didn't think you could do, or something that everyone else said couldn't be done. Well?"

About twenty hands went up. Brock directed his words at a woman in the front row. "Yes, Lynda, what was the difficult thing that you accomplished?"

"I quit smoking when most of my cigarette-smoking friends didn't think I could," smiled Lynda. "Actually, even I had serious doubts that I could quit."

"How long did you smoke before you quit?" asked Brock.

"About ten years, I guess."

"And was it easy to quit?"

"No, in fact, it was probably the most difficult thing that I ever did," replied Lynda, "Smoking was a mental curse on me, much more than a physical addiction. I tried quitting and went back to smoking after two or three weeks. This happened several times. I must have tried for three years before I finally quit for good."

"Did you feel a remarkable sense of achievement after quitting?"

"Very much so; I still do," Lynda said with great enthusiasm and pride. "This has to be one of the top three accomplishments in my life. It gave me incredible satisfaction and elevated my self esteem a few notches, because of the feat I accomplished."

Brock then interjected, "Lynda, no doubt what you accomplished is one of the most difficult feats for millions of human beings. Yet by undertaking the difficult and uncomfortable, you achieved a great deal of satisfaction from your accomplishment. This was The Easy Rule of Life in action. Of course, we can't forget all the benefits of quitting smoking, such as more energy, less coughing, fewer colds, fewer respiratory problems, and reduced risk of lung cancer. These benefits will make your life a lot easier and more comfortable in the long term."

"I strongly agree," smiled Lynda.

After two more trainees shared their personal examples of difficult undertakings that brought them immeasurable satisfaction and higher self esteem, Brock summed up the segment of the seminar.

"If you think that you can experience great satisfaction without any substantial effort on your part, you're in for one of the biggest surprises of your life. Sustained effort over a long period of time on a challenging project is indispensable to eventually experiencing the satisfaction that comes with a sense of major accomplishment. In fact, you will find, as Lynda did when she quit smoking, that the greatest satisfaction comes from doing what others say is too difficult or impossible.

"As human beings we are naturally inclined to avoid discomfort and pursue more comfort and pleasure. Unfortunately, true success, and the satisfaction and happiness that accompany it, require that we experience discomfort to some degree. Generally speaking, the higher the price we have to pay in discomfort, the greater the prize we attain in satisfaction. And since satisfaction is an important element of happiness, experiencing struggle and discomfort actually add to happiness.

"Most people today can't bear a little physical discomfort, dejection, or hard times without feeling hard done by. Don't be one of them. Learn to deal with discomfort, and you'll have an incredible advantage over most of the people living in North America and other Western nations. The more you can hold up to the trials and tribulations of life, the more successful and happier you will become."

Never feel guilty about experiencing a few comforts in this world.

Bear in mind, however, that comfort is a double-edged sword.

A little will increase health and happiness.

Too much, and it will destroy both.

****

Brock introduced the next topic, on how to avoid most of life's problems, by asking, "Does anyone have a special problem that you would like to share with the rest of us?"

Belinda, a dark-haired, attractive young woman, related how she got a $75 speeding ticket driving to the seminar. She blamed the police officer who issued her the ticket.

Brock responded with: "So, who caused the speeding ticket, Belinda?"

"The policeman," replied Belinda. "He was unfair. I was very late and I was in a hurry."

"So who's responsible for your being late? The police officer certainly didn't make you late. Being late is a choice. It may be an unconscious choice but it's a choice that you made. For some reason you believe that evil forces are creating your speeding ticket, and that you are so special and doing everything right. I can assure you that you aren't. I didn't get a speeding ticket coming here. Guess why I didn't get one?"

"You were lucky and I wasn't," stated Belinda belligerently.

"No, Belinda, not even close. The reason that Brock Mellor doesn't get speeding tickets is that he doesn't speed anymore," announced Brock. "About ten years ago he received three speeding tickets within a period of six months. In each case the police officer told him that they were allowing ten miles an hour over the speed limit. Brock Mellor eventually realized what a fool he was, and decided to take responsibility for his speeding tickets. He now doesn't have to pay speeding tickets and he has low insurance rates that are the envy of all compulsive speeders. Most important, his chances for getting in an accident are reduced immensely."

Brock continued, "Note that I didn't blame the police officers. I took responsibility and blamed myself. No excuses.

And guess what? Applying The Easy Rule of Life makes my life easy. I do the difficult and uncomfortable, and stick to the speed limits. Heck, I don't even have to stick to the speed limits because all the traffic police allow five to ten miles over the speed limits. And people like you still get speeding tickets and blame the cops for your predicament instead of yourself."

"I don't care what you say," snapped Belinda. "I'm going to fight the speeding ticket."

"Well, Belinda, go ahead and fight the speeding ticket but it will just drain you of time and energy that you could use in improving your life. You may even get lucky and win on a technicality. But it won't help you in the long run. You will still end up getting speeding tickets and paying high insurance rates. You may even cause a serious accident with dire consequences one day. You won't eliminate speeding tickets until you realize that you are the one and only cause of those tickets. You have to acknowledge that the cops are wonderful people for issuing you those tickets."

Avoid blaming other forces for your biggest problems and mistakes.

Otherwise you must also give these same forces full credit for your most cherished successes.

After Belinda, three more trainees each shared a personal problem. One trainee had wound up in a fight with her husband that morning, another had gotten fired from his job the week before for getting mad at the boss, and the third trainee couldn't pay his rent on time as a result of having spent more money than he earned. In each case, Brock emphasized that the trainee was solely responsible for her or his respective problem.

"As they say in the Southern States, the biggest troublemaker in your life is the person who you see in the mirror every morning, applying makeup to your face or shaving it. There shouldn't be any doubt that we are the authors of most of our personal problems. The consequences that we are experiencing are on account of our own behavior but too many of us are consumed with trying to pass the blame onto others. Unless we realize that we alone are creating our problems, we will have to keep paying for our actions over and over again.

"Believe me, whenever you're facing any predicament that you find yourself in, the best idea is to point the finger at yourself first. A number of your present problems are the result of decisions you made and things you did in the past. Many of the problems you will experience in the future will be dependent on decisions you make and actions you take today and tomorrow.

"Our actions in life have reactions in the form of penalties, which are sometimes much more than the action would seem to justify. Some people have difficulty in making a connection between their actions and the eventual penalties because the penalty isn't always obvious or immediate. If you fail to see these connections, you may end up living in misery for a long, long time.

"Action is required to rectify any shortcomings in your life. In many situations, standing around looking for someone to whom you can transfer blame can be extremely dangerous. For example, if you were to encounter a grizzly bear on a hiking trip, it would be idiotic to stand around figuring out who was to blame for your predicament. A much more intelligent response would be to find any means possible of rapid escape. Later, when you insist on blaming someone, blame yourself for putting yourself into that predicament.

"You aren't a helpless being, subjected to dark and mysterious forces. So, the next time that you catch yourself complaining about a traffic jam, blame the culprit who put you there — YOU! Also, consider that you are just as responsible for the traffic problem as all the other drivers on the freeway."

Brock paused and then stated, "Incidentally, you have a lot of control over this predicament. Does anyone know the best way to solve a traffic jam?"

Ting, the humorous Oriental man, wasted no time in responding to Brock's question. "The way to solve a traffic jam is to get yourself out of your car the first chance you get. Then you won't have any traffic problem."

"Ting, well done. This is precisely the answer I was looking for," Brock smiled in agreement. "When you stop blaming the rest of the world for your problems, you gain power and control over your life. It's wise to take responsibility for problems in every area of your life. Hold yourself accountable for getting yourself out of any predicament instead of looking to the circumstances and people in your life. You must be hard on yourself and gentle toward everyone else. Then you have a chance of identifying the true cause of your problems."

Erica, the jovial and radiant woman in her mid-twenties, who early in the session had questioned Brock about whether he was advocating excessive suffering with The Easy Rule of Life, caught Brock's attention and asked, "Aren't you liable to start hating yourself when you blame yourself for all your problems?"

"Erica, that's a very good point and I'm glad that you brought this up. I'm not suggesting that you blame yourself in a vicious and derogatory manner. The key is to take responsibility for your problems in a loving manner. Congratulate yourself for having created these problems so that you have the challenge and satisfaction of solving them. In this way, you will be creating the space for a life worth living.

"Let me sum up what it takes to reduce the number of problems that you have to solve. Above all else, the key to avoiding speeding tickets, angry spouses, getting fired from a job, financial difficulties, and most of life's other perplexities is to think about the consequences of your actions before you make them, instead of after it's too late. This will do wonders for reducing the number of problems you have to deal with. Reducing the number of personal problems is a simple matter of applying The Easy Rule of Life, along with continually reminding yourself that it's easier to stay out of trouble than to get out of trouble once you're in it."

Brock's last words, *"it's easier to stay out of trouble than to get out of trouble once you're in it,"* were important enough for Sheldon to record in his personal notebook, later that night. Mysteriously, he would also encounter these same words in *Life's Secret Handbook*.

Stay away from nasty people and
extremely dangerous situations.

All told, it's always easier to stay out
of trouble than to get out of trouble.

****

"Tonight, the last issue that we will address involves the application of The Easy Rule of Life as it relates to keeping agreements," announced Brock.

"The truth is, underachievers aren't good at keeping agreements. One of the most important reasons that your lives don't work the way you would like them to is that you choose to break agreements, not only with yourself, but also with other people. You are like the average North American, looking for as much recreation, entertainment, and cheap thrills as you can get at the expense of not keeping agreements.

"Needless to say, the reason that you break agreements is that it can be difficult and uncomfortable to keep them. More often than not, in the short term, it is easier and more comfortable to break agreements. Sadly, though, when you break agreements, you set aside accomplishment, satisfaction, success, prosperity, and happiness. In the long run, the more agreements you break, the more uncomfortable and difficult your life becomes.

"Here is a simple test to determine how committed you are to keeping agreements and making your life work: Do you do the things that you say you are going to do? In other words, do you keep your agreements with yourself and others? This applies to seemingly insignificant items like calling a person when you say you will. If you aren't doing the small things that you claim you will, it's highly unlikely that you will be committed to achieving larger goals in life."

Brock noticed a hand go up in the middle of the room and nodded toward the man. "Yes, Ron."

Ron, the bearded man with his hair tied back in a ponytail, who had earlier questioned Brock about what was wrong with wanting a comfortable life, now remarked, "I can see why I should keep important agreements with others but I'm not going to waste my time and energy keeping trivial or unimportant agreements."

"REALLY," scoffed Brock, putting down his glass of water with a thud to show displeasure at what he just heard. "RON, WHY DO YOU THINK SO MANY AGREEMENTS ARE BROKEN, CAUSING PEOPLE TO DRASTICALLY MESS UP THEIR LIVES? EVERY TIME SOMEONE WANTS TO BREAK AN IMPORTANT AGREEMENT, THEY AUTOMATICALLY DEEM IT AS UNIMPORTANT, TO ALLOW THEMSELVES TO FEEL COMFORTABLE WITH BREAKING IT.

"FOR EXAMPLE, IF SOMEONE OWES YOU $50, THAT'S AN IMPORTANT AGREEMENT. OF COURSE, IT SHOULDN'T BE BROKEN UNDER ANY CIRCUMSTANCES! BUT, IF YOU OWE SOMEONE ELSE $100, THIS EASILY BECOMES A TRIVIAL AGREEMENT! RIGHT, RON?"

Plenty of laughter erupted, causing Ron to blush a bit, and forcing Brock to pause a few seconds.

"Ron, I'm not implying to your fellow students that you won't pay me back a loan of $100 if I make it to you. I have no reason to doubt you or your payment. The point I want to emphasize is that people's minds have a tendency to evaluate the importance of an agreement on the basis of how much they feel like keeping it at the moment.

"The human mind will opt for the comfort of not having to go through with agreements, even if the long-term consequences are severe. The long-term consequences of breaking agreements with others can be a loss of integrity, reputation, and friendship. The long-term consequences of continually breaking agreements with yourself are just as serious and will include no true accomplishment, no satisfaction, low self-esteem, and little peace of mind."

To desire prosperity and riches
without having earned them
honestly through your own
creative efforts is to desire the
manifestation of a great mistake.

Brock then addressed the general audience, "Now, I would like every one of you to identify an activity that is important to you, something that will bring some major benefits to your career plans or to your personal well-being. At the same time, you must make an agreement or a contract with yourself to accomplish this within a certain time frame. It's important that you write down this agreement.

"If you are unclear about the type of wording to use, here is one of many agreements that I made with myself when I was first starting out as a seminar instructor and professional speaker."

Brock motioned for Sheldon to project the visual of sample agreement onto the overhead screen.

Personal Agreement

I, Brock Mellor, in pursuit of a more fulfilling life, do hereby agree to read one book every two weeks for the next year. My goals are:

1. To increase my knowledge of the world
2. To develop my career
3. To develop my ability to communicate with others
4. To learn what constitutes a bestselling book so that I can eventually write one myself

A few minutes later Brock looked around the room. Everyone was busy writing except Terry, the man who along with Joe had caused the disturbance earlier in the session.

"Terry, you aren't writing anything down," remarked Brock, as he edged away from the podium, closer to where the trainee was seated.

"It seems pretty stupid for us to have to write out agreements," declared Terry, "It's a lot of needless work that won't . . ."

"BE CLEAR ABOUT ONE THING REGARDING AGREEMENTS, TERRY," Brock warned. "WHAT I'VE DISCOVERED OVER THE YEARS IS THAT WRITING OUT AGREEMENTS SEEMS STUPID AND A LOT OF NEEDLESS WORK ONLY TO PEOPLE WHO ARE MASTERS AT NOT KEEPING AGREEMENTS."

A subdued wave of laughter broke out across the room.

After taking a sip of water out of his glass, Brock continued in a softer, more patient voice. "On the other hand, people who keep agreements have integrity and think that it's intelligent — and not much work at all — to write out their agreements. They record what is important to them and how they are going to attain it.

"By recording their agreements, they show commitment, unlike people who are too lazy to write things down. Therefore, Terry, if you want to get anywhere worth going in this world, I would suggest that you do what highly effective people do and not what hard-core underachievers and misfits do."

Terry, a little agitated, stared at Brock momentarily but said no more. After a few seconds, he started writing.

Later, after everyone had finished recording their personal agreements, Brock stressed that the trainees must do their best to keep their agreements. If they broke their agreements, they had to be hard on themselves and recommit themselves to those agreements. To increase the chances of achieving their goals, they were to place their contracts where they could see them every day. A good idea was to hang them on their bedroom wall by the light switch, or put them on their desks, where they would stare at them when they sat down.

"Agreements are made to be kept rather than broken," Brock was saying a few minutes later. "In case you haven't noticed, the road to mediocrity — and even hell — is paved with good intentions and broken promises. To avoid being on this road for the rest of your lives, you must develop the habit of keeping your agreements. This involves the issue of commitment, which is more than just saying that you're committed. Commitment is about keeping your word, no matter what happens. Being committed to your dreams means you have the intense desire to achieve them, regardless of what barriers appear in your way.

"The high achievers of the world know that they must have commitment to get satisfaction out of anything worth pursuing. It's one thing to talk about goals and dreams, and determine what must be done to achieve them. Most people can reach this point. Where most people fail is in keeping the agreements they make to pursue those goals and dreams. Inaction renders goals and dreams, and the ways for attaining them, worthless.

"Someone once said that after all is said and done, more is said than done. Without even looking for distractions, we will encounter many of them, to help us forget agreements that we make with ourselves and others. Consequently, you must let your integrity and priorities — not your distractions — determine your actions.

"What's the point of making promises and announcing your personal dreams if you aren't going to do anything with them? There comes a time when you have to realize that you have thought and planned and talked enough.

"The easy and comfortable part is to make promises and to talk about dreams. The difficult and uncomfortable part is to do something with them. Above all, remember that the day you start keeping your agreements, especially in the area of achieving goals and attaining your most precious dreams, is the day you start putting your mark on the world."

You may have a lot of life energy tied
up in your false beliefs about
successful people and your grudges
against them.

By letting go and detaching yourself
from these beliefs and grudges, you
get all that life energy back.

You can now use this life energy to
create achievement and prosperity
in your life – or you can use it to
make up even more mischief in
your mind.

****

"ARE THERE ANY QUESTIONS BEFORE I END THIS SESSION?" Brock asked suddenly.

Patrick, the large man in the leather jacket, posed the first question.

"Brock, earlier you said that we are largely responsible for practically all of our personal problems because of our previous actions. Isn't it possible that God predetermines most of the things that happen to us?"

Brock showed just a hint of a smile as he replied, "If you believe that most of life's events are preordained, then it's futile to spend time worrying about things that are beyond your control. Why not do your part and see what you *can* control? Don't leave everything in the hands of God. Buckle down and give him a hand with making your life work. Remember, he helps those who help themselves."

After answering a number of other questions posed by the trainees, Brock asked Sheldon to project the frame containing The Easy Rule of Life onto the overhead screen. Brock then proceeded with his summation.

"I suggest that you commit this diagram of The Easy Rule of Life, with its important message, to your memory. Never forget it. When something in your life isn't working the way you would like it to, think how you can use The Easy Rule of Life to get back on track.

"One or two of you may not accept The Easy Rule of Life today, or tomorrow, or in ten years, because it's easier to be a victim, and refuse to take responsibility for your lives. Nonetheless, some of you will accept it today and start seeing the results tomorrow. Some of you will resist this principle for a month or two. Then one day, you'll be walking down the street and The Easy Rule of Life will hit you like a ton of bricks.

"Then you'll realize that the degree to which you accept The Easy Rule of Life determines how much aliveness, accomplishment, satisfaction, and happiness you experience throughout your life. You'll start using it, and your life will change remarkably. You will want to kick yourself for having taken so much time to implement it. But at least you will have gotten your life to work at this point and you can go forward from here.

"Be clear that The Easy Rule of Life is unforgiving, especially to those with the victim mentality. Self-proclaimed victims seldom accomplish anything worthwhile. They put themselves through a great deal of disappointment and grief. Being a victim may make you feel secure, because it's familiar territory. Part of being a victim, and feeling secure about it, is using excuses. With an excuse — it doesn't even have to be a good one — you are set for life.

"There are no real payoffs, however, from offering excuses and maintaining victim consciousness all your life. These are just examples of focusing on the negative aspects of life, and there are two major problems with focusing on all the things that are wrong with the world.

"The first is that it simply doesn't do you any good. You can complain about the government or the unscrupulous corporations or all the alleged conspiracies or the super-rich people who control most of the money in this world. Nothing will happen, however, except that you'll waste a lot of time and energy by complaining.

"More important — much, much more important — is that complaining becomes an addiction. Once you get really good at complaining, you become a true professional and look for anything and everything to complain about. You get so immersed in complaining that it becomes a lifestyle, one devoid of creative accomplishment, success, and prosperity. In short, your life doesn't work and you are the sole reason — not the things you complain about — that your life isn't working.

"Being a victim is another negative path. It's a choice, just like being liberated. Being a victim is the easy choice, though, while being liberated is the more difficult, uncomfortable choice. The only way to liberation is through an altered state of mind, where we accept that it's not the circumstances that determine the quality of our lives; it's how we react to these circumstances.

"Liberation from recurring problems can be attained in all areas of your life. A major change for the better is possible if you are prepared to work for it by doing the difficult and uncomfortable.

"Whether it's changing careers, going into business for yourself, moving to another country, or finding a new mate, this liberation won't be easy at first. It will be a lot easier in the long term, however, than resigning yourself to a personal situation that leaves you somewhat comfortable, but without any liveliness or satisfaction.

"Keep The Easy Rule of Life in mind, and remember that there's no such thing as a free lunch. Everything worth having has a difficult and uncomfortable price. This includes friendship, love, financial independence, a balanced lifestyle, and freedom. Don't make the mistake of thinking that you can avoid paying the price or put it off until later. The sooner you begin paying the price, the sooner you will start enjoying happiness and satisfaction.

"Human beings are generally averse to undertakings that present the slightest of difficulties. Take advantage of this. Do a lot more difficult things and venture into the unknown, while other people are left doing the comfortable thing. Trust me, you will accomplish a lot. You will also experience a degree of satisfaction and happiness that escapes most people throughout their lives.

"Summing up, you must take responsibility for your lives if you want to create a paradise where you are happy and fulfilled. You have already taken a great deal of responsibility by choosing to be at this first seminar. One of my favorite authors, Richard Bach, stated, 'Every person, all the events of your life, are there because you have drawn them there.'

"Therefore, let's say that at some level you took responsibility and utilized your tremendous mental powers to encourage me to do this seminar for you. In other words, you created me being here. As a matter of fact, if it wasn't for all of you asking me to be here, I could be cycling around Stanley Park, wining and dining with my friends at Stepho's Greek restaurant on Davie, or working on my new book about The Easy Rule of Life right now.

"I'm glad that you created the opportunity for me being here, however. There is no greater satisfaction in my work than learning sometime down the road that people have received some real benefit from it. That has been the case with all the classes that I have presented in the past. I hope that this one is the same."

****

Attaining freedom in a generally unfree world is not well understood by less adventurous souls.

You experience your personal world – free or unfree – according to what you focus on and what you create for yourself.

After the session was over, Sheldon noticed that at least half of all the attendees came up to the front of the auditorium to compliment Brock for a job well done. This didn't surprise Sheldon. He didn't expect, however, to overhear half of these attendees go out of their way to praise Brock for handling the distraction caused by Joe and Terry effectively.

These attendees felt that too many of their previous seminar teachers hadn't done enough to create discipline in their classes. Sheldon realized that other teachers didn't work to create discipline because it was too difficult. He concluded that this example proved that Brock practiced what he preached. He certainly followed The Easy Rule of Life by doing the difficult and uncomfortable to get discipline in his seminar.

Overall, Sheldon was highly impressed with Brock's passionate approach and inspirational performance as a seminar instructor. Throughout the session Brock seemed to pay perfect attention to what everyone in the audience was saying. He seemed to be able to not only listen to the trainees' words, but also to understand the emotional basis for the words. Sheldon was also impressed with Brock's unorthodox presentation style, one that only a creative and bold person would adopt.

> If your success is not achieved
> according to your ideals, if your
> success is impressive to society but
> does not resonate with your psyche
> and spirit, then it is not true
> success at all.

Sheldon even got a big kick out of Brock's performance. He knew that he wasn't the only one; he overheard several female trainees expressing great admiration — even infatuation — for Brock and his self-confidence in handling himself in front of an audience. Again, Sheldon imagined what it would be like to be a professional speaker, but he had serious doubts that he could ever overcome his fear of public speaking.

> Those who are different change the world.
>
> Those who are ordinary do their best to keep it the way it is.

After all the trainees finally left, Brock brought out five new, crisp $20 bills and handed them to Sheldon.

"Sheldon, thanks for assisting me. You did a great job. Don't spend all this money in one place."

"Actually, I find it hard to believe that you're paying me $25 an hour to assist you. I'll have a hard time getting a full-time job that pays this much, even after I graduate."

Brock shook his head. "As I said in the session, be careful with your beliefs. You may not believe that you're worth $25 an hour, but there are people who will pay you even more, provided you always do a good job. In regard to graduating, I hope I'm hearing that you're going to finish your degree instead of quitting to get a full-time job and buy a car."

"Actually, I have decided," said Sheldon. He brought out his personal notebook to show Brock something he had written during the session.

Personal Agreement

I, Sheldon Brown, in pursuit of a more fulfilling life, do hereby agree to finish my college degree in the next five months. I also agree to:

1. Find a great job after I graduate
2. Exercise my will power by living without a car for a few more months
3. Increase my self-esteem and show my mother that I can accomplish something important
4. Buy a Mercedes 190 SL within five years

Brock and Sheldon carried on a friendly conversation as they packed up Brock's audio-visual equipment. When they were finished, Brock gave Sheldon a ride home in his Mercedes 190 SL, which he had brought especially so that Sheldon could enjoy the experience of riding in it. When he dropped Sheldon off at his aunt's house, Brock invited Sheldon to have dinner with him and his girlfriend at his home.

If it lacks integrity, it's not worth pursuing.

Success without integrity — isn't!

******* *****************

3

Experience your uncertain ventures with a good measure of glee.

To be delighted while on the rocky road to success and prosperity is not generally understood by less-adventurous souls.

They will think that you are crazy.

This is the fun part.

After Brock's first seminar, Sheldon felt a lot more positive about life. He was also more motivated to complete his marketing degree at City College. He was now attending all of his classes and forcing himself to study two to three hours every day. He still didn't find it easy to go to college, and it certainly wasn't easy being without a car by any stretch of the imagination. Still, he remembered something Reverend Thomas often used to say to him: *"Sure, life's tough. The question you have to ask yourself is, next to what?"*

On the Sunday following the first seminar, Sheldon traveled to Brock's house. It was a cloudy afternoon but at least it was warm and there was no rain. During the walk from his aunt's house in East Vancouver to the trendy Kitsilano area where Brock lived, Sheldon maintained a positive state of mind. He realized that it was only a matter of time until he was in a financial position to buy a car and not have to walk as much. This would only happen, though, if he finished his college program.

As Sheldon neared Brock's house on Ogden Avenue between Maple and Cypress streets, he recalled that he'd walked on this street two or three times before, wishing that he could live in this part of Vancouver. He had even thought that it would be nice just to know someone on this block so that he could visit one of the interesting houses, each worth well over $1 million.

When he arrived at Brock's address, Sheldon saw a modern two-story house with cedar siding, lots of windows, and skylights in the roof. It wasn't a mansion, likely only about 1,500 square feet. Nonetheless, it was a unique home, obviously custom-designed by an architect, with comfort and openness written all over it.

Sheldon climbed the steps and rang the door bell. A few seconds later, an attractive dark-haired woman, who looked to be in her late thirties, opened the front door.

"Hello, I'm Silvina. Brock calls me his girlfriend, though sometimes I wonder if I'm the only one," the woman joked. "You must be Sheldon."

"Yes, I am," Sheldon said as the two shook hands. "Brock mentioned you in the seminar. It's a pleasure to meet you."

"It's a pleasure to meet you too, Sheldon," said Silvina warmly. "Come in."

"Where's Brock?" Sheldon wondered out loud as he entered the living room.

"He's upstairs working on his new book while I prepare dinner. Usually when Brock and I have dinner here at his house, I let him cook and wash the dishes. I tell him that my contribution is my witty conversation," laughed Silvina. Brock unexpectedly walked into the living room, and Silvina continued. "Today, however, I'm preparing the meal so he doesn't get too overworked. You know it's really hard on Brock's ego if he has to work more than four or five hours in a day."

"Ha, ha, Silvina," smiled Brock. "Perhaps you should let me tell some of the jokes around here."

He then turned toward Sheldon. "Hi, Sheldon, I'm glad that you could make it. It occurred to me this morning that there was a small chance you might decide against coming to dinner tonight. I thought that perhaps seeing me again would be too difficult for you, especially after attending my first seminar."

"Yeah, copping out on coming to see you tonight did cross my mind," joked Sheldon. "But sometimes I allow myself to be a masochist. That's why I'm here."

"Never mind with the barbs," replied Brock. "Silvina already gives me a rough enough time. That's her idea of witty conversation — trying to run me off my rails."

"Don't worry about running him off his rails. He can take it," smiled Silvina on her way to the kitchen. "Let me go and make the salad now so he doesn't complain about having to prepare any of the meal today. In the meantime, he can give you a tour of his house, if you'd like to see the rest of it."

"Yes, I would," Sheldon agreed. "The house looks really interesting."

After Brock had shown Sheldon the other rooms, all tastefully designed and furnished, they came to his study on the second floor. It was furnished more lavishly than many executives' corporate offices.

"You have a beautiful house with a wonderful study for yourself," observed Sheldon. "How did you ever manage to get enough money to pay off this great home in just seven years? Most ordinary people take out a mortgage and don't pay it off for twenty or twenty-five years."

"It was simply a matter of applying The Easy Rule of Life to my career so that I ended up earning enough money, and applying it to my financial affairs so that I ended up saving enough," Brock said. "For several years I lived a simple lifestyle that most people would consider way below their comfort level. I drove rusted out cars and lived in cheap apartments that people wouldn't want to be caught dead in. While doing this, I was able to save more money than most people making three times as much as me."

"It seems like The Easy Rule of Life," remarked Sheldon, "can end up being an obsession."

"Indeed it can, but it's a good obsession to have," replied Brock. "Despite the fact it can become an obsession if you let it, using The Easy Rule of Life can be a guide for creating a better life. Following this principle is important for continually accomplishing bigger and better things than most other people, including paying off a decent home within a few short years."

"Easy for you to say, after you've done it," asserted Sheldon. "What can I do to pay off a house this quickly?"

"First, finish your college degree and then get yourself an enjoyable career, so that you end up making decent money."

"I'm not sure what sort of job will do that for me," shrugged Sheldon.

"What would you like to be doing more than anything else in this world?" Brock asked.

"Making a lot of money," Sheldon said at once. "Aside from that, I'm not sure."

"That's not good enough," advised Brock. "You have to be more specific. Take the time to discover what you really enjoy doing and then do it. This can be extremely difficult but that isn't a reason for not doing it.

"It's important to find work that you're enthusiastic about, without regard to how much money you can make in the first few years. People who are working at what they love, and developing as human beings at the same time, are naturally successful in their jobs. Eventually they end up making a lot of money, although this isn't their primary goal."

If you aren't as successful and prosperous in life as you would like to be, who do you have to become before success and prosperity flow easily into your world?

"Okay, the ideal for me is to be just like you," admitted Sheldon. "After watching you perform in your seminar, I would like to be a professional speaker. But I don't have the talent for it. That leaves me having to settle for second best, which is to get a full-time job in marketing once I graduate."

"Trust me," Brock insisted, "you have the talent to be either a professional speaker or a marketing specialist. It's a matter of learning what is necessary to be proficient at the work you choose to do."

"I don't believe that I could ever overcome my fear of speaking in front of a large group of people and become a professional speaker."

"Why not? You don't think that I was born a public speaker, do you?"

"Well," observed Sheldon, "you certainly have no fear of speaking in front of seventy-three people."

"I don't today," agreed Brock. "In fact, I could speak in front of ten thousand people and it wouldn't be any different from speaking to twenty. At one time, however, I was just as afraid of public speaking as you are now — possibly a lot more. I was too afraid to even speak up in my university classes, and there were only nine people in one of the classes. I lived in constant fear that one of my professors was going to ask me a question. The one time that one of them did, my voice quivered and I was shaking inside when I spoke a few words to answer."

"How did you get over your fears?"

"I simply did the difficult and uncomfortable. I didn't even go to Toastmasters like many people do. First, I applied to be a teaching assistant while I was working on my MBA. My job was to present a tutorial to ten undergraduate students. Although the students thought that I did a lousy job, presenting the tutorial was enough to ease my fear of speaking just a bit."

> You have dedicated the years you
> have lived on Earth so far to
> become the person that you are
> today.
>
> ## Has it been worth it?

Brock continued. "Later, when I landed an instructor's job at a private vocational school, I still experienced incredible fear, especially the first day when I walked into my first two classes. One class had eighty-five students and the other had seventy-nine. I was so terrified that I ended these two classes after fifteen minutes. When I got home that evening, I made a written agreement with myself, much like the one I showed in the seminar. My agreement was that come hell or high water — even if teaching these courses killed me — I would confront my fears and stick it out as an instructor until the end of the term."

"That must have been extremely hard to do," offered Sheldon.

"Yes it was hard but not nearly as hard or long as I figured it would be. Incidentally, this was when I first noticed the concept of The Easy Rule of Life and the power behind it. When I took the difficult and uncomfortable route, things turned out just fine. After only about a week, my fears greatly subsided. By the end of the term I was enjoying being an instructor so much, and doing so well, that I didn't want to quit. I even wound up with better student evaluations than all of the other instructors at the vocational school."

"So, being an instructor at a vocational school made it easy for you to enter the field of professional speaking?" asked Sheldon.

"It was a start, but it still wasn't easy yet. To be a professional speaker at conferences and conventions, you have to be a good speaker but that's not enough by itself. You also need a measure of fame."

"How does a person attain some fame?"

"If you aren't a sports, movie, or news-media celebrity, writing a book can get you there. In my case, having written *Thinking Big in a Small World* helped me get credibility with conference organizers."

"You mean that I also have to write a book to make it as a professional speaker?" asked Sheldon. "That definitely leaves me out of the picture."

"Why? At one time I didn't think that I could write a book either," Brock divulged. "In fact, I failed my first-year English course three times in a row. The university wouldn't allow me into my fourth year until I passed the course in summer school. As long as you're literate, you can author a book. A book is nothing more than a long essay or term paper."

"Aren't some people born with a knack for writing?" wondered Sheldon.

"No doubt some people are born with more talent than others. This superior talent gives them greater potential for excelling at certain things, including becoming an accomplished author. Nevertheless, writing a book is largely dependent on commitment and perseverance," advised Brock.

"Take me, for example. I know my limitations as a writer. My writing abilities will never approach those of George Bernard Shaw, Jean Paul Sartre, or any other winner of the Nobel Prize in Literature. Clearly, giving me the Nobel Prize for Literature would lead to rioting on the streets in all the world's major cities.

"But I won't allow my limitations to stop me from writing the books that I know I'm capable of writing. A week doesn't pass by where I don't meet someone much smarter and literarily more capable than I am. These people desperately want to write a book but haven't gotten around to it. Yet I have done it. What I realized some time ago is that I can't write a book on the same level as William Shakespeare but I can write a book by me.

"Above all, my writing accomplishments are a result of my agreement with myself to write a minimum of three hours a day. I try to write four pages during this time. These pages don't have to be masterpieces. Sometimes they contain some pretty pathetic writing, but at least I have four pages to work with. Even if I break my agreement to write three hours a day, and instead only write for fifteen minutes, I am still closer to completing a book than people who continually talk about writing one, but never get around to it. You may have noticed that it seems to take eternity to complete something you aren't working on."

"Can a person take a course on writing books?" asked Sheldon.

"Definitely! But it's not necessary."

"What's the alternative?"

"As the Nike logo advises, 'Just Do It,' " advised Brock. "In other words, do the difficult and uncomfortable and just start writing. Most famous writers never took a course on how to write books."

"Most famous writers are likely highly talented individuals. Therefore, they would find it easy to write books."

"Not at all," countered Brock. "Richard Bach wrote several bestsellers, inclu ding *Jonathan Livingston Seagull*, but he admitted that it was tough for him to write. Ernest Hemingway claimed that he often read his previous works to cheer himself up and remind himself how difficult and how nearly impossible it appeared sometimes. Joseph Heller, the author of *Catch-22*, summed it up very well when he stated that all great writers have difficulty writing."

"Then why do writers choose to write if it's so difficult?"

"If you truly want to be a writer, deep down, then not writing will eventually become more difficult and uncomfortable than writing. The same applies if you want to be a public speaker or anything else that provides a satisfying and fulfilling livelihood. As someone once said, 'It's not what you become but what you don't become that you will regret most in the end.' "

"Not all people who pursue their goals of being public speakers and authors attain their goals," noted Sheldon.

"Yes," agreed Brock, "but when you actively pursue what you truly want to do, you increase your chances for success infinitely over someone who just dreams and talks about it. Allow me to paraphrase Henry David Thoreau. If a person advances confidently in the direction of his dreams, and tries to live the life that he has imagined, he will meet with much greater success than those who haven't pursued their dreams at all."

At that, Sheldon posed another question. "Then why don't most people who dislike their jobs pursue more satisfying careers?"

"Given the choice between pursuing something better, or continuing on with a life of grindstone existence, most people opt for the grindstone existence. They will tolerate abusive bosses, lousy working conditions, and boring, dead-end jobs simply because it takes time and energy to find a better job.

"Furthermore, pursuing a better career requires change, risk taking, and other major sacrifices, such as having a lower income for a year or two. Most people find that it's easier to stay with the familiar, even if it offers nothing more than boredom and drudgery.

"Even so, many people are prepared to make the difficult and uncomfortable sacrifices in order to create an easier and more comfortable world for themselves some time in the future. For example, John Grisham certainly couldn't have attained his incredible success if he hadn't been prepared to quit his law practice so that he could pursue his dream of writing legal thrillers."

"It must be cool being a successful writer like him," Sheldon said wistfully.

"Wanting to be cool isn't a good reason to take up writing books," Brock countered. "People should write books because they like to write or because they have something important to share with others. Of course, there are many benefits from being an accomplished author, but I wouldn't count being cool as one of them."

"Making lots of money has to be the biggest benefit," offered Sheldon.

> Working strictly for money isn't the
> way to true success in life.
>
> Stop and ponder money in new
> ways and you will realize many
> aspects of it are totally absurd.
>
> You will also realize that after basic
> necessities are provided for,
> happiness cares little about money.
>
> So, why should you care so much
> about it?

"Far from it," Brock noted. "There is no question that being an author offers one an opportunity to make a great deal of money in a short period of time. There are much greater payoffs, however — adventure, personal satisfaction, acknowledgment from readers, and even self-enlightenment.

"Most accomplished writers profess that the biggest reward isn't financial. It's the thrill of sharing their views of the world with others and having others tell them that they experienced pleasure — even spiritual fulfillment — from reading their books. You can share in these benefits if you're prepared to do all the difficult things necessary to write a book and make it a bestseller."

"Even if writing books is difficult, though, writing your second book on The Easy Rule of Life must be easier than writing your first book on creativity," suggested Sheldon.

"Not at all," Brock revealed. "In some ways, I'm finding the second book to be even more difficult. Every second day I feel like quitting the project, but I still keep to my agreement to work at it for three to four hours a day. As a matter of fact, after working on this book for three months, one of the most difficult things about it is trying to come up with a good title. I've generated at least one hundred titles but none of them really stands out. Nonetheless, I know that if I do the difficult and uncomfortable and keep searching, eventually I will find one."

"Why don't you simply call it *The Easy Rule of Life?*" asked Sheldon.

"Too boring," Brock reasoned. "I want a title that has a lot more zip to it. In fact, if you can think of a blockbuster title and I eventually use it, I'll pay you a cool $500 for it."

"Five hundred bucks!" exclaimed Sheldon. "Are you serious?"

"Of course, I'm serious. A good title can make a big difference in whether people pick up the book in a bookstore and end up buying it," said Brock. "A great title is also important for generating publicity."

"Well, for $500, I'll certainly give it a lot of thought," remarked Sheldon.

"Just don't let this distract you from your college studies," warned Brock.

He paused and looked at his watch. "Hey, I think we've talked long enough about writing and public speaking. Let's go have dinner or Silvina will share it with the neighbor's dogs just to get even with us for being late."

Over dinner, Sheldon found out more about Brock and Silvina. Silvina was Latin-American, having moved to Vancouver from Buenos Aires. Silvina and Brock met while playing tennis on the public courts by Kitsilano Beach. They often dined out at fine restaurants and occasionally traveled together to destinations like Hawaii and Greece. They were both athletic, dedicating at least an hour and a half each day to vigorous exercise in order to stay fit and maintain optimum health. Because Brock and Silvina were both highly independent individuals, they also liked to spend time alone. Silvina owned her own house about half a mile away from where Brock lived.

After dinner, Brock and Sheldon washed the dishes. In answer to Sheldon's question about why Brock didn't have a dishwasher in his otherwise well-equipped house, Brock replied that he didn't need all the comforts in the world to be a happy person. He also found many luxuries a waste of money, and pointed out that the reason many people have money problems is that they purchase luxuries that they could easily do without.

Later, while Sheldon, Brock, and Silvina carried on a pleasant conversation in the back yard, Sheldon looked at Brock and said, "Brock, I was just thinking how much I would like to get myself a great girlfriend like Silvina."

"That can be dangerous," joked Brock.

"Seriously, you could give me a hand," suggested Sheldon. "You can't drive two sports cars at once. Why don't you lend me either the Mercedes 190 or the Porsche 924 for a week so that I can impress the women at the college? I might wind up meeting a funky girlfriend this way."

Brock gave Sheldon the type of look that made Sheldon feel good that the two of them were friends, and not enemies.

Before he could reply, though, Silvina spoke. "Sheldon, if you have to impress a woman with a nice car before she'll think highly of you, you don't want that woman as your girlfriend. In the long term, she won't do you much good. She'll depend on you for money, but deep down she won't really love you."

"Didn't Brock have a nice car when you met him?" asked Sheldon.

"When I first met Brock, he was driving an old Toyota Celica. It was the worst car in the parking lot, regardless of where we went," Silvina laughed. "Before I met him, I dated some of the brightest, most handsome, and wealthiest men in Vancouver. They all owned big flashy cars, wore expensive and stylish clothes, and took me to the trendiest restaurants. Yet none of them impressed me like Brock did. What I liked about Brock was that he was different. He did his own thing and didn't need a nice car or other possessions to feel good about himself. He would also take me to a good restaurant such as Stepho's on Davie, instead of one where people go to be seen."

Brock smiled in agreement. "Silvina said it more eloquently than I could. The truth is, you aren't going to get yourself a great girlfriend like her by driving someone else's car. Oh, and one other thing, you won't truly appreciate driving an exotic sports car unless it's your own and you've earned it, either through your own hard work or through your creative efforts."

"Yeah, right," Sheldon said quickly. "More of The Easy Rule of Life and all the stuff that it applies to."

"You catch on quick, kid," quipped Brock.

Don't be afraid to be outrageous.

Your critics will say nasty things about you whether you are outrageous or not.

And your supporters will love you for it.

While Sheldon, Brock, and Silvina continued their pleasantries, a nine-year-old girl entered the yard through the back gate. Because she was physically handicapped, and unable to walk without support for her legs, she was pushing a walking stroller.

"Hi Silvina! Hi Brock!" she said cheerfully, with a beaming smile.

"Hi Korina," Silvina and Brock responded in unison.

Several seconds passed as Korina, still smiling, made her slow and laborious way across the backyard. When she was within several feet of the group, she directed her inquisitive gaze at Sheldon.

"What's your name?" she asked cheerfully. "My name's Korina."

Sheldon smiled back. "My name's Sheldon. How are you?"

"I'm fine," she said. "I came to visit Brock and Silvina. Brock is my neighbor and he and Silvina are my good friends. What are you doing here?"

"Well, Brock and Silvina aren't my neighbors, but I hope that I'll eventually be considered a special friend of theirs, just like you obviously are," Sheldon answered.

"Korina isn't just our special friend," Silvina remarked. "She's also an incredibly intelligent and remarkable person to many people."

Suddenly Korina turned her head and pointed past Silvina. "LOOK AT THE BUTTERFLY . . . LOOK . . . IT'S BEAUTIFUL!" she called out, trying to chase it. "WOULDN'T IT BE GREAT TO BE A BUTTERFLY?"

This expression of joy and wonder was just one of many that Korina displayed during the next hour and a half. She had a way of drawing people toward her and Sheldon was no exception. By the time Korina left for her home across the back alley from Brock's house, Sheldon was in total awe of her. Not once did she mention her handicap or seem psychologically immobilized by it.

Brock and Silvina would later tell Sheldon that Korina always seemed to enjoy life more than anyone she met, whether the person was someone her age or much older than her. She refused to acknowledge her handicap as anything that would limit her in the present or later in life. Her mother told her that everyone had some sort of handicap, whether it was being poor, being obese, having a lower IQ than someone else, or not being as healthy as someone with optimum health. And since Korina was exceptionally gifted intellectually, as proven by her top standing in all her classes since she started school, most people were handicapped compared to her on this point alone.

After Korina left, Brock looked at Sheldon, and said, "Well, how many adults have you ever seen with good health, no physical handicaps, high intelligence, a great education, and much material wealth, who show as much love for life as she does?"

"None," smiled Sheldon in agreement. "It's unbelievable that she doesn't have any victim mentality, despite her handicap. It's too bad that you couldn't have captured her on video today to show to your seminar participants."

"Actually," Brock advised, "Korina has been bugging me for the opportunity to see what I do as a professional speaker, so Silvina's bringing her to the next seminar. The trainees will be able to meet her and see what a truly joyful person she is. Not surprisingly, many people are inspired to greater heights after meeting her for the first time. Even negative people, who don't see much joy in life, find her to be a breath of fresh air."

Living just to get by is not enough.

Just like the butterfly, an adventurous soul needs a varied and enchanting life — green grass and happy skies, freedom to go where it pleases, and joys that await it.

****

4

When money is lost, little is lost;

When time is lost, much more is lost;

When health is lost, practically
everything is gone;

And when creative spirit is lost,
there is nothing left.

Sheldon arrived at the second seminar with much less skepticism than he had felt at the start of the first one. He helped set up the audio-visual equipment for Brock and handed out the name tags to the attendees. Soon he overheard the attendees talking about what had happened in the first session and wondering whether everyone would show up for the second session. As it turned out, everyone did, including Joe.

Silvina and Korina arrived at the auditorium about fifteen minutes before the seminar was scheduled to start. Korina made her way slowly to where Sheldon was sitting, to say hi and ask him what he was doing. After Sheldon explained how he was assisting Brock by operating the laptop, Korina went to sit with Silvina at the back of the room. Most of the attendees watched curiously as Korina made her slow but steady and determined way across the room. She smiled at anyone who appeared to be looking at her.

> You can't truly start loving others until you love yourself.
>
> The God source is within you and not outside you.
>
> Trust it and your love, laughter, and life will reflect it.

****

"Brock began the session in a much more relaxed and subdued manner than he had started the first one.

"Greetings," he said with a smile.

The attendees responded with hi's, hello's, and smiles in return.

Brock continued, "Tonight we are going to spend a great deal of time applying The Easy Rule of Life so that you become more creative in generating opportunities in your work and personal lives — a worthy enterprise, you'll agree. Then we'll try to inspire you to fail yourselves to success. Before we start on the power of creativity, however, let's find out if anyone received any value out of the last seminar — especially out of The Easy Rule of Life as it applies to giving up being a victim of your circumstances, and taking responsibility for your problems instead."

Surprisingly, Joe, who along with Terry had created the distraction in the first seminar, was the first trainee to speak. First, he apologized to the other trainees for having caused the distraction and thanked Brock for having persuaded him to stay until the end of the first seminar. Next, Joe talked about how he chose the difficult and uncomfortable route when he risked being rejected by a woman who he was really interested in.

"The first time it was really hard," he said. "I walked up to her in the library and made small talk with her for only about two minutes. I left thinking that she must have thought I was a real idiot. The next day, I saw the woman again. I figured I had made such a big fool of myself the day before that it didn't matter if I did it again. So I talked to her this time for about twenty minutes. And then I talked to her a third time for about two hours. I still can't believe it, but I'm taking her to the Cactus Club on English Bay for dinner on Saturday night."

Applause broke out throughout the room, and then Brock responded, somewhat facetiously, "Gosh, Joe, I was expecting you to tell us how you used The Easy Rule of Life to make some extra money in a new way and not how to spend big bucks on a hot date. Seriously, though, thanks for showing us how you have to take risks to get what you want in life."

Several other attendees shared how they had put The Easy Rule of Life to use in their own lives. One woman expressed how she had taken the difficult and uncomfortable route by taking responsibility for her friend always being late. She let the friend know that she wasn't going to put up with having to wait for him all the time. The next week, he showed up early.

Then the older man named Ben, the one who in the first seminar unsuccessfully argued that everyone's reality was just as valid as anyone else's, shared how his rude boss wasn't that rude anymore because he had refused to be victimized by him. Ben came to realize that when his boss called him a jerk, he didn't have to take the man's words personally. Ben also realized that whatever anger he felt after his boss spoke was something that Ben was allowing to happen after his boss's words. Therefore, Ben was the source of his own anger, and not his boss. By taking responsibility for his own anger, Ben was able to do away with it.

Ting was the fourth trainee to speak. He shared how he had cut another driver off in traffic. The other driver started shouting at him at the next red light. Ting took the difficult and uncomfortable route by admitting that it was his fault. The other driver was totally surprised by Ting's actions and acknowledged him for having the class and integrity to apologize.

Belinda, the woman who had received a speeding ticket on her way to the first session, was the last to contribute. She revealed how she had started applying The Easy Rule of Life, as it related to avoiding being a victim, immediately after the first seminar,

"For the most part, I was feeling victimized by my recent divorce. However, after I left here two Tuesdays ago, I vowed to change that and become responsible for my happiness. I chose to take a positive path instead of a negative one. It's only been two weeks, and things are getting better and better by the day. When I start getting into a negative space and feeling like a victim, I just convince myself that I don't have time for this stuff. It was hard at first. But things are actually easier and so much better after only two weeks."

To this, Brock added, "Belinda, things will get even better if you keep working at it. Researchers tell us that it takes a minimum of three weeks of intense daily practice before a new way of thinking is ingrained in our psyche. So keep at it, and then you'll reach a state where your divorce affects you very little compared to how much it affected you three weeks ago."

Brock walked back onto the stage, where he paused, and then added, "I would like to thank those who shared their experiences. From these experiences, all of you should be able to see the power of The Easy Rule of Life as it relates to giving up being a victim and taking responsibility for your circumstances. It's not a case of whether or not you will experience major problems, bad breaks, discrimination, and other inequities; it's a case of doing your best to overcome them. This can be difficult and uncomfortable in the short term but it can go a long way to making your life easier in the long term.

"Taking full responsibility for your problems will make a big difference in how much accomplishment, satisfaction, and success you attain. For you hard-headed people who still don't get it, life is not complicated at all," declared Brock with a big smile on his face. "If life is one big pain in the ass, you're living it wrong. You're doing too much of the easy and comfortable. Start doing more of the difficult and uncomfortable and life will be much less of a burden.

"Now let's move on to The Easy Rule of Life as it pertains to utilizing your creativity and how to capitalize on more of the opportunities all around you."

Anybody can come up with an idea.

This is easy.

But to take an idea and run with it,
to do something with it, at the
opportune time, for the right
purpose, in the right way – is
what adventurous, prosperous
souls succeed at.

That is not even close to being easy.

During the next hour and a half, Brock covered several aspects of creativity and how the trainees should apply The Easy Rule of Life to be more creative.

He began by citing seven important creativity principles that are difficult and uncomfortable to follow, but contribute to personal success in the long term. These were projected onto the overhead screen by Sheldon, so that the trainees could record them in their notebooks.

- Choose to be creative.
- Look for many solutions.
- Do something with your ideas.
- Don't overlook opportunities all around you.
- Don't resist failure.

• Dare to be different.

• Be persistent and pay your dues.

Brock then tried to convince everyone in the auditorium that they had creative abilities that they weren't even close to fully utilizing. He declared that creativity is a million-dollar asset that most people don't know they possess. And if they do know that they possess it, then they don't know its true value, or how to use it properly. Brock assured the audience that if they used various techniques, anyone could learn how to be more creative than they were in the past.

It didn't take long for Brent, the young, bushy-haired, and bearded man who in the first seminar had questioned Brock about why people should always challenge their beliefs, to question him about creativity.

"How can you say that creativity can be learned?" he asked. "Either you're born with it or you don't have it, period."

"Brent," Brock responded as he moved to the edge of the stage, "you obviously have many hard-core beliefs about many things, including creativity. As I stated earlier, belief is a disease. Let go of your beliefs, or they'll run your life.

"Forget whatever romantic notions you have about creativity. Creativity isn't a gift from God, given only to certain artists and musicians. Creativity also isn't dependent upon a lot of suffering nor is it associated with a touch of madness. It is often thought to be a matter of special skill, ability, knowledge, or effort. In fact, not one of these factors is essential for creative success. If you take a hard look at creative people, you'll see that they are simply being creative.

"Researchers in the field of creativity have found that everyone is born creative, but most people unconsciously suppress their own creative ability. Researchers have also found that the older people get, the less creative they become. A forty-five-year-old adult is only 5 percent as creative as a six-year-old child. Yet adults don't have to be this way. All it takes is time and effort for adults to rediscover their creativity.

"Mark Twain said, 'Thousands of geniuses live and die undiscovered — either by themselves or by others.' These geniuses remain undiscovered because they're too lazy to use their God-given talents. In every uncreative person, there is a creative person waiting to break out and make a difference in this world. In fact, it's harder in the long term to suppress one's creativity than to use it, but most of us will utilize one or more ways to suppress it. The reason for this is that, in the short term, it's easier and more comfortable to suppress our creativity than to use it. No doubt the easiest way for us to suppress our creativity is to claim that we simply aren't creative."

Next, Brock discussed the barriers to individuals being creative. The barriers included societal pressure to conform, educational institutions teaching that there is only one right answer, corporations not supporting creative employees, and people's own self-imposed barriers, such as their fear of taking risks. He stressed that these barriers hinder people's creativity and ultimately stifle their goals, hopes, desires, dreams, and prosperity.

Then Brock used several visual and verbal exercises to show how the trainees were suppressing their creativity. The exercise that made the most long-term impact on Sheldon was one stressing the importance of looking for many solutions.

After he motioned for Sheldon to project a frame onto the overhead screen, Brock explained the exercise.

"Assume that the equation on the screen is made with matchsticks. Each line in the characters is one matchstick, including the vertical line and the horizontal line in the plus sign. The two horizontal lines in the equal sign are also made from matchsticks. As you can see, the equation utilizes Roman numerals. The equation is wrong the way it stands. In other words, 6 plus 2 is not equal to 6. I would like you to use your creativity to make the equation correct by moving just one, and only one, matchstick."

Brock then repeated the nature and purpose of the exercise, so that the trainees clearly understood what they were supposed to do.

After about five minutes, Brock noticed a number of the trainees had quit working on the exercise. At this point he asked:

"Okay, has anyone completed the exercise?"

Over half of the trainees put up their hands. Sheldon also put up his hand. He felt good about himself, considering that over a third of the trainees couldn't find a solution.

"Now, who of you proud people with your hands up has more than one solution?" said Brock with a half-smile on his face.

Not one hand remained up.

"It's interesting that not one of you has more than one solution," Brock announced. "Let's go back to the seven principles of creativity that are difficult and uncomfortable to follow, but are necessary for achieving creative success."

Brock again asked Sheldon to project the seven principles of creativity onto the overhead screen before he continued.

"You will note what the second principle is: Look for many solutions. WHAT WE REALLY HAVE TO BE CLEAR ABOUT IS THAT THERE IS ALWAYS MORE THAN ONE SOLUTION TO ANY AND EVERY PROBLEM THAT WE ENCOUNTER ON OUR JOURNEY THROUGH LIFE.

"Yet most of us solve our personal, financial, and workplace problems in exactly the same manner as we attempt to solve this matchstick problem. We come up with one solution; sometimes we extend ourselves and find two, but we don't look any further. Then, when these solutions don't work very well, or don't work at all, we start blaming the world for our all unresolved problems. We blame society, the government, our parents, and our bosses at work. We even blame the weather and the neighbors' barking dogs.

"The truth is that we should be blaming ourselves for taking the easy and comfortable route by looking for only one or two solutions to our problems. If we took the difficult and uncomfortable route, we would find many more solutions, some of which would be more workable than others. The thing to remember is that the workable solution, especially the blockbuster one that blows the socks off other people, is usually the fifth, or even the tenth one, and not the first or second.

"So, let's take another ten minutes to see if any of you can generate more than one solution to this exercise. Heck, let's make this interesting. The person who generates the most solutions will win a copy of my recent book on creativity."

As the trainees followed Brock's instructions, Sheldon tried his best to come up with as many solutions as he could. In the end, he came up with only two, which were later pointed out by one of the trainees. Even if Sheldon had generated a larger number of solutions, he wouldn't have announced it. First, he didn't know if he, as Brock's assistant, was eligible to win the copy of *Thinking Big in a Small World*. Second, he thought that it would be too weird to win a copy of the book after having refused a copy from Brock the day that he met him.

After another ten minutes, Brock asked if anyone had generated five or more solutions to the exercise. No one had five, but Ting had four. Brock requested that Ting share his solutions with the rest of the audience.

"For my first solution," said Ting, "I took the vertical matchstick in the Roman numeral 6 on the left side of the equation and moved it to the other side of the V. Then the equation reads 4 plus 2 equals 6.

"For my second solution, I moved the right matchstick from the Roman numeral 2 to the right side of the equation so that the equation reads 6 plus 1 equals 7.

"Of course, for another solution, I can move the left matchstick from the Roman numeral 2 to the right side of the equation so the equation again reads 6 plus 1 equals 7."

Brock interrupted Ting at this point and said, "That's very good, Ting. Most people wouldn't see these last two solutions as two separate solutions. You are certainly using your creativity."

Ting continued. "For my fourth solution, I moved the vertical matchstick in the Roman numeral 6 on the left side of the equation — the same one as in my first solution — to the far right side of the equation so that the equation reads 5 plus 2 equals 7."

"You did well," said Brock as he walked out into the audience to award the book to Ting. Then he walked back on the platform and addressed the general audience.

"I would like to point out that I found this exercise in a book on creativity the other day; yet it had only one solution. Apparently the author didn't search for more than one solution to the exercise. This doesn't make him that creative. Ting has already shown us that there are four solutions to the exercise. So far, I have generated the same four solutions plus one more, which in itself can lead to three more solutions.

Before I tell you what it is, however, I should give others a chance to share their solutions. Does anyone else have a solution that is different from the four Ting generated?"

"I do," revealed Belinda, "at least I think I do. If you remove the vertical matchstick from the Roman numeral 6 on the left side of the equation and place it over the equals sign, the equals sign becomes a 'not equal' sign. Then the equation reads 5 plus 2 is not equal to 6."

"Excellent, Belinda. This is precisely the solution that I was referring to, which leads to three more solutions," Brock revealed. "Of course, you can move the three other vertical matchsticks — either one of the two signifying the Roman numeral 2 on the left side of the equation, and the one in the Roman numeral 6 on the right side of the equation — to over the equals sign. This will give us three similar solutions using the 'not equal' sign. Therefore, this makes it another four solutions. When we combine these four with Ting's four, we now have eight solutions.

"Incidentally, does anyone else have any more solutions to this exercise? There has to be at least one solution that I haven't been able to see," Brock speculated.

No hands went up.

"Okay," said Brock, "You can see that we have eight solutions to an exercise that . . ."

"Wait a minute," interrupted Joe, "I may be able to make it nine solutions provided you accept one that just crossed my mind. Then again, you may not accept it."

"Well, let's have it, Joe. You know that I'm easy to get along with," joked Brock.

Joe offered his solution, "Why not take the top matchstick in the equals sign and move the right side of it down to touch the lower matchstick in the equals sign. This now looks much like, although not exactly like, the 'greater than' sign used in algebra. Presto! The equation reads 6 plus 2 is greater than 6."

"This is great stuff, Joe," Brock exclaimed. "Although we will have to use our imagination just a touch to have this 'greater than' sign look like the real thing, I can definitely accept it, as should everyone else in this room. The point is, using one's imagination is what creativity is all about."

Brock paused, and then continued. "All of us will probably agree that Joe has just come up with the blockbuster solution, simply because his solution is at least a little more imaginative than the other eight. As I said before, a blockbuster solution is normally neither the first nor the second one. In this case it was the ninth solution.

"By using this matchstick exercise as an analogy, we can see that getting a blockbuster solution to a problem involves putting in much more time and effort than it takes to get the first and second solutions. Only by doing the difficult and uncomfortable in the way of extra creative thought can we come up with blockbuster solutions to problems. This is true whether the problems are mathematical, financial, vocational, or personal. So the next time you have a lingering problem with no workable solution, spend more time and energy looking for more solutions. You'll generate more workable solutions, and one or two of them may be blockbuster solutions. The important thing to remember is that there are always more solutions to a problem, regardless of how many solutions you already have."

Twenty minutes later, after using more exercises to show the trainees how they could use their creativity to generate more solutions for their problems, Brock motioned for Sheldon to project another frame onto the overhead screen. All the trainees looked up to see:

OPPORTUNITYISNOWHERE

Brock asked, "What do the words on the screen mean to you?"

A number of hands went up. Brock pointed at Ursula, the trainee who had shown the most resistant to the material that Brock presented in the first session.

"Opportunity is NOWHERE," she said, confident that she had the right answer.

"It's interesting that you should say this, Ursula," remarked Brock. He paused, and then asked, "Does anyone see something different than what Ursula sees?

Before Brock could select any of the trainees, Korina called out from the back of the room, where she was sitting with Silvina. She used her stroller for support to stand up, and cheerfully said with a captivating smile, "Brock, I might be too young to say anything, but I see something different."

"Korina," said Brock, smiling back at her, "you may not be a regular seminar participant, but you are a special guest of mine, and that makes you a special guest of everyone else. On that basis, I think that everyone in this room will be glad to hear what the words on the screen mean to you."

Korina kept smiling her cheerful smile as she said, "To me, the words on the screen say 'Opportunity is NOW here.' "

"THANKS KORINA, YOU'RE GREAT," Brock offered enthusiastically.

He then paused briefly to collect his thoughts, not having expected Korina to be the person pointing out the alternative message in the words on the screen.

"First, I would like everyone to know that I was as surprised as anyone else by Korina's request to participate in this exercise. Undoubtedly, you can see that Korina cannot walk with the same ease as the rest of us. Even so, she shows an incredible zest for life that I haven't seen matched by anyone else in this city.

"I am quite sure — although I don't have scientific proof — that people like Korina, who have more optimistic views of life, are more likely to look at the words on the screen and see 'opportunity is NOW here' instead of 'opportunity is NOWHERE.' The point of this quirky exercise is to show us how easy it is to think negatively and not see the opportunity around us. Alternatively, it's just as easy to think positively, as Korina does every day, and see opportunities all around us. This can bring us from 'no where' to 'now here.'

"Sadly, many of us are unwilling to accept that the world just may be willing to give us many of the things we want. We don't want to accept that the world gives us opportunities to get these things. More than being afraid of failure, we are frightened by the possibility of success. Oddly enough, some of us don't want to give up the negative beliefs that have been a large part of our lives for so long. The log-standing behaviors of criticizing successful people, complaining about our lousy circumstances, and envying talented individuals would have to be sacrificed for a more positive view of the world. We find it easier to remain in a familiar, negative comfort zone than to opt out for a strange, positive one."

> The Universe doesn't reward you
> for the positive and valuable things
> you know.
>
> It rewards you for the positive and
> valuable things you act on.
>
> Taking positive action, even small,
> slow steps, is how you send signals
> to the Universe that you are
> inviting success and prosperity into
> your life.

A few minutes later, Brock was saying, "There is abundant opportunity for anyone in this room to make a difference in this world and get rich in the process, if that's what you want to accomplish."

Ursula, obviously a little irked by Brock's comments, put up her hand and stated, "I don't believe this. There's no opportunity in this world for common people to get rich. That's why so many people live in poverty."

"That's utter nonsense," Brock asserted. "Ursula, should you ever come to grips with reality, you will realize that the

Western world is full of opportunity. But don't think that I'm singling you out as the only person in this room who doesn't realize this.

"The most popular myth that adds to poverty consciousness — and keeps many people in poverty itself — is that all the good opportunities to make some real money have been exploited. Most people held this false belief fifty years ago, the majority of them agreed with it five years ago, and practically everyone clings to it today. I can assure you that this myth will also be the screaming rage in the future. It should go without saying that if you hang onto this myth, you are destined to miss great opportunities for the rest of your life."

Foster a curiosity for the uncommon, regardless of how unpopular it is.

The uncommon is where opportunity likes to hide.

"So where *are* all these opportunities?" demanded Ursula.

"The answer is everywhere, including your own backyard," advised Brock. "Every convenience in life that you see and touch was once an invisible idea, until someone decided to do something concrete with it. There are unlimited opportunities available today for new products and services. Numerous new careers and businesses are constantly being created. The rapid growth of technology and the Internet has generated new types of businesses that no one imagined possible just a few years ago. New products, services, and technologies emerge every day because someone has been creative and motivated enough to take advantage of opportunities."

Like most people, you undoubtedly have more than one remarkable idea on how to change the world and make it a better place.

Here is a sure way to make the best idea in the Universe totally worthless:

Don't do anything with it!

"Then why aren't more people capitalizing on all these opportunities and becoming rich?" asked Ursula.

"Ursula, I will venture to say that several people in this room personally know one or more individuals who have recently became wealthy over a relatively short period of time, but didn't have any great talent or advantage over anyone else. They merely spotted an opportunity and decided to capitalize on it."

Before Brock could ask if any of the trainees had any friends or acquaintances who recently become wealthy, Ting interrupted. "Brock, I myself know three people who have become wealthy in the last few years. My favorite example is Barry Ansetski, whose brother has a PhD in Geology, and is on welfare. However, Barry is a university drop-out who became a millionaire. I went to school with Barry, and no one ever thought that he would amount to much more than a nine-to-five blue-collar worker."

"How did he become a millionaire?" wondered one of the other trainees.

"The Asian computer company that Barry was working for in Vancouver wanted to pull out of the city because it didn't think that Vancouver provided a big enough market. So Barry asked if he could become the computer company's agent. He set up his own small company to sell and service the computer company's products here."

Ting continued, "I should note that Barry was formerly the company's service technician, and didn't have any experience at all in sales. He just went calling on potential clients in his blue jeans and cowboy boots. He told them about the equipment he was selling and the great service he could provide after they bought the equipment. Corporate buyers liked his low-key approach, his ability to service the equipment, and his honesty. In five years time, he employed ten people and sold more equipment than practically all of his competitors. Then the computer company paid him $5 million for his little company so that they could control the Vancouver market themselves. They even let Barry continue working for them at $150,000 a year as a consultant."

After Ting finished, Brock remarked, "Thank you for the great example, Ting. No doubt your friend Barry is a millionaire today because, first, he spotted an opportunity. Second, unlike most people who see an opportunity, Barry decided to pursue it. He had to risk his own time, money, and reputation to determine if he could make it selling the same computers that the company's own salespeople couldn't sell.

"This brings us back to the aspect of reality that I was just talking about. Opportunities drift in and out of people's lives every day. Unfortunately, these opportunities are seldom exploited, or, for that matter, even seen. Sadly, most North Americans won't pursue a great opportunity even when someone clearly points it out to them. Today's North American is too busy thinking about what sports event he should watch on television tonight, or what sort of makeup she should wear to the party on Saturday. With all the distractions at their disposal, most people find it much easier and more comfortable to complain that there aren't any opportunities available today for the common person — whatever that means.

"People turn their backs on potential fortune for a reason," Brock continued. "It was Thomas Edison who said opportunity is missed by most people because it looks like work. This gets us back to The Easy Rule of Life. It's easy and comfortable to say that there is no opportunity around us. This way, we don't have to make the effort to spot opportunities. Of course, capitalizing on opportunities doesn't just involve spotting them. Spotting them is just the first step. The more difficult and uncomfortable part is the time, effort, money, dedication, and other sacrifices required to make the most of any opportunity.

"The Western world will continue to offer great opportunities for individuals willing to give what it takes to sell ideas, advice, products, energy, enthusiasm, and services to those who need them. An unlimited number of problems exist in the world today. This translates into unlimited opportunities for those willing to solve those problems. More affordable housing, more efficient heating, more nutritious foods, cars that cause less pollution, better daycare, help in cleaning houses, techniques to relieve stress, and less expensive vacations are just a few examples of people's needs of today. Individuals in the hundreds of thousands have started highly successful part-time and full-time businesses solving these problems. If you want to be one of them, you must be able to spot the opportunities around you and do something productive with them."

Just before Brock announced a coffee break, he ended the segment on opportunity with these passionate words: "THIS APPLIES TO EVERYONE IN THIS ROOM. IT'S NOT A QUESTION OF WHETHER OPPORTUNITY WILL KNOCK ON YOUR DOOR IN THE FUTURE. YOU CAN REST ASSURED THAT IT WILL KNOCK OFTEN. THE MILLION-DOLLAR QUESTION IS: HOW OFTEN WILL YOU BE HOME?"

> A dramatically different tomorrow starts with a dramatically different you today.
>
> Inspiration manifests magic.
>
> And prosperity, too!

****

A good portion of the second half of the session was taken up with more exercises on how to be creative. Several exercises and techniques were used to show the trainees how to generate solutions to problems by thinking in different ways. Another five exercises were used to show the trainees how easy it was for anyone to overlook obvious solutions and opportunities.

The last thirty minutes in the session dealt with failure, and how people had to pay their dues if they wanted to be successful in their careers.

> Time and time again you will meet
> failure and every time the test will
> appear:
>
> Can you overcome adversity and
> continue on to become the happy
> and successful person that you
> want to be − the one making a
> significant difference in this
> world?

Brock emphasized that creativity and failure went hand in hand. Shortly after introducing the topic of failure, he declared, "If you want to be highly successful in this world, you must be an unqualified failure."

Brock paused briefly, while everyone pondered what he just stated. Then he continued. "You may be bothered by what I just said, to the point of thinking that my statement is pretty stupid. Nevertheless, I am going to repeat it. This way you get to be bothered and I get to be stupid."

A bit of laughter came from the back of the room.

"ONCE AGAIN," asserted Brock, now almost hollering for effect. "IF YOU WANT TO BE HIGHLY SUCCESSFUL IN THIS WORLD, YOU MUST BE AN UNQUALIFIED FAILURE."

Brock paused again, before he continued in a more subdued voice. "Can anyone clarify why I'm making this apparently stupid statement that is undoubtedly bothering a few people in this room?"

Joe, obviously by now much more receptive to the seminar content than he was at the outset, was the first to put up his hand and answer. "Your statement isn't stupid at all. Every successful person — even Steve Jobs and Bill Gates — experienced many significant failures, more so than the average person who doesn't accomplish anything significant."

"Precisely. Thanks, Joe," Brock stated. He directed his glance away from Joe and toward the audience as a whole. "What Joe is saying is that the road to success looks something like this."

He signaled for Sheldon to display the next frame on the overhead screen, and then pointed at the screen.

Failure. Failure. Failure. Failure. Failure. SUCCESS! Failure. Failure. Failure. Failure. Failure. Failure. SUCCESS! Failure. Failure. Failure. Failure. SUCCESS!

Raising his voice for effect, Brock continued, "SO, GIVEN THAT THE ROAD TO SUCCESS LOOKS LIKE THIS, WHAT'S THE EASIEST WAY TO DOUBLE YOUR SUCCESS RATE?"

Right on cue, a number of people, including Korina, called out in unison, "DOUBLE YOUR FAILURE RATE!"

"Absolutely! Easy how life is, isn't it?" smiled Brock. "You people are now really getting the drift of The Easy Rule of Life. We're on a roll now. Keep this up and I'll be reading about all of you in *The Who's Who of World Success* in no time."

One failure gets you started on the road to success.

A hundred get you there.

"As hard as it is to believe, the more successful you become, the more blunders you will have to your name," Brock continued. "On your way to better and bigger things in your career, congratulate yourself for the smallest of successes and for the biggest of failures. In Texas when they lose, they lose big, and they brag about it. To brag about your failures is to take responsibility for them — and to learn from them."

He paused, and then asked, "So why don't people fail more, if it's a matter of increasing our failure rate to be more successful?"

"People are afraid of failure," speculated Patrick.

"I don't quite agree with you, Patrick," Brock advised. "Are people really afraid of failure itself?"

"Actually it's not the failure itself, but the fear of what people will think of them that makes them afraid of failing," Patrick answered.

"Precisely," agreed Brock. "Most of us believe that there's a hierarchy, with geniuses on top, successful entrepreneurs and corporate executives just a notch below, moderately successful people a little lower, and fools on rock bottom. Needless to say, we don't want to be one of the fools. To avoid looking bad in the eyes of others, we resist taking risks that can lead to failure. Unfortunately, without taking risks, we can't become one of the successful entrepreneurs or executives. Needless to say, we also can't become one of the geniuses. Heck, we can't even become moderately successful.

"First, let's look at what it takes to become a genius. No doubt some of you think that geniuses are born. Not so. I agree with French feminist writer and existentialist Simone de Beauvoir who stated, 'One is not born a genius; one becomes a genius.'

"Consider Thomas Edison, who was regarded as one of the greatest geniuses of all time. He registered more than one thousand patents for his inventions. One of his best known inventions was the light bulb. Edison is reported to have conducted several hundred experiments in an attempt to invent the first light bulb. After about five hundred attempts, Edison's assistant asked him, 'Why do you persist in this folly? You have tried five hundred times and you have failed five hundred times.' Edison was quick to respond, 'Oh, but I have not failed even once. Now I know five hundred ways *not* to make a light bulb.' "

Laughter broke out in the audience.

"In due time, Edison's persistence paid off with a workable light bulb, and he was considered a genius for this invention alone. The moral of this story is that if we take a hard look at the apparent geniuses of this world, genius is nothing more than perseverance and persistence disguised. A genius is someone with a lot more persistence than you, who is following the difficult and uncomfortable route filled with a lot of failure.

"Now, let's look at what makes people successful as entrepreneurs and executives. Researchers in North Carolina did a study on highly successful executives to determine the one trait or quality — the one that stood above all the other traits and qualities — that helped make these executives highly successful. What do you think it was? Does anyone in the room want to take a stab at it?"

First, Patrick put up his hand and stated, "From the way you're setting this up, I have a feeling that I'm wrong, but off the top of my head I would say that it's their management abilities."

Then Christine, a woman sitting in the front row, remarked, "It definitely has to be their communication skills. You can't become a successful executive without the ability to communicate effectively."

After two more people tried to pinpoint the most important trait for achieving success as an executive, Brock continued. "The researchers found that the overriding trait of successful executives — the trait that stood above all the other important traits, such as management ability, communication skills, marketing aptitude, and leadership skills — was their ability to handle failure. Highly effective people celebrate failure and learn from it. Christine was right that it's virtually impossible to be a successful executive without communication skills.

But it's just as impossible to become a successful executive without the ability to handle failure.

"Successful people know that they may, and probably will, have to encounter a lot of failure to remain successful. This often involves being a fool. They also realize that there is one level on the hierarchy that is lower and worse than being a fool. It's being afraid of being a fool.

"Of course, as Patrick clarified for us, people who are afraid of being a fool are really afraid of what others think of them. If you resist taking risks and experiencing failure because you're afraid of what others think about you, I have some interesting news for you. In a study on people's thinking habits, researchers concluded that 80 percent of people's thoughts are negative, regardless of what they're looking at. So guess what? You may as well risk and go for it. What difference does it make? Most people are probably going to think bad thoughts about you, regardless of what you do or say."

The audience laughed.

Brock paused to acknowledge a woman at the back of the room who put up her hand.

Oriana, a woman in her early twenties, stood up and stated, "As human beings, we all want the love and affection of other people. So we're always going to be concerned about what people think of us. It's only natural that we resist being fools in the eyes of others."

"It's certainly true that as human beings we all desire some love and affection from other people," replied Brock. "But the problem with most people is that they want to be liked by everyone they meet. The late Herbert B. Swope warned us about this folly when he said, 'I cannot give you the formula for success but I can give you the formula for failure. That is: try to please everybody.'

"Perish the thought of trying to be liked by all people. Everyone — bar none — is a jerk to someone else. Of course, I realize that this even applies to me, especially after the incident in the first session," joked Brock. He glanced at Joe with just a hint of a mischievous grin.

After a few chuckles from the audience, he continued. "The desire for popularity is, in fact, a hindrance to personal success and well-being. Going through life trying to please everyone else will burn up a lot of time, energy, and money, which you could be putting to much better use. The end result is that you may please a few superficial people along the way. Sadly, you won't please the right people, nor will you please yourself in the end."

At this stage, Brock raised his voice for effect. "AGAIN, SPENDING YOUR ENTIRE LIFE TRYING TO IMPRESS OTHERS IS A WASTE OF YOUR PRECIOUS TIME, ENERGY, AND MONEY. IF YOU'RE GOING THROUGH LIFE TRYING NOT TO LOOK STUPID, AND NOT HAVING MUCH SUCCESS AT IT, THEN STOP TRYING NOT TO LOOK STUPID. IN CASE YOU HAVEN'T NOTICED, THE BEST WAY TO IMPRESS OTHERS IS BY BEING YOURSELF AND NOT TRYING TO IMPRESS THEM.

"Let's go back to the seven principles of creativity, which are difficult and uncomfortable to follow, but which can also bring us incredible results. Note what the sixth principle is: Dare to be different! Unfortunately, most of us do the opposite. We go through our entire lives trying to get respect and recognition by thinking like others and doing what everyone else is doing. This brings us dubious results, at best.

"If you want better results in the way of respect and recognition, take a look at Pablo Picasso, the Beatles, Madonna, Oprah, Margaret Thatcher, and Martin Luther King. They all made an incredible difference in this world. At the same time, they received incredible affection, respect, and recognition from hundreds of millions of people. My question to all of you is, did these remarkable individuals go through life acting like others, doing what others were doing, and worrying about what others thought of them?"

A number of "no's", "no way's", and nods came from the audience in response to the question.

Brock continued. "Of course, they didn't. Pay close attention, and you'll see that the most admired people on this planet do their own thing and ignore what other people say or think about them. These same people, who are loved by many, are also despised by many. The important thing is that even the people who dislike them respect and admire them.

"There's an important paradoxical lesson here: If you want to be admired and respected in this world, you must be too big and wonderful to worry about what people say and think about you. It's in your long-term interests to go out on a limb instead of being inhibited by all the things that deter most people from being successful.

"THE BOTTOM LINE IS, IF YOU WANT TO MAKE A BIG DIFFERENCE IN YOUR LIFE AND THE LIVES OF OTHERS, YOU CAN'T BE LIKE EVERYONE ELSE. YOU MUST BE WILLING TO RISK, BE DIFFERENT,

CHALLENGE THE STATUS QUO, AND RUFFLE A FEW
FEATHERS IN THE PROCESS OF LIVING. ONLY THEN
WILL YOU MAKE THIS WORLD A BETTER, MORE
INTERESTING PLACE."

*Why bother living a life devoid of
accomplishment, success, and
prosperity?*

*Adventurous successful souls create
their lives the way that spiders
build their webs – just the way
they want them.*

*Worthwhile dreams and inspired
action make the difference.*

****

Brock used a story to introduce his last principle of creativity.
"Two strangers were talking to each other in a local tavern. As
is usually the case, the conversation turned to the subject of
what they did for a living.

"One of the men uttered, 'I always wanted to work in a
circus. Finally, after two years of trying, I got a job with
Bailey's Circus. I enjoy it for the most part, but, it's tough on
me. I work fourteen hours a day, and only get paid for eight.
The pay is only $10 an hour. I have to wash trucks, sweep
floors, take out the garbage, and clean the elephants' pens.
One manager keeps telling me that he's going to promote me,

but he usually yells at me because he thinks I should work a little harder.'

"The other man replied, 'I wouldn't put up with that crap. Why don't you come and work with me? It's a union job, so it's an easy pace. They treat me really well and the starting pay is $25 an hour, with double time for overtime — all this for digging ditches!'

"Without hesitation, the circus worker responded, 'What? Dig ditches? And leave show business? No way!' "

Laughter was heard from some people in the audience before Brock continued. "The moral of the story is that you will have to pay a price if you want to enter any desirable career field, including show business. Reality will throw you for a nasty loop if you believe that everything is going to be easy . . ."

A trainee put up her hand and interrupted Brock.

"Shouldn't we select a vocation that we really enjoy?" asked Kirsten. "That way, we won't have to put up with difficulties and tasks that we don't enjoy."

"By all means, choose the most satisfying career you can find, instead of the one that pays the most money," replied Brock. "This will permit you to enjoy yourself in the present as much as possible. You'll definitely know that you're living your dreams and life's purpose when you learn to cope with — and even like — the difficult work, the responsibilities, the tedious tasks, and the dues that go with it.

"The point is, though, regardless of the occupation you choose, you can be assured that there will be trying times before you attain any measurable success. As you pursue your vocational dreams, you will find out — as I did — that creating a life worth living can be difficult at times.

"Before you make it to where you're comfortably living your dream, you may have to work at a much lower salary, and put up with undesirable tasks and unpleasant conditions. Perhaps you will have to tool around in a beat-up old MGB sports car for a few years, instead of that new Mercedes convertible. You may even have to work longer hours than you did in your last job. As they say, 'That's show biz.'

"It's not a case of whether or not you'll experience major problems, bad breaks, inequities, or even discrimination; it's a case of how you apply your creativity to overcome them. Hard times can be downright dejecting, but it's best to look at struggle as a natural occurrence in the process of life."

There will be days when nothing goes right.

But all is not lost.

Quite the contrary.

You will learn more from one day of difficulties than you will learn from a year of total pleasure and comfort.

Brock continued, "The seventh creativity principle — be persistent and pay your dues — will help you overcome whatever difficulties and setbacks you encounter. Like the other six creativity principles, it's difficult and uncomfortable to follow, but it will generate big results. People who do the difficult and uncomfortable, and hang on for another day or month or year longer, create the breakthroughs necessary for success in their ventures.

"Remember the guy who tried five hundred times to invent the light bulb, and eventually succeeded. The same guy — Thomas Edison — said that the most tragic failures are people who didn't realize how close they were to success when they gave up. About 95 percent of people's failures are the result of quitting too soon. Many of these people are quite close to success when they decide to quit important projects or desirable careers. Persistent people, on the other hand, know that they are nearing success when they reach the point where others are conceding failure.

"This leads us into another paradox associated with The Easy Rule of Life. Paying your dues isn't easy, but it's easier than not paying them. You will know that you deserve to be working in a challenging and rewarding career when you hit those tough spots and keep working right through them. Knowing that you have overcome the odds and have become one of the successful people in your field will make it all that more satisfying."

> Most successful, prosperous individuals at one time considered giving up on their dreams and aspirations.
>
> They decided against it, however.

At this point, Ting got Brock's attention and posed a question. "Brock, you imply that it took you at least two or three years before you started making it as a public speaker. How long does a person normally have to pay one's dues before attaining success as a public speaker?"

"There is no rule of thumb," answered Brock. "This applies to any occupational pursuit, whether it's being a restaurant owner, a management consultant, a financial advisor, a massage therapist, or a race car driver. Regardless of the occupational field you enter, you will always have to pay some dues before you attain some measure of success.

"But you don't necessarily have to pay the same time and energy dues that other people have to pay. The essence, the power, and the value of your creativity are not to be underestimated. You can climb the ladder of success rung by rung, or you can be creative and skip a number of rungs along the way. The fact is, creative people will achieve in two or three years what uncreative people may take ten or fifteen years to achieve, or may, in fact, never achieve.

"There are two important things to remember about paying your dues. First, when you're starting out in a new career, your greatest asset is your imagination. To gain any credibility in any new field, you will have to be ten times as creative as the veterans and experts. Luckily, this isn't all that difficult, simply because the veterans and experts are seldom creative. They find it easier and more comfortable to think that they know it all. This way, they don't have to put any effort into discovering new ways of doing things. If you put in the effort to think in new and different directions, you'll gain an incredible edge over the experts and veterans.

"The second thing to remember is that paying your dues can be difficult and uncomfortable, but it makes your life much easier and more comfortable in the long term. You'll find that when you start out in a new career, you'll be putting a lot more into new projects than you're getting out of them. You may be contributing five to ten times more time and energy than you're getting back in payments of achievement and money. After you pay your dues for two or three years, though, you'll start to break even. You'll start getting back achievement and money equal to what you're contributing in time and energy.

"There will come a time, however, when you're getting back ten to twenty times what you're putting into your career. Of course, people will then wonder why your life is so easy and comfortable. You can simply tell them that it's because you apply The Easy Rule of Life to everything that's important to you."

> The crisis of today is the
> inspirational story of struggle and
> accomplishment that you get to tell
> some time in the near future.

****

To complete the second session, Brock summarized the importance of following his seven principles of creativity. Abiding by these principles, he said, would ensure that the trainees lived the rest of their lives as overachievers rather than underachievers.

"THERE ARE TWO PRINCIPLES THAT GOVERN
INDIVIDUAL ACHIEVEMENT — ONE GENERAL AND
ONE DEFINITIVE. THE GENERAL PRINCIPLE IS THAT
EVERY PERSON ON EARTH HAS UNIQUE CREATIVE
ABILITY TO MAKE A BIG DIFFERENCE IN THIS
WORLD. THE DEFINITIVE PRINCIPLE IS THAT MOST
PEOPLE HAVE VOLUNTEERED TO BE EXEMPT FROM
THE GENERAL PRINCIPLE.

"Most people refrain from using their creative ability for a
reason: There is a price to pay for making the effort to be
creative, just as there's a price for anything worthwhile in life.
But rather than looking at the price you have to pay, consider
the many prizes that you'll get to enjoy. These include
increased self-esteem, personal growth, more enthusiasm for
solving problems, increased self-confidence to deal with new
challenges, and different perspectives toward work and
personal life.

"Never lose sight of your true worth as an income-
producing individual. Tap into your creativity every chance
you get. One good session of creative thinking can be worth
an extra $1 million to you sometime in the near future — not
to mention the satisfaction of coming up with something new,
interesting, and beneficial to humanity.

"Whether you're looking for an opportunity or a solution
to a problem, don't underestimate the power of your creative
mind. Put it to good use. Do the difficult and uncomfortable
instead of the easy and comfortable. Think. Think. Think.
Think. Think. And when you believe you've thought enough,
think some more. The blockbuster answer will appear if you
are willing to look for it. If you think sparingly, at least think

in new and different ways. Even a bit of creative thought will put you way ahead of the competition.

"There are just a few stumbling blocks in this world that can prevent any one of you from attaining most of your dreams. You are all human beings possessing incredible creative powers for overcoming the greatest obstacles on your journey through life. Aside from serious illness or death, all other obstacles — whether major problems, bad breaks, misfortunes, or discrimination — should be viewed as tests of your creativity.

"WHENEVER YOU ENCOUNTER AN OBSTACLE TO GETTING WHAT YOU WANT OUT OF LIFE, FIRST TRY GOING OVER THE OBSTACLE. IF THIS FAILS, TRY GOING UNDER IT; THEN TRY GOING TO THE RIGHT AND THEN TO THE LEFT. GET HELP TO ATTEMPT TO MOVE THIS OBSTACLE OUT OF THE WAY IF YOU HAVE TO. THEN TRY FLYING OVER IT.

"IF YOU STILL HAVEN'T SUCCEEDED IN OVERCOMING THE OBSTACLE, TURN 180 DEGREES AND GO IN THE OPPOSITE DIRECTION, ALL AROUND THE WORLD, TO THE OTHER SIDE OF THE OBSTACLE. ANOTHER SOLUTION IS TO THROW ACID ON THE OBSTACLE AND WAIT A DAY TO SEE IF IT IS EATEN AWAY. BURN IT IF YOU HAVE TO. YOU CAN EVEN TRY BLOWING IT UP WITH DYNAMITE."

With just a hint of a smile, Brock ended the session. "AND IF ALL THESE SOLUTIONS FAIL, USE YOUR IMAGINATION TO COME UP WITH SOMETHING TRULY CREATIVE."

Every soul – including yours – carries the seeds of remarkable accomplishment.

Motivate yourself, inspire yourself, dedicate yourself, and apply yourself.

Because without your best self, the rest of the Universe will be without the wonderful things that you are capable of creating.

After the session, a few of the attendees came to the front of the auditorium and asked Brock whether there were any good books on how to be more creative. Instead of recommending his own best-selling book, Brock told them that from a career and business perspective, Roger von Oech's *A Whack on the Side of the Head* was his favorite. Not only did it have a great title, the book was fun and easy to read. He also stated that if the attendees were looking for a more artistic approach to creativity, Julia Cameron's *The Artist's Way* was a great book. It would even help those who weren't particularly artistically inclined.

After all the trainees left, Silvina and Korina came forward to talk with Brock and Sheldon.

"So Korina, what did you think of what I said about creativity?" asked Brock.

"I liked how you used the exercise with the equation made out of matchsticks to show how there are many solutions to problems. All the solutions to the exercise were neat. But you know what? I thought of another solution, and I'm not going to tell you what it is unless you give me $20," Korina said playfully.

"Actually, I didn't even know that you'd learned about Roman numerals already, Korina. Even as an advanced student, you're only in grade five."

"I didn't learn about them at school," replied Korina. "Silvina taught me what Roman numerals are while we were doing the exercise."

"Wow, you learn fast," exclaimed Brock. "In that case, I would love to see your solution, but I'll give you more than $20. I'll be using this exercise in my new book about The Easy Rule of Life, and I'd like to have as many solutions as possible in the book. It's only fair that I pay you $100 for it."

"One hundred dollars! Really?" asked Korina gleefully.

"Of course. It's worth $100 to me for each new solution that I can use in the book, just like it's worth the $500 that I offered Sheldon if he comes up with a great title for the book."

Korina looked wide-eyed at Brock. "Will you give me $500 if I think of a good title for the book?"

"Definitely," replied Brock. "Why wouldn't I? But only if it's the title that I use. Only one of you can win the $500."

"Then can I also get in on the action if I think of more solutions to the matchstick exercise?" asked Sheldon.

"Sure, if either of you think of any new solutions, I'll give you $100 for each one," announced Brock. "Now, what's the solution you already have?" he asked, looking at Korina.

Korina smiled and proudly stated, "If you take the right matchstick out of the Roman numeral 6 on the left side of the equation and move it in between the two matchsticks that make the Roman numeral 2, you make a BIG FAT Roman numeral 1 out of it. Then the Roman numeral 5 plus a BIG FAT Roman numeral 1 on the left side of the equation equals the Roman numeral 6 on the right side of the equation."

"Wow! That is a brilliant solution, Korina! It's even better than the blockbuster one that Joe created," remarked Brock.

Silvina smiled at Brock and said, "I thought you'd like it. Korina stunned me when she came up with it."

Brock then looked at Sheldon, "See what I mean about there always being another solution — even another blockbuster one — to any of life's problems? Getting more and better solutions to any problem is no different from getting more and better solutions to this matchstick exercise. It's a matter of looking for them."

"Do you think there are more solutions to this exercise?" asked Sheldon. "I could use $100 to $200 extra."

"Sheldon, I can't tell you how many solutions there are to this exercise," answered Brock. "It's up to you to find out if you want to — in your words — make $100 to $200 extra. But don't lose sight of the true message of this exercise as it relates to what I said about creativity. Start applying your creativity to all areas of your life, and your life will change for the better in many ways.

"One of the benefits of developing your creativity is that you'll spot opportunities to make a lot of money. The $100 or $200 that you can make by getting more solutions to this exercise is insignificant compared to the money you can make by applying your creativity in a career or running a business. Remember, your biggest asset is your creativity. Whenever you list your financial assets, you should include your creativity as one of them, and then assign a value of $1 million to it."

"Don't worry," Sheldon assured Brock. "I haven't lost that message. You really piqued my interest in creativity and how to apply it to marketing and sales. I intend to be more creative, starting today."

****

> Live never to be astonished by the
> accomplishments of others.
>
> Live, instead, to be astonished by
> your own.

When Sheldon got home, he was bound and determined to find at least one new solution to the matchstick exercise. He was so impressed with Korina's blockbuster solution that he wanted to find his own. He looked long and hard at the exercise, moving all of the matchsticks in many different positions for over an hour. Once he felt that he was close to a new solution, but none appeared. After an hour, he gave up, somewhat disappointed.

Sheldon wished that he could start reading a book on creativity, like *A Whack on the Side of the Head* or *The Artist's Way*, to see whether there was something in these books to help him generate solutions to the matchstick exercise. He would even have read Brock's *Thinking Big in a Small World* if he owned a copy. He realized then that he would have to swallow a bit of pride and ask Brock for one the next time he saw him.

Then, on a whim, Sheldon picked up *Life's Secret Handbook* to see if there was anything on creativity that he hadn't seen already. The last passage that he read that night was inspirational, but the handbook had nothing about solving matchstick exercises.

You are the source of the miracles in your life.

Miracles go hand in hand with patience and commitment.

Remember not to quit just before the miracle is about to happen.

Just as Sheldon was about to call it a day, he remembered The Easy Rule of Life. He also recalled Brock saying, *"Think. Think. Think. Think. Think. And when you believe you have thought enough, think some more."* Motivated by these words, Sheldon did the difficult and uncomfortable: Although he didn't expect to get a solution, he decided to focus on the matchstick exercise for another minute or two before he went to sleep.

"If I move the vertical matchstick in the Roman numeral 6 on the right side of the equation from the right side of the V to the left side of the V, the equation reads 6 plus 2 equals 4."

"This certainly isn't a solution," Sheldon's thoughts continued. *"However, let me do something different. What if I look at this new equation in a mirror? It now reads 6 equals 2 plus 4."*

"AWESOME! I'VE GOT A BLOCKBUSTER SOLUTION!" Sheldon exclaimed to himself.

Instantly, Sheldon experienced the sense of *"Eureka!"* that many inventors experience when they get a major breakthrough. At the same time he also felt a great sense of satisfaction and self-esteem. Having come up with his own blockbuster solution to the matchstick exercise would have an incredible impact on Sheldon for the rest of his life.

The $100 that Sheldon would receive from Brock for this solution didn't even enter his mind as he went to sleep. It also didn't occur to him until the following morning that, with the $100 he earned assisting Brock at the seminar, he had actually earned $200 in one day. Until now, this was the most Sheldon had ever earned, and his creativity had played a big part.

****

5

Life is a game.

Happy people are the players.

Unhappy people are the spectators.

Which would you like to be?

Sheldon awoke early the next morning, thinking about the solution to the matchstick exercise that he'd created the night before. He spent a few moments basking in the satisfaction of having come up with a solution that no other participant in the seminar had generated, at the same time confident that Brock would label this as a blockbuster one.

After a while Sheldon wondered if he could find another solution. *"It would be nice to make another $100,"* he thought. Impulsively, he concluded that he couldn't generate any more solutions, especially after he'd already come up with a blockbuster one. To generate another solution would be a miracle.

*When the ship of the adventurous
soul hits the reef of criticism,
adversity, and failure – it's the
criticism, adversity, and failure
that are smashed to bits and pieces
– and not the adventurous soul.*

Then, as the night before, Sheldon heard Brock's voice in his mind. This time he heard Brock saying, *"The important thing to remember is that there are always more solutions to a problem, regardless of how many solutions you have."* Sheldon wondered if Brock's statement applied to matchstick exercises. Assuming that there were more solutions, he now fantasized about generating two more solutions so that he could earn another $200 in one day. From that moment on, for the rest of the day, Sheldon was obsessed with finding more solutions.

*Without problems, you wouldn't
have a means to earn a living.*

*Solving problems also leads to
experiences of accomplishment,
satisfaction, and abundance.*

*All told, problems are welcome
company for a fulfilling life.*

Whenever Sheldon got a spare minute that day, he tried to solve the matchstick exercise in a new way. At City College, he even chose not to have lunch in the cafeteria with his fellow students. For the first time since he'd started his college program, he spent the entire lunch hour in the library. At first, he felt that he might be missing out on some fun and games in the cafeteria, but he wanted to get as many solutions to this exercise as he could, and give it his best shot.

> Understand that most people don't
> spend their time on all things
> important.

> Just because a billion people pursue
> something doesn't make it
> worthwhile for you.

> On the contrary, it's usually a good
> sign of the folly of the pursuit.

By mid-afternoon, Sheldon still hadn't generated another solution. Nonetheless, he persisted. For inspiration he opened *Life's Secret Handbook*, which he carried with him whenever he attended college. The first two proverbs that he glanced at were enough to remind him of The Easy Rule of Life and motivated him to keep looking for more solutions.

> Be calm when things don't work out
> the way you would like.

> Failure is the Universe's way of
> ensuring that too much success
> doesn't happen all at once.

~

Never expect everything in life to be easy.

If you succeed on the first try, you can be assured that it won't happen again.

Either that, or what you have accomplished is not worth boasting about.

Later in the afternoon, after attending all his classes for the day, Sheldon started walking home. Soon it was pouring rain. *"What a lousy day!"* he thought. *"I spent the better part of the day thinking about this matchstick exercise, and I still haven't come up with another solution. Now I'm going to get wet and chilled in the rain."*

The severity of your problems is a matter of perspective.

Change your perspective and most of them become insignificant.

Some of them will no longer exist as big problems – but enormous opportunities instead.

After running in the rain for a few minutes, Sheldon spotted a Chapter's bookstore across the street. He decided to take refuge in the bookstore from the inclement weather outside. As he entered, it occurred to him that this would be a good time to check out the books on creativity that Brock had recommended in the seminar. Perhaps there would be something in the books that would help him find at least one more solution to the exercise.

> Adversity is not what it first appears to be.

> It's opportunity looking for some adventurous soul to take advantage of it.

Sheldon soon found a copy of *A Whack on the Side of Head* by Roger von Oech in the business section. He sat on a comfortable chair and started reading. As he skimmed through the book he came to a section where the author compared a computer to the human mind. It was this statement that influenced Sheldon to think about computers. He reminisced about some of the material from his first computer programming course at City College, which he then tried to apply to the matchstick exercise.

"If I move one of the matchsticks and place it over the plus sign, the plus sign now looks like an asterisk. In computer language an asterisk stands for a multiplication sign. Let me try moving the right matchstick in the Roman numeral 2 to over the plus sign to form the asterisk. Then, the equation

reads 6 times 1 equals 6. Hey! Awesome! This is another great solution!"

Again Sheldon experienced a great deal of satisfaction. He didn't think that this method of solving the matchstick exercise was as clever as the one he'd generated the night before, but it was another method that he'd created on his own. Moreover, he would ask Brock to pay him $200 for this method for solving the exercise, considering that it led to two separate solutions. Instead of moving the left matchstick in the Roman numeral 2, the right one could also be moved to form the asterisk sign.

Confident that he had earned at least $100, and in all probability $200 that day, Sheldon decided to purchase *A Whack on the Side of the Head*. It took practically all the money he had on him, but the book had already helped him be more creative, and earned him several times the cost of the book. He also decided that he would purchase Brock's *Thinking Big in a Small World* as soon as he got paid by Brock.

Surprisingly, when Sheldon walked out of the bookstore, the rain had completely stopped. He thought about how the rain ended up being a blessing in disguise, and thought that perhaps this was more synchronicity touching his life. It wasn't likely that he would have generated the two computer-related solutions to the exercise if he hadn't entered the bookstore and read some of the material in *A Whack on the Side of the Head*.

Be careful with your beliefs about what can't be done.

From a human perspective a robin shouldn't be able to find its way over 3,000 miles back to the same nesting place the next spring.

But the robin doesn't know that it shouldn't be able to do this.

So it does.

At home Sheldon forced himself to spend almost two hours on his college studies. After he finished, his mind jumped back to the matchstick exercise. While watching TV he skimmed through *A Whack on the Side of the Head*, hoping that he could find something else in the book that would trigger another solution.

Eventually he read from a part of the book where author Roger von Oech emphasized the importance of asking what-if questions. *"Asking 'what-if' is an easy way to get your imagination going."* This statement influenced Sheldon to say to himself, *"What if I do something totally different? What if I use a piece of paper to cover up some of the equation after moving one of the matchsticks? The only constraint that Brock put on the exercise was that only one matchstick could be moved."*

After moving various matchsticks and covering up portions of the remaining equations with a piece of paper for more than an hour, Sheldon's persistence paid off. He hit pay dirt again with another solution.

First, he moved the left matchstick that formed the V in the Roman numeral 6 on the left side of the equation to a horizontal position over the remaining matchsticks that helped form this Roman numeral 6. Then, by using the piece of paper to cover up a portion of the resultant illegible character, he was able to create the number 4 as it is normally hand written.

Sheldon immediately concluded, *"With just a bit of mental gymnastics, this is a solution. Mathematically, the real number 4 plus the Roman numeral 2 equals the Roman numeral 6."*

By now it was 10 o'clock in the evening. As the night before, Sheldon was on a mental high after generating this solution. Wanting to share his incredible experience of joy and accomplishment, he decided to telephone Brock to tell him about his four new solutions to the exercise.

It took only two rings before Brock answered the phone. Sheldon promptly told Brock that he had generated four new solutions to the matchstick exercise. Brock seemed a little surprised.

"Four new solutions? Are you sure that they're all valid?"

"Sure, I'm sure. Actually, it's three unique methods of solving the exercise, but one has two variations to it, just like the one that Ting had in the seminar. Two different matchsticks can be moved to get the same result," stated Sheldon confidently. He paused, then said. "What's the matter? Are you trying to get out of paying me $100 for each solution?"

"Not at all," Brock shot back. "I paid you immediately after you helped me in the first two seminars, and I'll pay you for any new solutions, just as I said I would. Look, why don't you meet me at the Naam vegetarian restaurant on West Fourth for dinner tomorrow night, and you can show me the solutions. Silvina and Korina are coming. I'll pay you for the four solutions at that time. I'll even bring some extra cash in case you get one or two more by then. I'll spring for dinner as well. How's 8 o'clock sound?"

"That suits me just fine," Sheldon remarked. "I'll go for a free dinner any day of the week, rather than preparing something myself."

"I'm looking forward to seeing the solutions. See you at 8," said Brock.

Competition is good for you in a Divine way.

Your competitors are your spiritual friends.

You learn best and most when you play with those who are much better and more successful than you.

****

It seems easier to live the comfortable and conventional, to fit in with the majority.

It's when you live the uncomfortable and unconventional, however, that you make the most of your talents, your creativity, and your actions.

That is also when your life starts being fun, satisfying, and meaningful.

The next evening, Sheldon arrived at the Naam restaurant a few minutes early, not wanting to be late. He recalled what Brock had said about the importance of keeping agreements, regardless of the significance of the agreement. When he arrived at the restaurant, Brock, Silvina, and Korina were already seated at a table.

After cordial greetings between Sheldon and the other three, the conversation turned to Korina and what she was doing in school. Sheldon was anxious to share his solutions to the matchstick exercise. Before he could say anything about them, however, Brock suggested that they wait until after they finished dinner. For the next half-hour Sheldon said little as Brock, Silvina, and Korina did most of the talking.

Halfway through dinner Silvina turned to Sheldon and asked:

"Sheldon, you're rather quiet. What's new and exciting in your life?"

"Nothing much," said Sheldon.

"Come on, there has to be lots of things that you aren't telling us," suggested Silvina.

"Well, okay. I wanted to tell Brock something, which he may find amusing coming from me."

"We would all love to hear it," said Silvina before Brock could respond.

"I phoned my mother today," divulged Sheldon, half smiling. "After saying hello, I asked her how she was doing. She replied, 'Oh, okay but I could be much, much better. It's the story of my life. Life is really difficult all the time. It's one big struggle and nothing else.'

"And you know what I told her? I said, 'Look Ma, life's easy. It will never be totally easy, but life can be a lot easier if you change your attitude and your behavior. You have to follow The Easy Rule of Life.' Then I told her about The Easy Rule of Life and how I was applying it in certain areas of my life, and how it was starting to pay off for me."

Sheldon continued, "I think she thought I was a little nuts because she didn't know what I was talking about. I intend to give her a better explanation of The Easy Rule of Life and how it could apply to her when I visit her next month. Maybe she'll start making some of the changes in her life that she's been talking about for so long."

At this point, Korina, who had wanted to speak for several seconds, gleefully interrupted with the same excitement as when she had seen the butterfly in Brock's backyard. "Brock, what Sheldon just said to his mom — that's a great title for your new book on The Easy Rule of Life."

"Oh yeah, what did he say to his mother that's so great, Korina?" asked Brock, a little puzzled.

Korina's smile was accompanied by a twinkle in her eyes, "Why don't you call your new book *Look Ma, Life's Easy?*"

"Hmmm . . . ," Brock paused while Silvina and Sheldon also pondered Korina's suggestion.

"*Look Ma, Life's Easy*," repeated Brock. "I think I like it."

"I love it," smiled Silvina. "I think it's a winner."

There was a little pause before Brock said, "I believe that you've just earned yourself $500, Korina. After all the time I've spent on it, I don't believe I can come up with a better title myself."

Brock paused, then turned to Sheldon and jokingly said, "Too bad that you didn't think of it, Sheldon. You're going to have to be more creative."

"Yeah, right," replied Sheldon. "This little creative wonder just took my four words and repeated them to earn $500 that I now can't earn for myself."

"As David Letterman would say," grinned Brock, looking at Sheldon, "there's no off-switch on Korina's genius machine. That's part of the creative spirit — spotting opportunities that others overlook and then taking advantage of them. As I often say in my seminars, pay attention to children. You'll learn a lot from them, especially about how to be more creative."

Korina then turned to Sheldon and happily announced, "Don't worry, Sheldon. When Brock gives me my $500, I'll give you half of it. You really gave me the idea for the title."

Before Sheldon could consider Korina's offer, Brock countered, "That's okay, Korina. I'll gladly give Sheldon and you each $500. Both of you were instrumental in coming up with *Look Ma, Life's Easy*. Having this great title is easily worth $1,000 to me, because I no longer have to rack my brains looking for a blockbuster title myself."

Soon after that, they finished their main courses. Brock ordered three glasses of expensive port wine for Sheldon, Silvina, and himself. He also ordered a special nonalcoholic drink for Korina.

> *If you can't enjoy spending money with the same degree of satisfaction that you experience while earning it, then your prosperity consciousness needs some serious work.*

Then he said, "I want to toast the team of Korina and Sheldon for creating the snappy title for my new book. There is no doubt in my mind that when *Look Ma, Life's Easy* is a big success, the title will have played a big part. I intend to credit both of you in the acknowledgments in the front of the book."

Then he asked, "So Sheldon, before I forget, what are your new solutions to the matchstick exercise? I may owe you some more money."

Sheldon took about five minutes to proudly explain his four new solutions to the matchstick exercise while Korina, Silvina, and Brock paid close attention. He had felt that Brock might question the validity of his second or third method of solving the exercise, but Brock was pleased with all of the creative solutions.

"These solutions are brilliant," he exclaimed. "You've certainly earned yourself another $400. See what I told you about taking the difficult and uncomfortable way to search for opportunity? It pays off, doesn't it?"

"Actually, it wasn't extremely difficult. It was challenging and time consuming, but kind of fun in the end. It was certainly satisfying and good for my self-esteem when I finally got the solutions, especially the first and last ones."

"No kidding. It's quite basic," said Brock. "Self-esteem is highly dependent on personal accomplishments. The more challenging and difficult a project, the more satisfaction you will experience from having completed it. And the more accomplishments to your name, the more self-confident you'll be. As I told you the day we met, it's amazing what you can create in your life when you're prepared to make it happen, no matter what it takes. Perseverance is one of the most important tools for creative success. Perseverance will always give you an advantage over the individual with greater intelligence and talent."

> When the quest doesn't involve considerable risk, time, and creative energy – and particularly if the doubters of the world aren't laughing at it – it's likely not worth pursuing.

"Hey, Brock," interjected Korina. "Do you think there are even more solutions to this exercise? I would like to make some more money too!"

"There have to be more, Korina. After seeing how many solutions Sheldon generated so far, there could well be an unlimited number. Just keep looking. Think way out in left field, and there's no telling what you might come up with."

Brock took nine crisp $100 bills out of his wallet and handed them slowly to Sheldon. "Here's $400 for the four solutions. Luckily for you, I brought some extra cash. And here's another $500 for having contributed to the title for the book."

Brock continued, "Korina, I'll have to pay you your $500 when we get home, because I didn't bring enough money. I didn't know that the two of you were going to cost me so much tonight."

"That's okay, I can wait," said a cheerful Korina.

As Sheldon put the $900 in his wallet, he jokingly said to Brock, "Thanks a lot for the megabucks. I now have real money that I haven't even spent yet."

"Right. It's probably burning a hole in your pocket," stated Brock facetiously. "On that note, will you do me and yourself a big favor?"

Sheldon paused for a few moments before he answered, "Maybe. What is it?"

"Instead of taking the easy way out and spending the $900 as fast as you can, why don't you hang onto the money until after the next seminar? The main topic will be applying The Easy Rule of Life to handling money, and how much money relates to happiness in life. You may want to do something with your new-found wealth other than blowing it on something like a new iPhone, which won't necessarily contribute anything to your happiness and satisfaction in the long term."

"Okay, I'll hang onto the bucks until then," agreed Sheldon. "What happens if I create more solutions to the matchstick exercise in the meantime? Do I get $100 and a week's use of your Mercedes 190 SL for every new solution?"

"I'll pay you $100 for every new solution that I don't have. That was the agreement. You should have noticed by now that I — unlike many people — keep my agreements. Forget about driving my 190 SL, however. I go by the principle that I should never lend my car to a friend. I could end up losing both if the friend smashes up the car and doesn't pay for the damages.

"Besides, now is the time to start saving for your own car with the money that I'm paying you. Just think, if you generate another ten solutions, that's an extra $1,000 you can use for purchasing a car. With the $900, that's almost half of what you need for a $4,000 car."

"I could put you into bankruptcy if I get on a roll with the matchstick exercise and think of one thousand more solutions. But then I'd be able to buy an exotic sports car like yours, and not just an ordinary set of wheels," pronounced Sheldon.

"Sheldon, you couldn't bankrupt me even if I had to pay you for ten thousand new solutions to the exercise," declared Brock as he motioned for the waiter to bring him the bill. "Remember, I would still have my creativity. I know it's worth at least $10 million, because I wouldn't part with it for such a small sum."

Strive for originality in thought and action.

Be first;

Be different;

And be daring.

Only then will you make a significant impact on this world.

You may even attain greatness.

As Sheldon started responding to Brock, Korina interrupted him again. "Brock, you're right! There has to be another solution to the exercise. I just thought of another way of getting one."

Brock looked at Korina and replied. "Shoot. Let's have it."

Korina smiled excitedly, "In the seminar you said that the equation is made of matchsticks. I can take one of the matchsticks, light it up, and burn some of the others and get a solution. This is only moving one of the matchsticks."

"Why didn't I think of that?" wondered Brock aloud as he looked at Silvina and Sheldon.

"And what solution do you wind up with?" asked Brock looking back at Korina.

"There has got to be one," claimed Korina.

"Okay, let's draw out the equation with matchsticks," offered Brock.

As soon as Brock was finished, Korina announced: "There, see it! Just take one of the matchsticks from the 2. Light it up and burn the one that's left, along with the matchsticks in the plus sign. Then throw the first matchstick away. Now the equation says 6 equals 6."

Brock was highly impressed. "This solution is amazing, Korina. Another blockbuster one that I wish I would have thought of by myself."

"I'll say," Sheldon nodded his agreement.

"Not only that," added Silvina, "Korina can move any one of four matchsticks in the 2 or the plus sign and burn the others to get the same result. These are four different solutions and Korina gets $400, right Brock?"

"That she does," Brock agreed. "These two geniuses are sure costing me a lot of money. Before they get through with me, I may have to sell 100,000 copies of the book just to break even. But at least I'll have a great title and 1,001 blockbuster solutions to the exercise."

Privately, Sheldon felt a bit of disappointment that he hadn't come up with Korina's latest method of solving the exercise. It wasn't only the extra $400 that he could have earned from the four variations. It was also that coming up with this method of solving the matchstick exercise was ingenious, but not that ingenious that he couldn't have come up with it himself.

Instead of being dismayed, just happily surrender when the world hasn't brought you what you want.

For everything you have been denied, the world has brought you something better.

It is your duty to discover what it is.

When Sheldon arrived home, he was still disappointed that he'd overlooked Korina's four blockbuster solutions involving burning the matchsticks. This motivated him to spend additional time on the matchstick exercise. Although it was difficult and uncomfortable to keep looking for more solutions until 3 o'clock in the morning, Sheldon generated three new solutions — all blockbusters — by the time he decided to call it quits.

This was the day when Sheldon realized that he was indeed highly creative, and that his creative talent, if put to good use, was worth $1 million. Over time it could be worth even $10 million. As Brock had said in the second seminar, *"It's better to have $1 million of thinking ability than $1 million. The $1 million can be spent or lost easily. Your creativity is always there when you need it."*

Just one great idea can change your
life dramatically.

Look for it.

It's there somewhere.

When he finally went to bed, Sheldon's thoughts, before falling asleep, turned to what he might learn in Brock's next seminar on applying The Easy Rule of Life to money and happiness.

Two life courses are available to
every one of us:

We can disappear into the main
stream.

Or we can be true to ourselves and
swim against the current.

One is a form of self-abandonment.

The other is an adventure into new
worlds and fascinating dimensions.

****

6

Your talent and creativity are gifts
that the Universe gave to you.

The inspirational and magical things
that you do with them are the gifts
that you give back to the Universe.

Brock began the third seminar by asking the trainees whether any of them had applied The Easy Rule of Life and his seven creativity principles since the last seminar. Zoria, a woman in her thirties, who hadn't spoken previously, was first to speak. She shared how she had used her creativity to help solve a family crisis. She didn't want to divulge the nature of the crisis, since it was deeply personal. It was a serious family matter that was causing an incredible amount of anxiety, stress, and anger for several members. There appeared to be no way to resolve the matter.

Zoria remarked, "I remembered what Brock said about there always being more than one solution to every problem, and how the blockbuster solution was normally the seventh or eighth solution. Although everyone else in my family had resigned themselves to a solution that didn't please anyone, I kept looking for new solutions. Three days into the crisis, I came up with a blockbuster solution. It resolved the problem to the satisfaction of everyone concerned."

Several more trainees recounted their experiences. Joe was the last one to share. He mentioned how he'd landed a job as an assistant manager at a sporting goods store. "Instead of taking the easy and comfortable way by doing what everyone else was doing, I did the difficult and uncomfortable," Joe said confidently. "All the other applicants sent in their resumes, hoping that they would get an interview and then convince the interviewer to give them the job. I could have done the same, but I decided to be different.

"I went down to the store and watched what was going on for two hours. I spotted several areas that needed improvement. Then I phoned the manager and let him know what I would accomplish if I got the job. He promptly asked me to come in for an interview, and offered me the job on the spot, without interviewing anyone else."

After Brock acknowledged the trainees who shared their experiences, he gave a preview of what was to come. "In this session, we'll address how the application of The Easy Rule of Life is the foundation for handling money, so that you don't have any serious financial problems. We will also see how The Easy Rule of Life relates to the degree of overall happiness you get to experience in your life."

Brock raised his voice. "LET'S START WITH MONEY.

"MONEY. MONEY. MONEY. PRACTICALLY EVERYONE ASPIRES TO HAVING PILES OF IT.

CLEARLY, IN THE WESTERN WORLD NOTHING IS DEEMED AS PRECIOUS AS MONEY. TO SOME PEOPLE, MONEY IS MORE IMPORTANT THAN LIFE ITSELF.

"YET MONEY CAN BE ANYTHING YOU WANT IT TO BE. MONEY CAN BE THE ROOT OF ALL EVIL. MONEY CAN BE SOMETHING THAT ANSWERS ALL THINGS. MONEY CAN BE SOMETHING THAT BURNS A HOLE IN YOUR POCKET. MONEY CAN BE A MEANS TO FREEDOM; MONEY CAN BE AN INTERESTING CONCEPT — IT CAN EVEN BE A STUPID CONCEPT.

"Whatever you cause money to be, remember that you created the concept. If money is evil to you, you caused it to be evil. If money is a problem to you, you caused it to be a problem. If money is precious to you, you caused it to be precious. If money is joy to you, you caused this concept. You must take full responsibility for your concepts about money. Be clear that these are just concepts — nothing more and nothing less. Concepts are beliefs. And remember, unchallenged belief is a disease.

"We've already discussed how important it is to undertake the uncomfortable task of challenging our most cherished beliefs. Needless to say, our beliefs about money are the ones that we tend to hang onto more than any others. Whatever beliefs you have about money and what it's going to do for you, I would suggest that you set them aside, at least for the remainder of this seminar.

"No doubt money can do a lot for us, but we allow it to have too much control over our lives. The problem is that most of us don't acknowledge the truth about money. Some of us may not know the truth, and we don't want to hear the truth. Others know the truth deep down, but are in denial about it. Accepting the truth would destroy the one big fantasy about money — the one about how it will save our hides.

"We cling dearly to our beliefs, attitudes, and assumptions about money, regardless of how much contradictory evidence the world brings our way. This keeps us locked into an unhealthy relationship with money. Unfortunately, unhealthy and unrealistic attitudes toward money lead to financial problems that can complicate all areas of our lives.

"To have a good relationship with money, it's important to put money in its place. The truth about money is that the lack of it for the basics in life can make us unhappy, but obtaining a great deal of money won't make us truly happy by itself. This sounds contradictory, but it isn't. We'll discuss why obtaining a great deal of money won't guarantee true happiness in the latter part of this session.

"To start with, I think that everyone will agree that a lack of money for the important things in life can detract from our happiness. This being the case, in order to have sufficient money, we must handle it properly. This is where The Easy Rule of Life comes into the picture again. For those of you who may have already forgotten The Easy Rule of Life, let's display it again."

Sheldon turned on the computer to project the PowerPoint image onto the screen.

THE EASY RULE OF LIFE

Brock pointed to the left side of the diagram. "As in all other areas of life, 80 percent of us take the easy and comfortable way insofar as handling money. Needless to say, being in the 80 percent means that life is financially difficult and uncomfortable. To put it another way, we end up with money problems. Worse, we are in denial about who caused these problems."

"These are some things we do that are initially easy and comfortable, but create money problems for us in the long term," added Brock. He motioned for Sheldon to project a new frame onto the screen.

It's Easy and Comfortable but Financially Damaging to:

- Rely on others for our prosperity.
- Do what practically everyone else is doing.
- Spend all the money we earn.
- Spend all the money we can borrow.
- Opt for instant gratification.
- Forget about creating wealth for the future.

After Brock read what was on the screen, he stressed why the trainees should take responsibility for their money problems.

"If you want life to be easy and comfortable financially, the first difficult and uncomfortable thing that you must do is accept responsibility for your money problems — today and for the rest of your life. You must point the finger at yourself, as hard as it may be. Placing blame on outside forces will ensure that you continue to have money problems, regardless of how much money you earn.

"People who take the easy and comfortable way blame their money problems on not having enough money. This ensures that they continue to have money problems. They become victims of their own shortcomings, and never escape their financial difficulties."

Shona, another woman who hadn't spoken in the first two seminars, raised her hand. Brock turned and acknowledged her.

"I disagree with you. Not having enough money to pay your bills will lead to money problems, not the fact that you won't blame yourself for them," argued Shona. "Obviously, people who have attained financial freedom don't have money problems. Not everyone can make $500,000 a year and attain financial freedom in the process. People who are on the lower income levels are all going to have money problems, and people who make $500,000 a year won't."

"I can assure you that there are tens of thousands of people who make $35,000 a year who don't have any money problems to speak of," came the swift reply from Brock.

"On the other hand," he continued, "there are many people who make $500,000 a year, and still have serious money problems, to the point that many creditors are scouring the bushes looking for them. Many high-income earners end up declaring personal bankruptcy several times in their lives, while millions of low-income earners don't ever have to declare personal bankruptcy. Isn't this at least some indication to you that there is something more to avoiding money problems than how much money you earn?"

"I suppose, but it's certainly easier to eliminate money problems when you attain financial freedom," insisted Shona.

"Let's be clear about something, Shona. In order that we can attain financial freedom, it's important that we first clarify what financial freedom is. True financial freedom isn't about how much money you earn. Financial freedom is nothing more than having more money coming in than going out. If you earn $1,500 a month and spend $1,450 a month, guess what? You have attained financial freedom because you don't have money problems. So the key to financial freedom is to continually have more money coming in than going out."

"This usually involves having to earn more money. That's a lot easier said than done," sighed Shona.

"No doubt, it is, Shona. That's what The Easy Rule of Life is all about — doing the difficult stuff instead of the easy stuff. We already covered how we can use creativity and opportunity to earn more money. Of course, it's easier to gripe about money than to go out and create it. But it doesn't serve any purpose to have belief systems about how society and the system are putting it to us in the area of money. We end up with a bag of excuses about our lack of money, instead of learning the techniques for obtaining the amount we need to let it serve us in living a satisfying life."

Brock now addressed the entire audience.

"There's no doubt in my mind that everyone is this room has the ability to earn a decent income. As underachieving adults, you have a choice: You can spend all your time debating esoteric subjects with the pseudo-intellectuals at the local coffee bar, or you can utilize some of that time working on creative and constructive projects. The latter produces satisfaction, happiness, and wealth; the former leads to confusion, frustration, anger, resentment, and, in many cases, poverty.

"There's nothing wrong with taking it easy. In fact, I, more than most people, advocate a healthy balance between work and play. However, devoting all of your time to nebulous activities leaves no time for the constructive and creative activities that are so extremely important for producing financial results. Once you put your creative talent to work, earning sufficient money for the basics is relatively easy. Actually, it's nothing to brag about, given that a large majority of people in Western society earn a decent income.

"So, let's all agree that we're going to sooner or later put our creativity and talent to great use, and earn a decent income. After we earn our money, spending it wisely is the magical accomplishment. Any fool can spend money, but it takes responsibility, will power, wisdom, and genius to spend a portion of it on things that bring you true satisfaction, and to save the rest of it for things that will make a big difference in your life sometime in the future. This is the way to financial freedom, and the way to avoiding money problems."

Brock paused briefly to look at his notes on the lectern. "Let's look now at one of the most difficult things we must do to avoid money problems. We must get in touch with our emotions and find out why we mistreat money. Unless we address and rectify these emotional problems, we'll always have money problems."

"You make it sound like we're all neurotic," interjected Joe with a smile on his face. "What sort of emotional problems are you talking about?"

"The emotional problems that cause us to spend money that we don't have, and to spend money on things that don't bring us any satisfaction," specified Brock. "Perhaps you've noticed that many of our spending habits are beyond the comprehension of common sense. Will Rogers said it more eloquently than I could: 'Too many people spend money they haven't earned, to buy things they don't want, to impress people they don't like.' "

A few chuckles were heard as Brock continued.

"I believe that practically everyone here will agree that there's a bit of this financial insanity in all of us. The only way to change this type of irrational behavior is to get in touch with our underlying emotional desires, and then fulfill them in ways that money can't. Money can buy us cars, houses, trinkets, fleeting sex, shallow companionship, cheap attention, and superficial status. Money can't buy us peace, love, or happiness, however."

Brock then spent over twenty minutes explaining that unconscious psychological motivators, along with a poor sense of reality, are normally responsible for people's irrational monetary behavior. Behind every irrational spending urge is a profound emotional desire that requires attention. It can be power, status, fame, freedom, revenge, respect, security, or self-respect. It can even be love.

Not just one, but several of these unfulfilled emotional desires in conjunction with each other, normally drive people to purchase something they don't need, and likely can't afford. People need to be able to deal with these emotional desires head on, because in most cases more material goods aren't going to make things any better. A feeling of inadequacy can keep people making irrational purchases for the rest of their lives.

Instead of admitting what is driving their spending habits, most people rationalize their expenditures. Brock used the example of a person who impulsively buys the latest model of computer for $3,000, despite having spent $2,000 for a new one just a year earlier. He tells himself that the new computer is going to make him more productive with the work he brings home from the office. This rationalization is somewhat muted, given that he uses the home computer for pleasurable Internet encounters 95 percent of the time. The underlying reason that he wants the new computer is his fear of losing the respect of his friends, who always have the latest models.

Another example Brock used was a woman who, on the verge of completing an MBA degree, exceeded her credit card limit to buy herself a $3,000 Cartier watch. Despite having $45,000 in student loans, and no job lined up, she justified the large expenditure by telling herself that the watch was a reward for how hard she had worked to complete her degree. In this case, a lack of self-confidence was the underlying emotional problem driving her irrational spending tendencies.

She was striving for status to compensate for a weak self-image. Brock cited studies that confirm university students majoring in business are more likely to buy expensive watches, pens, and briefcases when they have lower grades and face uncertain job prospects.

Brock summed up this segment by saying that money is a means through which people channel their deeper wants, needs, goals, hopes, and dreams. Unfortunately, emotional desires such as a sense of accomplishment, happiness, and peace of mind cannot be satisfied through money. These desires can only be satisfied through outer creative efforts and inner growth.

Forget about destiny.

You don't need destiny to soar to greater heights.

You need to tune into higher frequencies.

Brent, the young bushy-haired, bearded man who had questioned Brock about beliefs in the first seminar, and about creativity in the second one, again challenged Brock about people's needs and wants.

"How about our levels of needs as described by Abraham Maslow? We have many unfulfilled needs that relate to physical and security aspects. These all require money. This is why people purchase many of the things they purchase."

"Indeed, we all have basic needs relating to water, food, shelter, and security," Brock agreed. "Beyond that, it's a question of how much food, shelter, and security we actually require. People's desires to upgrade their food, shelter, and security are wants. What we are talking about are unfulfilled wants and not unfulfilled needs. A want is different from a need. In fact, upon close scrutiny, you'll find that all your needs are presently satisfied."

"No they're not," protested Brent. "I have a lot of needs that are unfulfilled."

"Brent, you're fooling yourself about your unfulfilled needs," Brock countered. "Not only are all your needs satisfied today, they have been since birth. Otherwise you wouldn't be alive at this moment."

Most of the other trainees smiled, but Brent frowned. He thought carefully for a few moments before he answered. "Okay, it's a case of semantics. What I do have is a lot of unsatisfied wants."

"Big deal," snapped Brock. "So does everyone else on this planet. Economists tell us that human wants are insatiable. This means that all our wants are impossible to satisfy. If your wants are impossible to satisfy, you must get them under control. Otherwise, you're destined for financial ruin. As the graffiti writer declared, 'You can never get enough of what you really don't need.' "

Brent shrugged his shoulders, but didn't say anything.

"Brent, don't get me wrong," Brock resumed. "There's no harm in having material wants and satisfying these wants if you can afford to. What gets people into financial trouble is buying things that they can't truly afford. And sadly, people don't even truly want many of these things. They just *think* they want these things because advertisers have convinced them that they'll be happy if they acquire the best junk money can buy.

"Let's look at how to avoid falling into the trap of buying things that you don't need and don't even truly want," he said as he walked back toward the platform and addressed the whole audience again. "This is the most effective way to handle your wants, so that you don't end up in a financial mess, and at the same time end up possessing a lot of personal belongings that do you absolutely no good.

"When purchasing something, you must take the difficult and uncomfortable route. You must confront your wants. It's a case of taking some time to think about all your intended purchases. Ask yourself what benefit or how much satisfaction you will truly receive from the item or service you intend to purchase. Always be honest with yourself, and you'll end up purchasing a fraction of the things that you would have purchased if you hadn't taken the time to question the benefits you had hoped to receive."

Just as important as deciding what you want in life is deciding what you don't want.

Allow yourself to let go of those things that don't make you happy.

Oddly enough, they aren't always the easiest things to give up.

Erica, the radiant and positive woman in her mid-twenties, who had in the first seminar indicated that she didn't want to suffer all her life because of The Easy Rule of Life, now protested again.

"Brock, I don't think I want to stand in stores and question everything I buy. This would take the fun out of shopping, and make it a tedious and unhappy experience. I bet you don't always take the time to think about all your purchases. Don't you ever impulsively buy anything?"

"Naturally, I buy a few things on impulse," admitted Brock. "But these things normally cost less than $20. Keep in mind that I can afford to do this with cheaper items, because I make an income significantly above the average. For purchases over $20, I routinely evaluate what benefits I will get out of the intended purchase. And guess what, Erica?"

"Okay, I'll bite. What?" Erica asked cheerfully.

"I invariably find that my best purchases are the ones that I never made," smiled Brock.

There were a few chuckles throughout the room.

"What's the point of not spending your money? Isn't there ultimately only one purpose for money — to spend it?" mused Ting mischievously.

"Definitely. I couldn't agree with you more. I wouldn't have to question any of my purchases if I had unlimited funds. But really, who has? Therefore, I have to save money for future expenditures. Someone once said that to buy what you don't need is to steal from yourself. You have probably found this out many times: It's impossible to spend your money on something important after you've done something else with it."

"I have to confess that this has happened to me several times," laughed Ting.

"Allow me to say one more thing about how to keep your spending in check by controlling your wants," said Brock. "With just a little will power, you can do without most wants for at least a week or two. And with a little more will power, you can do without them for a month. You'll find in most cases that if you go without a want long enough, it normally goes away."

For the better part of two hours Brock discussed several principles of good money management, such as the merits of avoiding credit cards as much as possible. He advised the trainees that they could not spend themselves to self-respect, happiness, and prosperity. In addition, he warned the trainees about spending money they hadn't earned.

"The financial stress of having to pay for something expensive that you bought some time ago, and didn't even enjoy, is unquantifiable," he told them.

"'It's a simple fact. Your financial position is governed by how you treat money," he added. "It's healthy when you're responsible and respectful of your money. When you treat it with disrespect, you are also being disrespectful to yourself. And when you show little respect for yourself, you repel the good things in life, including wealth.

"The fact is, most people spend their money in ways that they hope will please others, so that they'll be accepted by them. The alternative is to spend money to please only yourself. You'll have to spend a lot less when you get over trying to please others and being accepted by them.

"The key here is to be an in-tune person. In-tune people have a sense of being in touch with their inner selves, and know that they don't need to impress others. As I said in an earlier presentation, the best way to impress others is by not trying to impress them. By developing your inner self, and not needing to impress others, you won't need nearly as much money to function in the outer world. In fact, just ten minutes of quiet reflection each day will mean you need thousands or tens of thousands of dollars a year less to operate financially."

Brock also emphasized that the trainees should take the difficult and uncomfortable route and save a portion of their money, regardless of how little they earned. "This is where The Easy Rule of Life really applies," he stressed. "It comes right back to the importance of keeping agreements with yourself. There's a price to be paid for saving for the future; however, there is an even bigger price to be paid for spending all your money today.

"Once you set money aside for a particular purpose, make sure that you don't touch it. Label these funds as untouchable. If you take the easy way out, you'll spend this money when the first temptation for instant gratification hits. Unfortunately, instant gratification has a big price on it, and leads to financial pain down the road.

"If you take the difficult and uncomfortable route, you will resist any and every temptation to touch those funds. By routinely saving a portion of your income, and watching your untouchables grow and grow, you'll find that there's nothing like having a nice little nest egg to give you a sense of financial freedom. Remember the difference between spending 10 percent more than you earn and spending 10 percent less than you earn. The first translates respectively into financial chaos and eventual personal bankruptcy, versus the second, which translates into financial satisfaction and personal freedom.

"If any of you think that your income is far too low for you to save any money, you may want to take a lesson from Oseola McCarty. She was a washerwoman with a grade-six education. In 1995, when she was eighty-seven years old, Ms. McCarty became a folk celebrity after she gave $150,000 to a scholarship fund for poor blacks at the University of Southern Mississippi. I might add that she had never visited this university previously.

"Oseola McCarty's donation later gained her an honorary doctorate degree from Harvard University. She also received praise and acknowledgments from President Bill Clinton and the United Nations. Not bad for a woman with a grade-six education, earning an income that most of us would reject as too low to live on.

" 'So, how does a low-income washerwoman amass a $150,000 fortune to give away to a university?' all of you should be asking me." Brock paused briefly.

"Simple but not easy," he continued. "Ms. McCarty took the difficult and not so comfortable route with her money. Being a responsible person, she saved a good portion of it instead of blowing it on things that she didn't need or truly want. She actually managed to save over $250,000 from washing and ironing other people's clothes in her home. Needless to say, her house wasn't air-conditioned. And her income was far lower than every one of you is capable of earning with just a little bit of effort.

"As a tribute to Ms. McCarty, I would like to end my spiel on handling money by quoting her. In 1996, after she gave a good portion of her nest egg away, she actually wrote a book called *Simple Wisdom for Rich Living*. In her book, Ms. McCarty advised us, 'It's not the ones that make the big money, but the ones who know how to save who get ahead.' This may sound like unsophisticated wisdom, and it is, but it's powerful wisdom. Above all, I hope that all of you learn enough from the story about Ms. McCarty to never have serious money problems. She never had another money problem, because she followed her own advice."

By the time Brock ended the part on money management, there were forty-five minutes left in the three-hour seminar. He announced a fifteen-minute coffee break, and stated that the last half hour would be devoted to how the trainees could attain true happiness for the rest of their lives.

****

> Being happy in this world is not your right.
>
> It is your duty and responsibility, however.

"Okay," Brock announced in a loud but somewhat mild voice to start the last part of the seminar. "Now that all of you are on track to getting rich and handling your riches wisely, the last thing we're going to handle is how to apply The Easy Rule of Life to happiness. Some of you may think that once you attain wealth, you automatically attain happiness.

"Nothing can be further from the truth. The truth is, after necessities are provided for, happiness doesn't seem to care that much about money. Wise people have been saying that money can't buy happiness for ages, but no one, especially in the modern world, seems to believe it."

Michelle, a woman sitting in the middle of the crowd, was quick to offer her opinion about money and happiness. "I agree that a lot of money in itself won't make me truly happy. But I believe that having the money to do the things I want to do will make me happy."

"What sorts of things?" asked Brock.

"Well, for example," replied Michelle, "I am very unhappy living in Vancouver. I would like to have the money to buy a nice-sized acreage in the country, where I could experience a state of bliss and happiness that I can't attain in a big city."

"Perhaps you will be happy in the country, perhaps not. Good luck, anyway, Michelle," stated Brock.

> *Everyone seems to want to be somewhere they aren't.*
>
> *Choose to be where you are right now and you will be happier than 90 percent of humankind.*

Surprised by Brock's response, Michelle indignantly asked, "What's wrong with believing that I would be a lot happier if I lived in the country instead of a big city?"

"Don't be so sure that you'll be any happier in the country," advised Brock. "I can guarantee you that there are thousands of unhappy people living in the country right now, who think that they would be happy if they could live in a big city such as Vancouver. Ultimately, it's not city or country living that determines whether people will be happy where they live."

"Well, what is it, if you are so smart?" asked Michelle. "I'm certainly not happy living in Vancouver, because it's a rat race I could do without."

"To be peaceful and happy living wherever you are," Brock said to the doubtful Michelle, "you must be able to experience gratitude. But I detect that you're not very good at this. I'm not saying that you can't be happy living in the country. Ultimately, you may actually find that country living is much better for your peace of mind and health than living in a big city. But, until you've learned to experience gratitude and be happy in the city at least half the time, there's a good chance you won't be truly happy in the country either.

"On that note, Michelle, do you want to know how to guarantee that you'll be happy when you move to the country?"

"Okay, how?" asked Michelle doubtfully.

"Follow these two rules of happiness," said Brock matter-of-factly. He then asked Sheldon to project a new frame onto the overhead screen.

RULE #1

Be happy with who you are, where you are, with what you have.

RULE #2

When you find yourself unhappy with what life brings your way, go back to Rule #1.

After everyone in the audience had a chance to read what was on the screen, Brock looked back at Michelle.

"In other words, Michelle, you must start experiencing the city as a happy place. If you do, you'll have no problem in the country. Think that the city is a lousy place all of the time and you're likely to think the same of the country once you live there for a while. The Buddhists have a saying that no matter where you go, there you are."

> The only way to win and be
> successful, sometimes – is just to be
> happy and blown away with what
> you already have today.

"Much of our happiness is dependent upon our ability to be grateful for what we have," Brock continued, now addressing everyone in the audience. "Let's get back to what I previously said about happiness not caring that much about money after the basics are provided for in life.

"The way I see it, if you are grateful and happy for what you have on a low or modest income, you'll also be happy when you have a lot of money coming your way. But if you are miserable and unhappy with a modest income, then you certainly won't be grateful and happy, even if you acquire $10 million. You'll still be miserable and unhappy, but with a lot more style and comfort."

A few smiles and chuckles came from the audience.

"Indeed," Brock continued, "you may be even more miserable and unhappy than before you acquired the $10 million. You'll no longer be able to say that you're not happy because you don't have enough money. There will be nothing but unhappiness and misery to look forward to."

Ron, the bearded man with his hair tied back in a ponytail, who had first questioned Brock about what was wrong with wanting a comfortable life, and then about the purpose of keeping trivial agreements, now vigorously confronted Brock again.

"I can't let you keep repeating this nonsense without speaking up. I just won't let you!"

"Go ahead, Ron. You have the floor," responded Brock.

"Your claim that money can't buy happiness is garbage," said Ron angrily. "I know it isn't true. You agreed that a lack of money will make you unhappy. Obtaining a lot of money, then, has to make you happy."

"Fine, do you have more proof than this?" Brock asked gently.

"As a matter of fact, I do," uttered Ron. "Studies show that rich people are happier than poor people. This proves that money can buy happiness."

"No it doesn't," said Brock, a little louder. "The problem is that you're hanging onto the best belief system that your mind can create in regard to money and happiness. You'll accept any little bit of information that supports you, just to protect your beliefs about what money can do for you, and disregard anything significant that is counter to your beliefs.

"Look, Ron," Brock continued, "I agree that certain studies show rich people are generally happier than poor people. But it doesn't mean that all rich people are happy. First of all, many rich people are in a neutral state, where they're not unhappy. But they aren't happy, either. In the neutral state, they may be happier than most poor people, who are having difficulty paying for the basics of life. That doesn't mean that these rich people are truly happy.

"In fact, let me cite the findings of Ed Diener, a researcher at the University of Illinois, who specializes in happiness. He found that 30 percent of the top income earners aren't as happy as the average American. This study in itself should be enough evidence that money can't buy happiness. Ron, be patient. We will do an exercise shortly, and it may help change your mind, if you're willing to be open minded and suspend your beliefs about money and what it can do for you."

"I can hardly wait," said Ron facetiously.

Be unduly mindful of what you perceive as a happy life.

A happy life isn't the absence of unhappiness.

Unhappiness will sneak into your life whether you want it or not.

So will happiness.

What you choose to do with either is up to you.

Just as Brock was about to continue, Ting put up his hand to offer his thoughts. He started speaking before Brock was able to acknowledge him.

"Brock, there's a point I would like to make in regard to the studies Ron cited."

"Let's have it," said Brock cordially.

"Studies may show that rich people are happier than poor people, but that doesn't in itself prove that it's the money that makes them happier," suggested Ting. "There's no proven cause and effect relationship. This may be a case of which came first — the chicken or the egg? Perhaps many people became wealthy because they were essentially happy even when they were poor. The fact that they were happy and positive about life when they were poor may have helped them to become rich. Poor people who are unhappy about life and gripe about it, never doing anything about it, are more likely to remain poor and unhappy."

"That's a very good point, Ting. To be honest, I wish I would have thought of it myself," Brock said.

You will be able to tell when you have attained true happiness.

Real happiness doesn't cost much.

Unworkable substitutes do.

Brock walked to the lectern and quickly glanced at his notes before he resumed.

"For interest's sake, if for nothing else, I would like to cite some more of the research findings by Ed Diener. He's the University of Illinois psychologist specializing in what makes people happy. After conducting several studies, he concluded that money can add some more pleasure to people's lives, but won't bring the true happiness that comes with self-respect, accomplishment, and satisfaction.

"In one research project, Diener found that lottery winners may have had some sense of happiness for a while; however, they were no happier one year after their good fortune than they were before winning the jackpot. In other words, if people were miserable and unhappy before winning the lottery, it didn't take them that long before they became just as miserable and unhappy again."

Ursula, the blonde woman with a Dutch accent, who had in the first seminar claimed that she had been deprived of love in her childhood, and blamed her parents for some of her shortcomings, now spoke vehemently.

"I don't care what some arrogant academic at some two-bit University says. Money can buy you long-term happiness, it can buy you peace of mind, and it can even buy you enlightenment. You can't have any of these when you're poor or have financial problems."

Brock didn't say anything, but the look on his face said, "*I don't believe that you're even close to getting it.*" Instead, he thought for a brief moment and then addressed everyone else in the audience.

"Who here thinks that Ursula would be a genuinely happy person, way into eternity, if she won $10 million in a lottery?"

An eerie silence swept over the room. Not one hand went up. Even Ron and Michelle didn't put up their hands.

Soon Ursula blurted out, her voice rising with the heat of anger, "Everyone here is wrong. If I won a $10-million lottery, I'd be the happiest person in the world. I'd prove that a lot of money can buy happiness."

Brock paused again, and then spoke in a loud voice briefly for effect, "THAT'S UTTER NONSENSE, URSULA. HAPPINESS CAN BE EARNED, CREATED, AND EXPERIENCED, BUT IT CAN'T BE PURCHASED, REGARDLESS OF HOW MUCH MONEY YOU HAVE.

"If acquiring lots of money led to long-term and genuine happiness, the wealthy of this world would be walking around with perpetual smiles on their faces. The last time I checked, they didn't appear to smile that much more than the rest of us. Far from it. In fact, I know a few wealthy people who seem to be in pain whenever they manage a smile. My guess is that these people also once thought that they would the happiest individuals on Earth if they attained substantial wealth."

Some of the audience smiled while Ursula, obviously taken aback by his comments, just glared at Brock.

"Ursula, don't think that I'm making fun of you. We all fall into the trap of believing that a lot of money will bring us happiness," added Brock. "In fact, I would like to acknowledge and thank you, as well as Michelle and Ron, for your opinions about money and happiness. Your contributions are an excellent lead into my exercise, which challenges the folly of believing that genuine happiness can be attained through money.

"Now, I would like everyone to take the time to list the elements of happiness that money *can't* buy. I'm talking about priceless things that contribute to happiness, which can't be purchased regardless of how rich you get. And there are more than just one or two of these elements."

After giving the participants five minutes to reflect on their own, Brock asked them to share their answers. Sheldon recorded the entries in the computer, and then projected the list onto the overhead screen. Soon the number of priceless elements of happiness grew to thirty-seven.

Elements of Happiness That Money Can't Buy

Health	Street Smarts	Luck
Longevity	Patience	Charm
Self-reliance	Physical Fitness	Gratitude
Creativity	Compassion	Self-esteem
Real Friends	Empathy	Time
Achievement	Emotional Stability	Greatness
Satisfaction	Spiritual Fulfillment	Wisdom
Loving Family	Money Management	Warmth
Integrity	Money Appreciation	Humility
Reputation	Sense of Humor	True Love
Peace of Mind	Enjoyment of Leisure	Courage
Great Character	A Good Night's Sleep	Generosity
Respect of Others		

Brock then stated, almost hollering, "THIS IS DIRECTED AT ALL OF YOU INDIVIDUALS WHO STILL THINK THAT MONEY CAN BUY HAPPINESS. WE'VE NOW LISTED THIRTY-SEVEN ELEMENTS OF HAPPINESS THAT MONEY CAN'T BUY. NOW, IF HAPPINESS IS A BY-PRODUCT OF ALL THESE THINGS, AND THESE THINGS CAN'T BE PURCHASED WITH MONEY, THEN HOW CAN MONEY BUY HAPPINESS?"

Brock paused briefly. He then asked, gently, "Can anyone not see this?"

There was silence in the room. To no one's surprise, no one challenged him.

Silence – don't shun it.

Embrace it.

Silence is not only golden.

It is the universal refuge.

That's where you go for calm, peace,
self-love, creativity, and energy.

After a brief pause, Brock proceeded to end the seminar.

"You can resist the truth as much as you want, but the truth doesn't care how little you believe in it. Ultimately, happiness is a choice you make. The size of your bank account and the number of expensive material possessions have nothing to do with living a happy and joyful life. This planet is inhabited by many unhappy millionaires and billionaires who think that they may find happiness with more wealth. Unfortunately, they will never find true happiness, unless, of course, they change their ways.

"There is one more priceless element of happiness; it's so important in your life's journey. It's called 'purpose.' Take a close look at the great people of the world — Mother Teresa, The Dalai Lama, Nelson Mandela, and Mahatma Gandhi. These remarkable individuals lived with little in the way of money and possessions. Yet they experienced happiness, joy, and self-fulfillment throughout their lives. They weren't pursuing happiness and self-fulfillment as goals in themselves. Happiness and self-fulfillment were the result of having a higher purpose, one that involved working toward the common good of humanity and making a big difference in this world.

"The truth is, for practically all of us, that the greatest joys in life aren't derived from money, power, or prestige. They come from experiencing satisfaction as a result of total immersion in something worthwhile. Instead of money, or some other end result derived from it, a worthwhile activity — either work-related or a personal pursuit — becomes its own reward."

If only one impassioned adventurous soul works diligently to create a world that he or she believes in — one that is full of love and joy and decency and creativity and integrity and freedom and opportunity and self-sufficiency and excellence and truth and justice — and if he or she fails to come close in manifesting this kind of visionary world before he or she passes away to a different dimension, it's not this one impassioned adventurous soul who is crazy.

It's the rest of humanity.

197

"This may come as a surprise," continued Brock, "but you will all have to follow The Easy Rule of Life for the rest of your lives if you want to be happy. You must have a purpose or an important mission that offers some risk and challenge. This is vital if you want to continually experience the accomplishment and satisfaction that lead to true happiness."

"I would like to conclude by saying that it doesn't matter so much what you do for a living, or how much fame and fortune you attain, so long as you are enjoying peace, health, and love. If you don't possess these, what can replace them? Never lose sight of the fact that happiness is not an end in itself, but a by-product of a job well done, good health, doing your duty, pursuing your goals, accepting the inevitable, loving the world, showing gratitude, helping others achieve happiness, and living fully.

"By all means, spend a good portion of your life attaining all the personal success you would like to achieve. Make sure, however, that you have a full, relaxed, satisfying, and happy life along the way. Whatever success means to you, the journey toward it should feel better than the arrival. And if you're doing what's right for you, you won't have to pursue happiness. It will find you."

Prosperous

and

Free.

You can't be one — without the other.

****

The most ambitious destination can
be the easiest.

Pursuing your wildest dream does
three things:

It gives you flight.

It keeps you young.

It makes you highly creative.

Not to mention, there are other
rewards that are just as delightful.

After all the trainees left, Brock paid Sheldon $100 for his work at the seminar.

"Believe it or not, you owe me another $300," grinned Sheldon.

"And why's that?" Brock asked curiously.

"I generated three more solutions to the matchstick exercise on Monday night after I got home from meeting you at the Naam."

"No way!" exclaimed Brock. "Let's see what you've come up with this time."

After Sheldon had shown his new solutions to the matchstick exercise, Brock complemented him, and then gladly paid him.

"Now, does anyone have to tell you what a genius you are and what you're capable of when you set your mind to it?" asked Brock as he looked in his wallet.

This comment made Sheldon think about a passage he had read in *Life's Secret Handbook*.

> Surround yourself with individuals
> who support and encourage you,
> who are genuine voices of praise.
>
> Words that inspire the human soul
> are more precious than money,
> diamonds, and gold.

"I can give you $100 in cash," Brock continued, "and I'll have to give you a check for the other $200. Just out of curiosity, do you still have the $900 that I gave you the other night at the Naam?"

"It's all in the bank. I'm saving for a car. To use your term, it's in my untouchable account. I'm going to put another $300 of today's take into the car account and spend the other $100 frivolously," replied Sheldon.

"As I said before, you catch on quick, kid. Let's go and grab a coffee at the Bread Garden. I'll give you a lift home later," offered Brock.

"Great idea," agreed Sheldon, "especially the lift home. Too bad you couldn't just give me one of your cars — either the 190 SL or the Porsche would do just fine."

"Never mind," replied Brock. "You will have your own car in due time."

Today's happiness has no past and no future.

It is what it is.

Experience it while you can.

Happiness not enjoyed today is lost forever.

It was a warm and pleasant evening as Brock and Sheldon walked out of the Landmark Hotel onto Robson Street. Parked half a block away was Brock's Mercedes 190 SL convertible. Brock first put the top down. Then, much to Sheldon's surprise, Brock asked him if he would like to drive.

Sheldon truly enjoyed driving the Mercedes. Being a 1959 model, it was rather slow for a sports car, but gave him a sense of pleasure that he hadn't experienced driving any other car. Brock let him drive it to the Bread Garden, and then from the Bread Garden to Sheldon's home.

Later, in his aunt's house, Sheldon fantasized about how great it would be when he finally had enough money to purchase a Mercedes 190 SL for himself. He also thought how neat it would be if he ever earned as much money as Brock, and could buy many of the things he'd always wanted.

A few minutes later, Sheldon randomly opened *Life's Secret Handbook* to two pages near the end. Two powerful reminders of what Brock had emphasized appeared on the left and right pages. These proverbs struck a chord deep inside his heart. Sheldon would remember them, and quote them to others, for the rest of his life.

In the game of wanting to be
   rewarded for making a difference
   in this world, you ultimately end
   up with only one of the following:

1. Results.

   or

2. Reasons why you didn't get
   results.

~

Reasons only help you sound
   reasonable.

They have nothing to do with
   manifesting achievement and
   prosperity in your life.

****

7

You have two choices in your pursuit
of what's important to you:

Make bold moves today, knowing
most things won't work out, but one
or two may.

Or make no moves, knowing nothing
will ever work out.

The weeks passed into months and the months into years as Sheldon applied The Easy Rule of Life to all areas of his life, especially his career, his health, his physical fitness, his financial affairs, his family, and his social life. He also read a passage or two from *Life's Secret Handbook* every day, to give himself an emotional lift.

Ten years after meeting Brock, Sheldon was happily married and had a six-year old son. He lived in San Francisco, but still kept in regular contact with Brock, Silvina, and Korina. Brock had married Silvina and they remained in Vancouver. *Look Ma, Life's Easy* went on to become an international bestseller. Korina was now twenty years old and studying anthropology at one of Vancouver's universities.

Thanks to his application of the principles associated with The Easy Rule of Life, Sheldon was living a full, relaxed, happy, and satisfying life. His accomplishments made Brock truly proud. He had graduated from college and started work at a San Francisco based company. By utilizing Brock's seven principles of creativity, Sheldon had become the top salesperson for his firm for two years running.

Invite more mentors into your life.

Hang out with accomplished individuals – the passionate, the innovative, the risk-takers, the well-intentioned, the doers, and the truly prosperous – those who create value for the Universe and get rewarded handsomely for it.

Allow their spirit to strike a bright light within you, to make your own difference in this world, so that your legacy inspires those adventurous souls who live here after you to do the same.

A year later, Sheldon was promoted to marketing manager. He even completed an MBA degree via an evening program. When his employer expected that Sheldon work an average of sixty hours a week, he realized that The Easy Rule of Life also applied to people who were working too hard.

Sheldon came to grips with the fact that he was doing the easy and comfortable by staying with the company for the high salary and security that a regular job offered. The difficult and uncomfortable aspect of remaining with the company was that his life was unbalanced, and he couldn't spend as much time with his wife and son as he wanted.

He remembered Brock saying that a person had to do the difficult and uncomfortable if he or she ever wanted to get to the position that Brock himself enjoyed. Consequently, to the surprise of his friends and colleagues, Sheldon quit his high-paying job to pursue what he dreamed about most — to become an author and a motivational speaker.

> You don't have to deny yourself the prosperity and personal freedom that you would like.
>
> Live in the realm of already having the prosperity and personal freedom that you would like – and pay whatever price is required to live that way.

Because he had learned how to use his creativity as his biggest asset, it took Sheldon only a few years to establish himself as one of the top conference speakers in North America. He was paid up to $10,000 a speech.

Although it was possible for him to speak at 300 conferences a year, he only accepted a maximum of fifty paid speeches, so that he could lead a balanced life. He also donated his time to conduct ten life management seminars a year for various nonprofit organizations that specialized in helping disadvantaged young men and women.

As the international best-selling author of a book titled *Work at What You Are and Not at What You Ain't*, Sheldon was now a highly respected global authority on peak performance and life management. He was also a highly recognized media personality, featured in hundreds of publications ranging from *Success* magazine to *USA TODAY*.

> There is a Spiritual realm that
> encompasses all Beings.
>
> Embrace your guardian angels, who
> will be out of sight, but always
> there to assist you.
>
> Make good use of their assistance
> while creatively pursuing your
> dreams.
>
> Your success and prosperity will come
> much easier.

Sheldon's book sales helped him achieve a measure of financial independence and personal freedom that he had never thought possible. Indicative of his mastery at applying The Easy Rule of Life to his financial affairs, Sheldon purchased his own dream home in the Pacific Heights area in San Francisco. Unlike Brock, he first obtained a mortgage. He had the house fully paid for in seven years, however.

Sheldon also acquired his own older sports car. It was a black 1960 Mercedes 190 SL, with red interior and a black hardtop, purchased only three years after meeting Brock. Sheldon and his wife also shared a new Lexus sedan and a Porsche Boxster convertible.

Sheldon often reminisced about how Brock had insisted that if Oprah could face all the adversity in her life and still make a difference in the world, then Sheldon could do the same. Although he hadn't reached the stature of Oprah, Sheldon had come a long way. He had even become moderately famous, mainly through hosting a weekly personal development program for young adults on PBS Television. As a matter of course, The Easy Rule of Life was mentioned a lot on the show.

The Easy Rule of Life was also one of the main principles emphasized in the seminars that Sheldon presented for disadvantaged young adults. To emphasize the incredible opportunity in this world for anyone who looked for it, Sheldon also used Brock's matchstick exercise as an analogy. Incredibly, Sheldon now had a collection of thirty solutions to the exercise.

Although Sheldon had his own best-selling book, he still incorporated many of the maxims from *Life's Secret Handbook* into his speeches and seminars. One of his favorite passages was used to inspire his students to risk and try new things in life.

"So hard, so difficult," we say.

Things aren't difficult because we
   have tried them and found them to
   be so.

Things are difficult because we
   haven't tried them and continue to
   think that they are.

Another passage was used when Sheldon stressed the importance of having quality friends.

Make no mistake about it.

The degree of your success and
   happiness will be determined by the
   company you keep.

Keep good company and you shall
   become like them.

Keep bad company and the same
   applies.

Sheldon also used his own words to bring home this message. "If you have always wanted to become a degenerate, but have never quite been able to make it, then hang around with a bunch of degenerates. And if your goal is to be average, then hang around with people who are content to be average. However, if you aspire to greatness, then hang around with people who are doing difficult and uncomfortable things, and in the process are making a big difference in this world."

As an example of how much a disadvantaged person could attain if she was willing to give up being a victim, Oprah was mentioned a lot in Sheldon's speeches. He stressed that there were many things people could do to overcome being a victim of circumstance. They could psychologically, emotionally, and spiritually change the way they approached life. Sheldon also cited his own success as proof of what could be accomplished by disadvantaged individuals.

Not that there weren't any difficulties and major hurdles along the way to Sheldon's success. Brock had warned that using one's creativity and paying one's dues were necessary to get to places worth going. So did *Life's Secret Handbook*.

Never be discouraged because others
are more privileged or talented
than you.

You can always make up in creativity
what you lack in good fortune.

Playing the game of life is like
playing poker.

Playing three aces badly won't get
you as far as playing a terrible
hand well.

Achieving success wasn't easy. Sheldon had to overcome many difficulties and setbacks along the way.

What most people think is important for creative success is not so significant after all is said and done.

And what most people think is insignificant is vastly more important than most people could ever imagine.

To be more successful, learn to distinguish between the truly unimportant and the truly important.

Eventually you will be considered not only a genius, but a Master as well.

Brock had also warned that successful people have just as many problems as anyone else.

Be careful with success.

It's best to stop and ponder what it all means once you acquire it.

Success can also cause misery and
dejection.

Don't be surprised when you learn it
doesn't bring you all the happiness
and peace of mind you thought it
would.

One of the problems that Brock mentioned was that successful individuals should expect resentment from envious people who hadn't done their part to attain a share of success.

You will know when you are doing
something good, right, or important
in this world.

The amount of criticism you receive
will be deafening.

You will acquire more enemies as
well.

Sheldon often thought about how much satisfaction and joy he would have not experienced if he hadn't encountered The Easy Rule of Life and *Life's Secret Handbook*. Clearly, he may never have become a best-selling author, renowned public speaker, and high-profile media personality. He may have wound up like several of his old acquaintances, living an unfulfilled life and blaming society for it.

You alone get to decide how much
prosperity and personal freedom
you experience in life.

To depend on other forces —
including friends, relatives, society,
government, and chance events —
is to be a slave.

To depend wholly on yourself is to be
a Master.

So, slave or Master?

It's your call.

In his seminar presentations to underprivileged young
adults, Sheldon stressed that they should pursue their
vocational dreams instead of the career that pays the most
money. He also emphasized that they themselves should
decide what career to pursue, and not their parents, school
teachers, friends, or a school career counselor.

Most people go to their graves
regretting things they haven't done.

The easiest way to become like them
is by joining society's chorus instead
of singing your own songs.

Unlike many people, Sheldon had given up trying to figure out why life wasn't fair to everyone in this world. *Life's Secret Handbook* had put this matter in proper perspective.

Think often, but not too much.

And not too deeply.

Life is meant to be lived.

It isn't meant to be figured out.

Instead of trying to figure out why life wasn't fair, Sheldon decided to do his best and live life to the fullest, in spite of any disadvantages and prevailing negative circumstances he might face. This helped him achieve personal success that he had at one time felt was impossible. Ironically, by society's definition of success, Sheldon had actually become more successful than Brock.

Much more important than the fact that he had attained a good measure of fame and fortune, though, Sheldon was happy. He had achieved peace of mind because he lived a full, relaxed, and satisfying life, and was extremely grateful for having achieved it.

Identify all that is wrong in your life.

Then do what must be done to
correct it.

You cannot afford not to.

****

Now, almost ten years to the day after meeting Brock and finding his copy of *Life's Secret Handbook*, Sheldon was presenting one of his seminars in Oakland to a group of disadvantaged young adults. His assistant was Eduardo, a twenty-four-year-old Mexican and landed immigrant, who Sheldon had met just two days before. There was some irony in how he'd met Eduardo. Sheldon had just parked his Mercedes 190 SL on Polk Street in San Francisco. At the same time Eduardo stopped to admire it.

As Sheldon got out, Eduardo observed, "That's sure a nice old sports car. I sure wish I could own a car like that one."

"Why don't you?" asked Sheldon with a big smile.

"This isn't possible for a young Mexican like me, who has just moved to the United States. I am just starting out and struggling to make a living. So you see, Señor, owning an expensive car is an unattainable dream for me," reasoned Eduardo in his Mexican accent.

"Why is it an unattainable dream? I was raised in the ghettos of Los Angeles by a single mother, and faced with many disadvantages when I started out. If a black man like me with a disadvantaged past can own an older sports car, so can you."

"How? Did you win a big lottery?" wondered Eduardo.

"Not at all," smiled Sheldon. "By the way, my name is Sheldon. Let me tell you about The Easy Rule of Life."

Half an hour later Sheldon invited Eduardo to be his assistant at his seminar in Oakland. He also lent Eduardo his copy of *Life's Secret Handbook*. Eduardo curiously and

slowly opened the handbook toward the end and glanced at
two of the last few passages.

Look at the world around you.

It may seem like a hard place to live,
and a harder place to be happy.

It is neither.

With the right attitude – and your
God-given talent – you can make
it a Paradise unto itself.

~

Always do your best to make a big
difference in this world.

When you live your best, and
always do your best, the results
that you attain are, in fact, perfect.

Whatever the results – they couldn't
have come out any better.

****

ABOUT THE AUTHOR

Photograph by Greg Gazin

Ernie J. Zelinski is an international best-selling author, prosperity life coach, innovator, speaker, and unconventional career expert. Ernie has helped thousands of individuals from all walks of life in their major career transitions and retirement planning through his life-changing books.

Ernie's fifteen creative works — published in twenty-two languages in twenty-nine countries — have sold over 900,000 copies worldwide. His two international bestsellers *The Joy of Not Working* and *How to Retire Happy, Wild, and Free* have been featured in major international media such as *The Wall Street Journal* and have sold a total of over 575,000 copies.

Ernie's core message — that we all can be much more creative and really live life the way that it was meant to be lived — is at the heart of all his work. Ernie believes in the powers of common sense and creativity — instead of hard work — as the most important elements for achieving true success, financial independence, and personal freedom.

A SPECIAL REQUEST FROM THE AUTHOR

Ernie J. Zelinski would like to hear how *Look Ma, Life's Easy* has affected your life. Please share your success stories, insights, and experiences. Do you have a tip or excerpt that resonated with you big time? Let Ernie know about the positive difference that the book has made in your life. Ernie will make every reasonable effort to respond with a personal note and even send you an autographed complimentary copy of one of his other books. You can contact Ernie at:

Ernie J. Zelinski
c/o: Visions International Publishing
P.O. Box 4072
Edmonton, AB
Canada   T6E 4S8
Email: vip-books@telus.net

Virtual Gods

Tal Brooke
GENERAL EDITOR

HARVEST HOUSE PUBLISHERS
Eugene, Oregon 97402

Contents

92607

Introduction
Tal Brooke

More than once, a giant man-made beast has stood in the town square of history with the claim that it could change the world. In its bargain, it offered people something unique that they considered invaluable while firing their imaginations with the wonders it could perform. If it succeeded, the people would be compelled to magnify it to greatness while giving it the world to change in return. Such a beast entered history early in the last century. If we can understand it, we can also understand the beast that now inhabits the town square of history.

If you asked people in the early 1800s what machine had recently appeared that was changing their world, they would tell you it was the giant steam locomotive. In its heyday, nothing else captured the public imagination quite like the train. It became almost a national obsession with its power to travel great distances and move cargo across the land. Part of the train's allure, on the human end, was the thrill and mystique of the great railway journey so often described by the great writers and poets over the past century—from Mark Twain, Carl Sandburg, John Steinbeck, right up to Paul Theroux (author of *The Great Railway Bazaar*).

Consider the timeless image of the grand nineteenth-century freight trains thundering through small-town rural America with awed onlookers wishing they could climb aboard, on the wave of an impulse, and ride across America's vast expanse. The giant hissing locomotive was something that could take them to exciting places beyond the colorful descriptions handed down by travelers. It could take them through real country—into the wide-open prairies of Montana and Nebraska, the high mountain passes of Colorado, past the huge riverboats rolling down the Mississippi, through the country of Louisiana, and finally on to such great cities as San Francisco, New York, and Boston. During the train journey, the texture of life would unfold outside the car window as scenery, dialects, fashion, and weather changed constantly to form a rich narrative of life.

The romantic mystique of the locomotive journey viewed the traveler as expanding with each journey. Railway travel created rich perspective by quickly telescoping many of life's points of reference. The journey itself became a kind of exotic and liberating rite of passage. If urbane and sophisticated people became that way by having far more points of reference than ordinary folk—much of it gained through travel—*so could others*. And the same idea of inward expansion through travel remains to this day. At its heyday, the train was the beast in the center of the town square.

The train continues to be exciting—the point of Paul Theroux's best-selling narratives. But other mechanical beasts have filled the town square of history since the era of the railroad. Some have been smaller, such as the television and the automobile. Others have been far larger, such as the space shuttle and the Atlas rocket (seen through the eye of the television by most of today's onlookers).

Today, however, a new mechanical giant looms imposingly in the town square. It has entered our world with as much fanfare as the locomotive of the last century, dazzling the imaginations of those standing at the end of the twentieth century.

This new mechanical giant is called cyberspace. The inhabitants of today's global village are looking upon this new leviathan with growing amazement and expectation. Truly, it is the beast at the end of the twentieth century.

If we recall, one of the "miracles" of the train was that it carved up the world, for the first time connecting villages, towns, cities, and even nations. Now cyberspace is connecting the world in a wholly new way. Its omnipresent hardware already covers the earth like a vast neural network. The electronic components of cyberspace literally crisscross and mesh around the surface of the planet, creating an immense human-computer interface. The Internet is only a part of it—a starting point.

Many believe that the present beast will take the human race on a journey through far more exotic terrain than its counterpart of the last century. Many—the youth above all—look at cyberspace in wonder. The fascination of our youth with cyberspace was the inspiration for William Gibson's novel, *Neuromancer*. Gibson passed a digital arcade and saw the new generation reflecting the electronic digital world of computers as colored light and patterns rippled across their faces while they went on imaginary journeys in the arcade. This represented the crudest beginnings of virtual reality. And, indeed, this vision had the future written all over it.

Cyberspace, however, deals not only with travel, but with knowledge and information as well. Beyond the elements it has in common with the railway, cyberspace has even greater affinities with one of the greatest beasts ever to enter history—the printing press. The press inaugurated the original information explosion. It also occupied the town square for hundreds of years.

The printing press was a thing of wonder. The Gutenberg press stormed the world in the early fifteenth century and opened an unprecedented information gateway into the heart of the medieval world, thrusting history into the next age, the Renaissance. For centuries the vast cross-section of people had lived in the darkness of the Middle Ages. Serfs and artisans who were illiterate and ignorant suddenly had access to knowledge and information that was never before available. This single invention changed the social order forever, intersecting human need and human vulnerability while firing the imaginations of people with the wonders it could perform.

Now, on the eve of the next millennium, cyberspace is bringing change in the wind—global thinking and global technology—with amazing synchronicity. Asked at the start of 1997 what big news loomed ahead for the coming year and beyond, the editor of *Time* magazine stated that without a doubt cyberspace and the digital revolution would set the course of the world into the future (*Larry King Show*, CNN, January 3, 1997). This is not just the "smoke and mirrors" of media hype or a new fad, as some claim, but something that has left a tangible footprint across the earth.

Why this immense effort to wire the earth? Is it blind curiosity, or the endless hunger for knowledge? Is something eating away at the soul of man that cannot stop until some hunger is satisfied—maybe a hunger that started in Eden? And where will this quest take us—this limitless hunger for knowledge and experience? Are there other reference points in history that might give us a handle on today's quest?

As in the days of Babel, when men built the great tower with a view to storming heaven, we are today storming heaven once again. Beyond the ceramic, metal, and silicon building blocks of the present undertaking is the ageless desire to push the human race toward new realms of consciousness and human potential. Like the ancient Tower of Babel, the present undertaking is a quest for global unity—even a return to one language, as once existed on the ancient plains of Shinar.

Cyberspace is a beast with unique promises. It portends to be an instrument that can amuse, educate, and expand the boundaries of knowledge and experience. Yet, the very instrument that can invade the mind enough to bring a cornucopia of sensate delights could also enter the hidden recesses of the mind and its most private thoughts. As well, it could have the power to corrupt, deceive, control, police, and perhaps even enslave someday. It is not an instrument to be taken lightly.

When the door into digital history is fully opened it will be a one-way affair. We can never retreat back to the moment before the door opened. That is the nature of such historical doors, as John Milton illustrated in *Paradise Lost*—the first door being in Eden, causing history to cascade.

As we behold cyberspace, we do not want to enter the next age blindly, being carried into some technological future—a kind of Babylon of wires and electrodes—having been told we were destined for some utopian promised land. If the emerging digital frontier promises to bring heaven on earth, as some futurists boast, we must look at other challenges that lie ahead. We must see what lessons history has shown us in the past so we might resist the terrible dictate of George Santayana who repeatedly warned that "those who cannot remember the past are condemned to repeat it."[1]

We must therefore peer across this vast new electronic horizon with the help of a source older than time itself.

— Tal Brooke
Berkeley, California

PART ONE

Cyberspace—
The New Frontier

1

CYBERSPACE: STORMING DIGITAL HEAVEN

Tal Brooke

———————————— OVERVIEW ————————————

This chapter provides a panoramic view of cyberspace—what it is and how it "feels." It portrays what it is like to experience the various elements of cyberspace: from the Internet with its World Wide Web to virtual reality. It also unveils the engines that power this technology. It shows how cyberspace has grown from its earliest beginnings to the present—and where it is headed. Only then can we appreciate the need to plumb the depths of this electronic ocean—going through the inviting and dazzling outward ripples to those deeper regions that will mold the future.

A vast formless, machine is quickly wrapping itself around the earth like a "virtual glove." It is being built from an endless array of electronic components whose power, range, and size is far greater than the sum of its parts, which weave across the planet like a neural network. This titanic but largely hidden structure is the nervous system of "cyberspace." Like the human nervous system, much of it lies underground, hidden in the flesh of the earth.

For the first time, this maze of electronic hardware extends the human nervous system across the globe. Its potential for altering the course of human history could echo that of the Gutenberg printing press which, for the first time in history, provided books to the masses. Until then, only royalty, the church, the aristocracy, and the academy had books—unique, rare, and penned by human hands. With the press, literacy expanded geometrically through this public conduit of information and ideas. Medievalism and feudalism were replaced by the Renaissance as the social order of the West changed. Today, computers, cyberspace, and the information superhighway (the Internet) could again change the social order, catapulting present-day society fully into globalism as spatial distances collapse between previously divided groups.

The more rudimentary ancestor of cyberspace began in the last century with the telegraph machine laboriously sending out pulses of Morse code along analog wires at so many words per minute. Later came the analog telephone system for voice transmission, allowing significantly more words per minute with the added quality of mood and personality infused into the transmission. The telephone started the great task of wiring the globe. Then microwave towers, satellites, and grand trunk cable emerged on the scene to make possible the transmission of vast amounts of information across continental divides. Computer data entered this bit-stream. More recently fiber-optic cable has come on the scene to replace copper wire. This amounted to replacing a digital capillary tube (the copper wire) with an oil pipeline (fiber optic), upping the transfer rate, by analogy, from thumbnail amounts to millions of gallons per minute.

The powerful hardware that awakens the mechanical nervous system of cyberspace is the computer, the final interface with the human nervous system through eyes, ears, hands, and brains. Yet the hardware is lifeless without the human interface. Consciousness is the key.

In the words of *Time* special editor Philip Elmer-Dewitt, wires and cables and microwaves are not really cyberspace. They are the means of conveyance, not the destination; they are the information superhighway, not the bright city lights at the end of the road. "Cyberspace, in the sense of being 'in the same room,' is an experience, not a wiring system. It is, like Plato's plane of ideal forms, a metaphorical space, a virtual reality."[1] Yet this new technology is only in its early hours of infancy on the earth.

The term "cyberspace" was coined by William Gibson, a 44-year-old American science fiction writer living in Vancouver. Wandering past the video arcades around Vancouver's Granville Street in the early 1980s, Gibson saw teens intently hunched over video machines—and the idea of cyberspace hit him. Their eyes seemed frozen by this pale otherworldly light. Gibson turned the disturbing image into a novel, *Neuromancer*, the first novel to win science fiction's triple crown award. It became a cyberpunk classic, attracting a computer-savvy youth audience. According to Dewitt, "Critics were intrigued by a dense, technopoetic prose style that invites comparisons to Dashiell Hammett, William Burroughs and Thomas Pynchon. Computer-literate readers were drawn by Gibson's nightmarish depictions of an imaginary world disturbingly similar to the one they inhabit."[2]

In Gibson's fictional realm, cyberspace is a computer-generated landscape that characters enter by "jacking in"—sometimes by plugging electrodes directly into sockets implanted into the brain. What they see when they get there is a three-dimensional representation of all the information stored in "every computer in the human system"—great warehouses and skyscrapers of data.

In *Neuromancer* cyberspace is described as a place of "unthinkable complexity," with "lines of light ranged in the non-space of the mind, clusters and constellations of data. Like city lights, receding."[3] This is an idealized vision of where cyberspace is heading.

At present, cyberspace teems with many millions of inhabitants all over the globe who send billions of signals across its electronic synapses. It includes, in the images of Dewitt, the rapidly expanding wireless services; microwave towers that carry great quantities of cellular phone and data traffic; communications satellites strung like beads in geosynchronous orbit; and low-flying satellites that will soon crisscross the globe like angry bees, connecting those who are too far-flung or too much on the go to be tethered by wires. Someday even our television sets may be part of cyberspace, transformed into interactive "teleputers" by so-called full-service networks like the ones several cable-TV companies (including Time Warner) are building along the old cable lines, using fiber optics and high-speed switches.

A Cornucopia of Information

What can cyberspace really do in its touted ability to transmit and navigate through oceans of information across the world?

In the spring of 1995 I traveled from Berkeley, California to the Cambridge University library in Cambridge, England, a trip that usually takes at least two days, using cars, planes, trains, and subways. I made the same trip by cyberspace, entering the same library in seconds through the Internet. The cyberspace visit cost pennies and was near instantaneous. The physical visit and flight to England cost far more (yet had different and tangible rewards). Of course there were differences. In the real world I parked behind the Cam River on the back side of Trinity College and wandered around the perimeter of Clare College to the library. Books could be held and retrieved, but this took time. In cyberspace, sifting through large numbers of books is much faster. Rather than writing a quotation on a note card in the stacks, scratching it out with pen or pencil, one can download (electronically transfer) the text "on-line" in a fraction of a second. Still, the Cambridge library—like our own Library of Congress—is far from getting all of its books in digital format, though the catalogs are digitized.

It is through the World Wide Web (WWW)—the most powerful and sophisticated of the Internet gateways—that it becomes simple and commonplace, for instance, to go from Berkeley to a town in Finland, to Rome, then Paris, *all in a matter of seconds*. This is called "surfing the Net." A work about Austrian poet Rainer Maria Rilke or French author Louis F. Céline at the Sorbonne can be found through cyberspace in far less time than crossing Paris on the Metro and working through the Sorbonne library system in person.

In cyberspace, a 100-page book, a color photograph of the Great Pyramid, or a small software program can be "downloaded" into a computer's memory in well under a minute (via a 28,800-baud Global Village Teleport Platinum modem connected to a Power Macintosh 8100 that has 32 megabytes of RAM, and a one gigabyte hard drive—yes, a new "computerese" language is emerging). That is the magic genie aspect of cyberspace—seemingly instantaneous access to knowledge in bit-streams of data that can lure you all over the world. (This is where less prepared minds can get trapped in cyberspace, as we will see later).

Yet this is only the beginning of the information explosion from the world's storehouse. A new interactive, indeed tactile, universe is emerging through cyberspace's most complex doorway—virtual reality. Rather than the still color images that most people get on the World Wide Web at the moment, one day a full immersion into a computer-generated alternate reality will be possible. What the mind thinks, reality will become. What is presently holding things up is that computers need much more data access to bring this off. Right now, the World Wide Web can only provide miniature "Quicktime" movies on a computer screen. But one day anyone will be able to put on a helmet and see wide spatial distances in full color in three dimensions—and maybe they won't need the helmet!

Perhaps the most powerful and immersive means of entering a virtual reality experience will not be by using a helmet, with its limited and crude screen and grainy pixel depth. Instead, it might be by means of a beam of cold laser light. This laser light will be beamed directly onto the retina. In that beam will be carried the full pixel depth of the outward world—50 million polygons a second—coming from a computer. (It has been alleged that in a high-secrecy military experiment, using the cold laser on the retina, a full 360 degree immersion took place and the subject experienced being in a simulated world that was as real as being in the real world.)

Then three-dimensional town meetings will take place, with levitating participants from around the world meeting in an electronic designer universe with any kind of backdrop conceivable. Although the participants may be in cities ranging from New Delhi to Bonn, they will be able to assemble together in a vast virtual space like Hindu gods gathering on some *Bardo* plane. Participants might decide to appear in designer-bodies—for instance, the CEO of a global database corporation "morphed" partway into an ancient Boddhisatva ("enlightened one") from Tibet meeting another software giant who is "morphed" into Zeus, and so forth. All of this lies in the near future as central processors—the brains behind computers (such as the Pentium and the Power PC)—become much more powerful, and as storage and transmission become truly immense. We are already partway there.

The Exponential Process

If a Power Macintosh RISC processor 604 alone has more power than 10,000 archaic Univac computers combined, what happens if millions of these RISC processors are connected? Few can sum up the vast scales of amplification that lie behind this new universe of digital power—utterly unknown in the 1940s—better than futurist George Gilder, a kind of dean of the technological edge. Gilder notes that we have seen the power of the computer chip not just in the individual case, but now interlinked as cells to a greater meta-chip. He gives the following example:

> The Emperor of China was totally infatuated with this new game of chess that had been invented for him. He was so grateful to the inventor that he came to him and said, "I'll give you anything you want in the kingdom as a tribute for this wonderful game you gave me."

> And the inventor said, "Well, I want one grain of rice. I want one grain of rice on the first square of the chess board, which has sixty-four squares, then I want two grains of rice on the second square. Four grains of rice on the third square, eight grains of rice on the fourth square and so on."

> In other words, this is an exponential process.

And the Emperor happily granted this apparently modest request, and everything went fine for the first thirty-two squares. He could produce the several billion grains of rice fairly well on a quarter square mile of rice fields. But after the first thirty-two squares, things began to get interesting.

There are two ways the story ends. One is, the Emperor went bankrupt because after sixty-four squares, this was several billion trillion grains of rice, which would take the entire surface of the earth, plus the oceans times two to produce. The other end of the story was that the inventor lost his head.

But in any case, to get some perspective on how this applies, Kurzweil estimates that by 1993 there had been exactly thirty-two doublings of computer power since the first digital computers were invented in the early 1940s. So we've now completed the first half of the chess board, where things really become interesting and where the Emperor began to take notice of this process.[4]

Rather than grains of rice, Gilder tells us that microprocessors are on the chess board—increasing in quantity and power:

As we proceed into the second half of the chess board, as Ray puts it, the personal computer is just going to blow away television and all these broadcast technologies associated with it.

. . . Early in 1993, both Bill Gates and Andy Grove, the world's leading experts on computer production, essentially, both projected a great year. . . . Worldwide computer production in 1993 was nearly fifty million, almost 4 percent greater than most projections. This is a tremendous upside surprise.[5]

The fundamental particle of cyberspace is not the atom but the bit—the binary digit, a unit of data usually represented as a 0 or 1. Nicholas Negroponte, director of M.I.T.'s Media Lab, observes that information may still be delivered in magazines and newspapers (atoms), but the real value is in the contents (bits). Bits are different from atoms, Negroponte observes, and obey different laws. They are weightless. They are easily (and flawlessly) reproduced. There is an infinite supply. And they can be sent across cyberspace at nearly the speed of light. When it comes to moving bits across the earth in this new nervous system, barriers of time and space disappear.[6] Hence the Rilke passage from Paris to Berkeley is accomplished in mere minutes, reproduced on the screen and downloaded, all in digital form. Pictures can be made digital as well, whether it is a "home page" on the World Wide Web with graphics and pictures (scenes out of the movie *The Net*, for example), or NASA's Jupiter probe sending close-ups of Jupiter in streams of digital data back to earth to be assembled from the outer reaches of cyberspace. NASA bulletin boards in cyberspace carry the latest space shuttle photographs. Indeed, there are now declassified photos from several U.S. spy satellites available on the World Wide Web.

The Origins of Cyberspace

Thirty years ago, in "The Computers of Tomorrow" (*Atlantic*, May 1964), Martin Greenberger wrote about an earlier prediction of computers:

> Nineteen years ago, in July, 1945 . . . Vanneva Bush predicted that the "advanced arithmetical machines of the future" would be (a) electrical in nature, (b) far more versatile than accounting machines, (c) readily adapted for a wide variety of operations, (d) controlled by instructions, (e) exceedingly fast in complex computation, and (f) capable of recording results in reusable form.

This 1945 prediction has more than come true. Such machines are the basis of the Internet, which could not exist without them. How do such machines link together to create the Internet?

The Internet evolved from a computer system built 25 years ago by the Defense Department to enable academic and military researchers to continue to do government work, even if part of the network were taken out in a nuclear attack. It eventually linked universities, government facilities, and corporations around the world. They all shared the costs and technical work of running the system.[7]

Unlike most telephone transmissions, the Internet works on a "packet-switching" protocol. A packet-switching network is so decentralized that it is practically indestructible—which is the reason the Defense Department paid to create and expand the Internet, starting in the 1960s. Each message sent over the Internet is broken into its constituents—that is, into small units of data, or "packets." Each packet sent from your computer may take its own independent path to its destination, through different phone lines and connected computer networks. On arrival the packets, from a few to many hundreds, are reassembled into a complete message. This is a technical marvel, and it keeps the entire network as bottleneck-free as possible, since each packet follows a path that is, at the instant it departs, less crowded than all the others.[8]

The scientists who were given free Internet access in its early days quickly discovered that the network was good for more than official business. They used it to send each other private messages—electronic mail or e-mail—and to post news and information on public electronic bulletin boards known as USENET newsgroups. Over the years the Internet became a favorite haunt of graduate students and computer hackers, who loved nothing better than to stay up all night exploring its web-like connections and devising new and interesting things for people to do. They constructed elaborate fantasy worlds with Dungeons and Dragons themes. They built tools for navigating the Net—such as the University of Minnesota's "Gopher," which makes it easy for Internet explorers to tunnel from one place on the world network to another, and various other programs that can locate a particular word or program from vast libraries of data available to Net users. More and more newsgroups were added until the bulletin-board system had grown into a dense tangle of discussion topics with bizarre

computer-coded titles, such as *alt.tasteless.jokes, rec.arts.erotica,*
and *alt.barney.dinosaur.die.die.die.*[9]

Virtual Communities

What more than 30 million modem-equipped computer
users around the world have discovered is that cyberspace
allows them to leap over barriers of time, place, sex, and social
status and connect with strangers who share a particular
obsession or concern. "We're replacing the old drugstore
soda fountain and town square, where community used to
happen in the physical world," says Howard Rheingold, a
Berkeley-based author who has written a book on what he
calls "virtual communities."[10]

Along with Rheingold, the Bay area is full of cyberspace
visionaries, from Jaron Lanier, inventor of the term "virtual
reality," to the two main cyberspace magazines, *Wired,* based
in San Francisco, and *Mondo 2000,* based in Berkeley. A large
percentage of cyber-visionaries worldwide happen to live in
Berkeley. Many have their own habitats not too far from the
Spiritual Counterfeits Project (SCP). Inventive anarchy has
always been in the air of Berkeley (which is why SCP remains
in the belly of the beast). Berkeley also has a large population of computer wizards, hackers (programmers), and software gurus. The joke is that many of Berkeley's advanced
hackers who barely know or talk to one another when they
pass on the street probably gush with intimate confession
once they meet anonymously over the Net—perhaps
thinking the other person is in Norway rather than being a
neighbor around the corner. (A gasp heard at Berkeley's
Cafe Strada: "You mean you're the *Nirvanic Liberator?* And
that's *Commander Cody?*)

There has never been anything like this. People can be
totally vulnerable with utter strangers. They can also project
various kinds of assumed identities into this new social realm,
like folks at a perpetual *Beaux Arts* ball changing masks,
accents, and stories while constantly moving through faceless

crowds and encountering an unending stream of strangers behind changing masks. *You can be virtually anybody.*

But these virtual communities in cyberspace have quickly created rapidly expanding virtual red-light districts, ghettos of depravity, with meetings and deals being made. With an open gateway and no age limit, anyone can get in, as the cover of *Time* shows in its cyberporn issue. Curious young minds can see it all. It is far worse than a preteen walking down Hollywood Boulevard and seeing open displays of hard-core porn. This stuff is live and interactive, with predators on the loose reaching vulnerable young kids with names right out of *The Exorcist:* "Hi, Melinda, this is Captain Howdy." They might meet in kid cafes or one of countless conference rooms set up to discuss a range of topics.

This has created yet another social phenomenon—*cyberspace runaways;* not just kids leaving home, but this time kids being sent bus tickets by adults to rendezvous at secret locations. This is especially true among homosexual virtual ghettos. A "chicken hawk" on the Net can stake out some vulnerable lad with indeterminate sexual boundaries—another symptom of our permissive era with its broken families and open-mindedness about "alternative" lifestyles. Soon the child is recruited and initiated.

A 12-year-old boy flew from Seattle to San Francisco after being mailed a ticket by a gay pedophile. They met over the Internet. It probably went something like this: "Hello there Jeremy. This is Batman looking for Robin. I have a picture in your mailbox." Jeremy then downloads a hexadecimal GIF file [*alt.binary.erotica.pedophilia*], watches it through a graphical interface, and ends up blanching like the kid on the cover of *Time.* It might be a scene of sodomy or something worse, a shot of a San Francisco gay bathhouse in full swing ("anal justice," "rimming," and so forth). Jeremy can then be instructed to go to various global bulletin boards that carry thousands of pictures that would not be allowed even in the most hard-core adult stores in America. The stuff from Amsterdam and

Copenhagen is especially bad. It's all available: bestiality, bondage, sadomasochism, and kid porn. Jeremy's life suddenly takes a new turn, and he may never recover. *He is defiled.*

Time's cyberporn issue (June 26, 1995) gives one of many examples:

> Ten-year-old Anders Urmacher, a student at the Dalton School in New York City who likes to hang out with other kids in the Treehouse chat room on America Online, got E-mail from a stranger that contained a mysterious file with instructions for how to download it. He followed the instructions, and then he called his mom. When Linda Mann-Urmacher opened the file, the computer screen filled with 10 thumbnail-size pictures showing couples engaged in various acts of sodomy, heterosexual intercourse and lesbian sex. "I was not aware that this stuff was online," says a shocked Mann-Urmacher. "Children should not be subjected to these images."[11]

How available is cyberporn? Martin Rimm, a Carnegie Mellon research associate working on a study of pornography in cyberspace, discovered the answer. He used Carnegie Mellon computers to download 917,000 dirty pictures that ranged "from simple nudity to pictures of men and women having sex with animals. He tracked how often the pictures had been downloaded, or called up by a computer user—6.4 million times."[12] And that is not all that is on the Internet, not by a long shot.

The world's galleries in cyberspace bustle with activity like Manhattan on a Saturday night, with everybody up and partying. It seems a perfect cure for loneliness. Singles can meet over the Net. Or, you can surf through the various conference rooms, clubhouses, and gatherings and end up in the strangest places. A curious teen can plug into a bulletin board called "alt.witchcraft" and attend a virtual coven. He can also find out where a live coven meets in his geographical locale. It is an instant connection, a sort of Manhattan transfer, from gallery to gallery. Those who want to check out satanism, discover where to buy the drug "ecstasy," or find out where the next all-night

Rave concert is in Menlo Park can do it. This push to explore the Net is partly driven by the fact that everybody is faceless, anonymous. Like the Billy Idol song, the participants are "eyes without a face" and remain truly anonymous until they decide to meet in the flesh.

While anonymous intimacy grows on the Internet, friends and intimates in the *real* world are often put on hold as a new sort of addiction grows among those who have tasted the Internet. Irwin Winkler, who produced the movie *The Net*, which is among a new wave of cyberspace intrigue films released in the summer of 1995 (others are *Virtuosity* and *Johnny Mnemonic*), now describes himself as an "Internet widower." He says his wife has been disappearing for long hours on the Net. Once greeted cheerfully with martini and meal prepared, Winkler is now all but ignored by his wife when he comes through the door. His wife stares transfixed at a computer screen, while navigating the World Wide Web, barely acknowledging his presence.

Governing Anarchy

Computer wizards subscribe to a somewhat anarchistic ethic, stated most succinctly in Steven Levy's *Hackers*. Among its tenets are: 1) Access to computers should be unlimited and total. 2) All information should be free. (This is where software piracy comes in; one student at M.I.T. posted copyrighted software, giving away millions of dollars of it before he was busted.) 3) Mistrust authority. 4) Promote decentralization.

This "ethic" has the feel of a 60s cliché. Nevertheless, the Internet was built up by people who lived and breathed this hacker ethic—students at Berkeley and M.I.T., researchers at AT&T Bell Laboratories, and computer designers at companies such as Apple and Sun Microsystems. "If there is a soul of the Internet, it is in that community," says Mark Stahlman, president of New Media Associates, a research firm in New York City.

Originally a relatively small community, the Internet could be self-policing. Anybody who got out of line was shouted down or shunned. But now that the population of the Net is larger than most European countries, those informal rules of behavior are starting to break down. "The Internet is becoming Balkanized, and where the mainstream culture and hacker culture clash, open battles are breaking out."[13]

One area of contention is the commercialization of the Net. There are also arguments over taste, ethics, and "netiquette." New usurpers on the Internet are disdained even more. A good example is found in two lawyers from Phoenix, Laurence Canter and Martha Siegel, who advertised their wares on the Internet (getting aliens green cards for the right fee) by "spamming"—a way of mass-posting information to tens of thousands of global bulletin boards. In response, the two lawyers were "flamed" by vast numbers of angry Internet fire ants who found interesting ways of punishing them; reportedly bombarding their Internet mailbox till the regional system overloaded, locking up their hard drive, sending computer viruses downstream hidden in responses, getting their fax machine to spew out reams of paper, sending them hideous messages, and so forth. One Norwegian hacker devised a program that would hunt for their messages on the Net and destroy them. (Keep in mind that most gifted hackers are on the far right of the bell-shaped curve.)

Also keep in mind that significant damage can be done by gifted hackers in cyberspace. On-line crimes include illegally transferring electronic funds, debiting visa cards and bank accounts (major banks report that millions are being stolen every day this way), raiding the Pentagon computer and stealing defense secrets, messing up flight schedules of commercial airlines, confusing air traffic controllers, changing college grade point averages in university central computers, and the like. Many in the media are alleging these and more serious "terrorist" crimes, indicating a real need for greater policing of the Net.

An early cyberspace film entitled *War Games*, starring Matthew Broderick, was based on a young whiz kid who used his home computer to electronically tap into the North American Air Defense Command (NORAD), then tricked the defense computer into "believing" (we are forced into using terms that apply to human cognition) that a nuclear confrontation was taking place between America and the former Soviet Union. Things escalated quickly, once the computer's codes were set in motion, to the brink of nuclear war. A vast arsenal of missile silos opened, with jet engines beginning to whine. Only a computer genius could reverse the process. With seconds left in the countdown, the earth was spared. But the movie message is clear regarding the threat of computer-savvy minds entering into forbidden places. The plot was not solely fiction.

Computer hackers have already penetrated NORAD, the Pentagon computer, the Central Intelligence Agency's Langley complex, and many other security-tight computers in the public sector. On the other side, the military is dreaming up new ways to engage in cyber-warfare. Military hackers could disable phone systems, commerce, airport control towers, defense computers, and so forth. There have been rumors about the CIA's advanced hackers transferring funds from Swiss bank accounts of political enemies. Fiction author Tom Clancy has written about such things.

Clifford Stoll, a University of California (Berkeley) physics faculty member and BMUG (Berkeley Macintosh User Group) hacker, discovered that an East German spy ring had gotten into a number of America's defense computers via the Internet. (I was at the BMUG meeting where Stoll told his story.) The hacker jumped from computer to computer, figuring out passwords and hiding out inside each one. Then onward he would go, camouflaging behind names the computer knew. Stoll's slightly fictionalized account of finding the cyber-spy ring, entitled *The Cuckoo's Egg*, was on the *New York Times* bestseller list. Stoll has also unmasked the darker side of cyberspace—its depersonalization and perversity—in his book *Silicon Snake Oil.* Related to this, Stoll remarked in an interview, "People don't like it when you spit at the god's eye, especially when they think you're one of them."[14]

Dreams of Godhood

The idealized utopian hope of cyberspace is that it might enable the human mind to be amplified by machine in the same way that machines, from bulldozers to jets, amplify human physical abilities. An athlete who can run only 20 miles per hour can move thousands of miles per hour in a supersonic jet. Bulldozers and cranes enable people to lift tens of thousands of pounds, far beyond their natural abilities. No one really knows where the cyberspace phenomenon is going. But at its root is human consciousness operating the machine. What will happen to human consciousness during this strange marriage is the issue at stake.

Some anticipate that cyberspace will become a true planetary nervous system, an electronic ocean of digital consciousness, where human minds enhanced by computer technology form a godlike alliance. They hope a global mind will appear through this and bring to fruition Marshal McLuhan's metaphor (McLuhan, a Canadian academic and author of *The Medium Is the Message*, coined the term "global village.") It will be a dream come true for those who believe in the awakening consciousness of the earth into the goddess, Gaia. Others look to the vaunted paradigm shift of the cosmic millennium. But it could equally become the new tower of Babel—bringing unity to the world electronically—and a doorway into techno-tyranny. It is by no means inconsistent that it could be both at the same time. A utopia for one can be a hell-on-earth for another. The two are not mutually exclusive.

A Darker Future

A perfect example of the dark side of cyberspace appeared almost 50 years ago in a futuristic novel. George Orwell's literary classic *1984* introduced the concept of a two-way television that looked back at the viewer. It was interactive and would constantly monitor everything that happened in the private dwelling of every viewer. Anyone whispering or conspiring, or who looked circumstantially guilty of "thought crimes," had only moments between the suspicious event "seen" by the TV and the arrival of State police in full force.

Winston, the main character in *1984*, was utterly diminished by the two-way television overlooking his room. He was forced to duck around a slim section of wall out of its view to find his diary hidden behind a loose brick. He was permitted no solitude and had to scrounge for brief interludes of privacy. If he was out of view for more than a few seconds—one of his few remaining strands of liberty—the screen would bark at him. If the techno-eye of Big Brother was not satisfied with his response, he knew it could order storm troopers. It would begin with threats, such as when he refused to do his morning calisthenics. Winston was reduced to a number, a mere cog in the State machine. In the end, another monitoring device reported him to the central system, and he was sent to be brainwashed. Winston the individual was erased. There was no room for an independent mind in the collective State, which needed intrusive and interactive ways of monitoring its human fold behind every wall.

Such a device exists today. In fact, it resembles the two-way TV in *1984*. It is merely the Orwellian application that is lacking. For now, you can order pizza or tickets to a sporting event if you are in Europe. But there are ways, "for the good of the many," to bring in-house monitoring on a mass scale— for example, to keep intruders from breaking into your house. Other crimes can be "seen" as well. If the TV sees an "ecological" crime, such as pouring solvent down a drain, in comes the State apparatus. Not police at first. Perhaps, rather, notification of a fine is sent in the mail or debited from the offender's account. In time, more and more parameters of an individual's life would be under observation—again, for the good of the many.

Singapore has already embarked on this course. Today it could be described as a "benign techno-dictatorship." Singapore's proposed National Information Infrastructure (NII)—which aims to wire up every home by the year 2005 with optical fibers of almost unlimited carrying capacity—offers various attractive options from this new technology. Patients will be able to stay at home while linked to the hospital by a bedside terminal that monitors their progress and transmits the results. Dynamic road signs will automatically warn drivers of conditions ahead. Bus stops will display the expected arrival time of the next bus. The NII will also be used for watching sporting events around the world, viewing the treasures of the Louvre or the Smithsonian Institution, playing long-distance interactive computer games, and downloading video rentals.[15] Of course, it could be used to watch other things as well—*its own citizens*. The techno-eye can go both ways. And it has in Singapore.

In what the media call "another of Singapore's experiments in social engineering," taxis are soon to be monitored by satellite. "Cablink" will ensure that taxis work to maximum efficiency with minimum cruising time. (If this works it can be extended to all automobiles, and why not?) Already taxis are outfitted with alarms that activate when they exceed 80 kilometers per hour. Of real concern, however, is the thought that Singapore is trial-testing a system destined for the industrial nations of the West during the promised era of the world order. Some social planners really do think that far ahead, as does Singapore's Oxford-educated leader.

Aldous Huxley's *Brave New World* portrayed a different type of techno-dictatorship than Orwell's. It was less austere and less blatantly cruel. It used the pleasure principle rather than punishment as the prime motivator of the docile masses. The citizens were manipulated through controlled economy and entertainment, "bread and circuses." If Singapore embodies the Orwellian approach as far as rules and punishment and disdain of the corrupting influence of the pleasure principle are concerned, the West could head—indeed *is* heading—in the Huxleyan direction, through permissiveness (a perverse redefinition of real freedom), pleasure, and guaranteed welfare.

A Ghost in the Machine

Consider this haunting image: It is a rock concert of the future, perhaps around the year 2000. An audience of more than 100,000 people are on custom "dental-style" reclining chairs in a vast underground stadium that has been laser-melted. Concertgoers can look out at a broad expanse where they can see the rock band live if they choose not to use special viewing goggles. Within the vaster expanse above the band, holographic images of gigantic proportions are projected in empty space. The audience is fed designer drugs of choice through tubes. They are also wired to body-sensation devices incorporating what we would now call virtual reality headgear. The sound system is incredible—fully digital. Rock music, designer drugs, and electronics, all for the total experience that completely overwhelms the individual.

The concert's underground laser-melted arena is a kind of replica of the human lung. Just over the coliseum, a giant metallic-grey command tower rises above ground, surrounded by a landscaped rustic wilderness. The only clues to the underground auditorium are the modern subway-style escalators that emerge at tunnel entrances away from the tower. The tower harbors the technological engines that run the rock concert. Vast cables go in and out of it. The tower also performs another function, of which the audience is oblivious. It probes concertgoers through brain-body sensors in their hi-tech body gear and can look back *into their minds.*

Now the image takes a strange turn. Powerful entertainment moguls in the tower, far from public view, surround a supercomputer that is far beyond the CRAY computer (one of the world's fastest, most powerful computers). What is of terrible concern is that a massive spiritual force—a demonic presence—is mind-melding with the computer that is the interlink between the human controllers and the audience. In the digital feed of rock lyrics, the words are being interpolated on a higher level and somehow carry morpheme and phoneme messages to the inner minds of the listeners. They are being invaded with some deeper message. Beneath the entertainment are behavior and personality modification. The audience of mostly youth have become clay in the hands of the triumvirate of powers in the grey tower. Distracted by pleasure, defeated in spirit, they are being prepared for something other than entertainment. In a strange way, they are being domesticated. Perhaps, in the days of Babylon, we would say enchanted.

The above image was a visionary awake-dream I had in Costa Brava, Spain, months before going to India where I spent several years with an Indian power yogi. It took place at the exact time of the Woodstock concert in America. I learned this two days after the dream when I saw the cover of *Time* magazine. I felt a strange kind of shock when I read about this concert in upstate New York, with half a million or so of my generation. Far from an ordinary dream, I remembered every detail. It will be curious to see how far it approximates real history.[16]

A Giant Digital Ganges

During the mid-1980s, when Mitch Kapor and Bill Gates were America's young software prodigies, Kapor named his software company Lotus—simple, elegant, and quietly reflective of his spiritual leanings. The lotus is the flower upon which the Hindu god Vishnu reclines as "preserver of the cosmos." In real life, Kapor's Lotus 1-2-3 is a powerful spreadsheet program that has become something of an industry standard. (Meanwhile, Gates founded Microsoft, a global corporate empire.) In 1990 Kapor and Grateful Dead lyricist John Barlow started the Electronic Frontier Foundation to defend the civil liberties of hackers in cyberspace. They also shared a similar worldview common in cyberspace.

Robert Wright of *Wired* magazine makes this observation about Kapor and Barlow:

> Kapor is being true to hacker culture, which exudes a nearly mystical faith in the benign force of uninhibited information. Barlow often cites Pierre Teilhard de Chardin, the Jesuit priest who envisioned the technological assembly of a planetary "noosphere," a global brain that would seal humanity's spiritual destiny: Point Omega. "Whether or not it represents Teilhard's vision," he has written, "it seems clear we are about some Great Work here—the physical wiring of collective human consciousness. The idea of connecting every mind to every other mind in full-duplex broadband is one which, for a hippie mystic like me, has clear theological implications."[17]

Cyberspace, by its very unitive structure, tends toward a functional pantheism. Besides that, the reigning beliefs of cyber-culture are post-Christian, globalistic, and unitive. It is a demographic of the young, privileged, and bright who are demonstrably post-Christian. To them, this electronic plane functions like a giant digital Ganges—unifying people, nations, thoughts, and concepts almost mystically.

India's great river is its living symbol of an ancient belief— Hindu, Advaitist, Vedantist, monist, Yogic—that all things are one and that all things return to the final source, *the One*, from which they are said to come. The Ganges is India's natural symbol—its living metaphor—of this process. For this ancient river is seen as the collector of lesser rivers and tributaries, and the body into which all things flow and join. It becomes in some ways the great repository of Indian civilization down through the millennia. Pantheism, by its very nature, finds unity at the lowest common denominator, at the base of existence. Unity, to the Eastern mystical mind, is the great center of existence. But for those who see Hinduism up close (such as myself, having once converted to it) this unity comes at a terrible price, for it is built upon the oldest spiritual lie—that we shall be as God. The Ganges, upon closer inspection, is able to unify, but only on a baser level.

To one pilgrim from the West, this unity at the bottom of the universe is also visually evident in the ebb and flow of the Ganges river, which he describes with rare lucidity:

> We reach the Ganges and take a boat ride. All the buildings we can see from the river are in various stages of dilapidation. The heat and the moisture have eaten into stone, brick, and plaster; everything is pockmarked, with that leprous aspect that overtakes even decently constructed buildings when, in tropical lands, nobody cares and everything decays.
>
> On the steps leading down to the river and on the stone landings are masses of people. Pilgrims and locals doing their . . . well, what should one call it?—acts of private life. The dirty green river becomes bathroom, toilet, mouthwash, laundromat, drinking place for animal and man. Fully or half-immersed, people wash their hair, their underwear, rinse their mouths, and defecate, as the freely floating dung testifies. All this with the utmost matter-of factness, without embarrassment. Our oarsman, sweating under the beating sun, leans over the side and slurps palms-full of water.
>
> On this horrifying boat ride, I no longer know whether we are navigating the River Styx or gliding with Dante in a liquid hell. We come in sight of the funeral pyres. On the way to Benares we had passed trucks loaded with white wrapped bodies, corpses brought by families from distant villages. All day the pyres burn, and every three hours or so a white or red-clad, garlanded, cadaver is laid on top. There it burns for hours.
>
> . . . What attracts and keeps them here is the degradation: of reason, of self esteem, of vital forces, of faith in God and man. Here they find innumerable gods and none at all; everybody may do his thing just like the monkeys and the cows, sinking slowly toward the Ganges or Nirvana. Intelligence and purposefulness dissolve on the trashheap, the body rots until it becomes one with the road, the grass, the dung. The great nothingness envelops all, and the ashes go into the river.[18]

Cyberspace, in some ways, reminds me of a giant digital Ganges. Like the timeless river crossing India, it promises to unify. And no doubt it will create the appearance of unity as it flows along the digital plane, but perhaps at a great price—by absorbing the lowest elements of human nature, that substrate of human desire and experience that occupies an expanse of darkness. Like the Ganges, where things decompose then converge back, so too with the digital plane. Unity will come through a convergence of substrates—and that is one of the most ancient themes of the occult, its dark secret where unity and power meet at the bottom. We will look into this theme at varying times throughout this book.

2

WELCOME TO THE CYBER-MILLENNIUM

Donald L. Baker

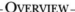

OVERVIEW

As we approach the twenty-first century, change is accelerating rapidly due to the unique interplay between the technology that has created cyberspace and the changing worldview of the West. The West is suddenly crossing over from Modernism to Postmodernism, ending Modernism's several-hundred-year reign. If the result of all this is a new sort of cyber-millennium by the twenty-first century, will this new social order be driven by such forces as global economics and entertainment, or forces much deeper? This chapter calls it a "high-stakes battleground in an amoral and postmodern society." Will the new cyber-millennium keep out the knowledge of God, like some new despotic Roman emperor, or will there be new entranceways into this vast global network through which its inhabitants can be reached? Such issues are vital right now.

We are entering an era of electronically extended bodies living at the intersection points of the physical and virtual worlds, of occupation and interaction through telepresence as well as through physical presence, . . . and of new, soft cities that parallel, complement, and sometimes compete with our existing urban concentrations of brick, concrete, and steel.[1]

–William J. Mitchell, *City of Bits*

T he great work[2] of the cyber (third) millennium—networking the world for digital cyberspace—is underway. The governments of the United States, Western Europe, Japan, and China are pushing it; businesses are hoping to make money through on-line commerce and on-line banking; cyber-savvy Americans are snapping up computer hardware and software for home use, while the kids are accessing CD-ROMs and Internet-based resources at school. Brick by digital brick, the city of bits is being erected before our eyes.

41

People still ask whether it's inevitable? In a word: *yes*. The acceleration of worldwide digitization and networking is approaching escape velocity, pulling free from the material world into cyberspace. Nothing will deter our society's trajectory into the electronic ether. The recent expansion of world markets has made competition and communication only more intense. There will be fits and starts, missed deadlines, and the inevitable glitches inherent in software development. But the final result is virtually inescapable; it is in many senses already here.

CyberWhat?

The cyber-millennium dawned in 1989[3] in the wake of the fall of European communism with its dogma of centralized social and economic planning. In the post-postwar New World Order, Asian communist nations—China, Vietnam, and North Korea—are tottering. Their obsolete authoritarian structures will, the cyberphiles* say, eventually collapse as their citizens enter the decentralizing city of bits. *And enter they must.* The world's nations know they must upgrade their telecommunications networks lest they be left behind in the datacloud.[4]

Crossing into the cyber-millennium, we have left the 20th century and with it, Modernity. We remember Modernity, vaguely—the Enlightenment project founded on the replacement of Christendom with a utopia of humanity redeemed and transformed by reason and science alone. With the failure of overweening Modernity and the arrival of postmodernism, we have reached the moment (to borrow H. G. Wells's phrase) of the "mind at the end of its tether."

A Word About Postmodernism

Postmoderism was for several years the playground of art historians, philosophers, and professor-novelists who noted the shift in Cold War culture away from modernist faith—

---

*Cyberspace enthusiasts.

democratic and Marxist—in the absolute truth of progress through reason and science. The failures of Modernity (for example, The Somme, Auschwitz, Prague 1968, Brasilia, *Challenger,* Bhopal, Gorbachev) confounded atheist academics, who began first to believe and then teach that with God "dead" and Modernity fatally flawed, why not ditch the lot, and believe all facts, all reality, to be relative and social constructions. The postmodernist result, notes Gene Edward Veith, is that "intellect is replaced by the will. Reason is replaced by emotion. Morality is replaced by relativism. Reality itself becomes a social construct."[5] Suspicion that something is not right becomes pervasive. Recent generations, tutored by their professors, rejected not only Modernity but the entire Western heritage propagated by those infamous dead, white European males. The baby-boomers' sense of mission has ensured that these radical theories trickle-down to the elementary schools.[6]

It is no small matter that the technologies of cyberspace have arrived at precisely the same historical moment that communism has fallen to secular capitalism, and Western culture—even the United States—has rejected not only belief in God's active reality, but also the anti-Christian Enlightenment project. While Western corporations are busily establishing trade with former enemies and other rapidly developing nations, postmodernist theorists are teaching students to deconstruct the entire infrastructure of reason-based reality, and to replace it with a pastiche of multiculturalism, premodern (but non-Christian) religion, and new ideas about what it means to be human in an age of silicon-based machines.

Just as Renaissance Europeans projected their own hopes and fears as myths about the New World, various groups are struggling to establish and control the underlying myths of cyberspace. Of these groups, the post-Marxists are the greatest enemy of the kingdom of God. For while the capitalists will accommodate us (so long as they turn a profit on our business), and the personal-freedom zealots will defend our right to Net access (so long as we do not stuff Jesus down their throats in the *alt.sex.stories* newsgroup), the postmodern neo Marxists and their fellow travelers are overtly hostile not only to the gospel of Christ, but also to our personal and social practice of Christian morality.

Why? Because Christianity is anathema to postmodernists. It stubbornly proclaims a the reality of overarching truth: that there exists one true Father God (not mother goddess) who must be worshipped and obeyed (eliminating many alternative lifestyles), and who can be approached and known only through submission to Jesus (yet another male patriarchal figure).

Reaching the Millennial Generation

The colonization and definition of cyberspace is *not* primarily a leisure pursuit, but very much a conscious project of organizations and individuals who view cyberspace as a tool to advance toward particular goals. Since its origins, cyberspace has become indispensable as a medium for managing the increasing complexity and data necessary for business, science, and the military to function. The balance of cyberspace-related industry, however, has developed either 1) to make money providing new consumer products and diversions, or 2) to advance transformative social agendas. It is the second goal I will focus on here.

The cyberspace industry eagerly awaits the first cyber-generation. In a *Ministries Today* article, Michael Thompson describes the kids born from the 1980s to the year 2000. Three of nine "sociological shapers" that Thompson says distinguish this generation from baby-boomers and the so-called Generation-X concern their heavy involvement in electronic technologies (media saturation, technological advancement, and the global village). Thompson notes:

> The Millennial Generation is literally addicted to visual and audio media. . . . Fifty percent of these kids own an

answering machine or a CD player. Ninety percent own a stereo. Three out of 10 own their own personal computer. They are mesmerized by technological advancement.[7]

In the dawning cyber-millennium, efforts to make new disciples of Christ will soon shift from baby-boomers and Generation-Xers to include the millennial generation. Thompson says it is essential to understand this group in light of their affinity for electronic media. While F2F (netspeak for "face-to-face") will no doubt continue to be the most common mode for personal evangelism, an increasing amount of seed-sowing will be accomplished on-line, in electronic agoras and on digital Mars Hills. This is why we should know something of the hidden building blocks of cyberspace.

City of Bits: Frontier Town?

In 1990, gentleman rancher, Grateful Dead lyricist, and Internet enthusiast John Perry Barlow wrote:

> Cyberspace, in its present condition, has a lot in common with the 19th century West. It is vast, unmapped, culturally and legally ambiguous . . . hard to get around in, and up for grabs. Large institutions already claim to own the place, but most of the actual natives are solitary and independent, sometimes to the point of sociopathy. It is, of course, a perfect breeding ground for both outlaws and new ideas about liberty.[8]

Later that same year, in a manifesto announcing their creation of the Electronic Frontier Foundation (EFF), Barlow and Lotus 1-2-3 inventor Mitchell Kapor called cyberspace

> a frontier region, populated by the few hardy technologists who can tolerate the austerity of its savage computer interfaces, incompatible communications protocols, proprietary barricades, cultural and legal ambiguities, and general lack of useful maps or metaphors.[9]

In the mid-1990s, cyberspace is still "up for grabs." But little else of Barlow and Kapor's description has remained unchanged. The Internet, once the government-supported research and communications domain of university and military researchers, now supports an estimated 50 million users worldwide, with thousands of "newbies" coming on-line every day. The two leading on-line service providers, America Online and CompuServe, have linked their private networks to the Internet and now claim more than 12 million subscribers together. Software behemoth Microsoft is joining the fray with its own on-line service linked to Windows 95. New software tools such as Yahoo and Netscape have made it much easier to navigate and publish on the Net.

But is cyberspace really being settled like a frontier region from the Old West? No—not if one examines the historical record. Most Western settlement was accomplished not by isolated individuals "lighting out for the territory" like Huckleberry Finn, but by families and communities who built towns and neighboring farms. Settlers were usually not solitary, independent, or "sociopathic" outlaws, but *conservative* folk hoping to reproduce the culture of the towns they had left behind. "Colonization by congregation and kinship groups . . . refutes the argument that the pioneers were champions of 'individualism,'" notes historian Page Smith. "The lonely, wide-ranging frontiersmen bulk large in historical fiction and in the popular mind, but they counted for little in comparison with the town-builders of the covenant."[10]

In truth, cyberspace more closely resembles the 19th century *urban* West—mapped and promoted by profit-seeking investors (America Online, electronic shopping centers), and settled primarily not by individuals but by corporate and academic communities. Many settlers—particularly on the Internet—behave as inhabitants of a postmodern urban landscape (which, of course, most of them are in real life). The Internet in particular is an unzoned megalopolis where pornographers hawk their wares across the street from schools and meeting halls, and wild-eyed anarchists distribute electronic pamphlets alongside the new CommerceNet shopping center. In seconds, a World Wide Web surfer can double-click from "Thomas," the Library of Congress home page, to the *Hustler* magazine site—and much worse.

Why, then, did Barlow and Kapor deliberately engage the attractive imagery of the frontier in describing cyberspace? Perhaps it was because their inaccurate reading of history was a good fit for the Electronic Frontier Foundation, which helps channel political debate of cyberspace toward guaranteeing the greatest amount of legal protection for cybernauts' file transfers and personal communications. This agenda includes drafting laws, or amending old ones, to eliminate legal gray areas when adapting traditional business practices and the Bill of Rights to the city of bits.

Barlow and Kapor's choice of "hot-button" Old West imagery to describe cyberspace to the TV generation was a shrewd, largely successful attempt to garner support for their free-speech agenda. They devised "a mythical history and an impossible origin in emptiness,"[11] while soft-pedaling what many netizens (Internet citizens) had half-forgotten: the Internet's roots as a U.S. Government-funded, defense-related computer network used by thousands of workers in the Cold War military-industrial-educational complex.[12] The frontier (or "backward-looking") model of cyberspace is aimed at those netizens to whom on-line access and activity are rights to be protected and expanded, not controlled by government.

While Barlow admits, "I certainly don't claim we're creating a [cyberspace] utopia,"[13] other netizens do. The following manifesto, penned by one S. Boxx of Denver, Colorado, is typical of the genre:

> The ideology of "electronic democracy" [electracy] is that a vast cyberspatial revolution and renaissance is in progress at the very moment, stealthily bubbling beneath our noses. While it appears that there is no orderly progress taking place on the Internet, it is actually brimming with vast

forces of creativity and ingenuity. These forces are almost
about to be unleashed in an unprecedented explosion of
light and heat. . . . Today only a few isolated visionaries are
aware of the vast, untapped force of this lumbering, slum-
bering giant. But soon the Savior of Cyberspace will be
making his appearance. . . . [14]

Some of these screeds are indeed "brimming with vast
forces of creativity and ingenuity," thereby inviting further
interchange (mostly the abuse known as a "flame"*) concerning their total loopiness. One cannot have a postmodern
city, however, without a Hyde Park (or, I would argue, a Mars
Hill)—and it is good for us that the city of bits has any
number of such places, and their defenders.

. . . Or Locus of Control?

As cyberspace becomes an essential workplace for more
people worldwide, its reality as a *city*—not a frontier or village—of bits becomes more evident. The complexity of transactions and communications drives the need for more market
and storage space. Growing risks from muggers (computer
hackers), vandals (computer viruses), and perverts (on-line
creeps) spawns a growing need for order and control. This
city model promotes cyberspace as a realm created to store,
control, and manipulate the overload of data. In this forward-
looking model, the focus is on creating rather than discovering an electronic realm; on its use primarily by government
and business rather than by individuals; and on data manipulation and control rather than personal freedom. This cyberspace model favors regulating and restricting on-line
communications and uploaded content, rather than the frontier model's freedom to communicate with anyone desired
and to access and download any type of on-line file. Calls for
the regulation or elimination of on-line smut (how can such

---

*A hostile, nasty electronic message sent via e-mail.

regulations succeed in a worldwide network of the unre-deemed?) assume this model of cyberspace.

The backward-looking frontier model attracts the free-speech utopians, while this forward-looking city model attracts those who believe that on-line data-sifting and manip-ulation will somehow produce knowledge and wisdom. The trend today is not to teach children facts—which in post-modern society are suspect anyway—but instead to train them in information retrieval and sorting. Derrick de Kerckhove, director of the University of Toronto's McLuhan Program, puts it this way:

> Why bother learning all this stuff yourself if you have access to it when you need it? Quite the reverse, you might find value in not knowing something, as the very process of dis-covering anything may be more useful and exciting than the content of the discovery. With real expert systems, improved by sophisticated neural networks with rapid learning curves, you don't need to be an expert in anything.[15]

You don't need to be a learner at all, I suppose. Just the ticket for kids who cannot place the Civil War in the 19th cen-tury! The assumption is that if those of the millennial genera-tion are trained in data manipulation rather than stuffing their heads with useless old facts and other lessons from human experience, they will somehow be able to make sense of retrieved on-line information. Langdon Winner calls this wrongheaded belief "mythinformation," and points out:

> What is the "information" so cherished as knowledge? It is not understanding, enlightenment, critical thought, time-less wisdom, or the content of a well-educated mind. Looking closely at the writings of computer enthusiasts, "information" means enormous quantities of data manipu-lated by various kinds of electronic media. . . . [16]

If students have no underlying factual structures and value systems through which to contextualize and evaluate newly acquired information, how can they possibly ascend the slope that leads from unorganized information to synthesized knowledge, and finally to clearheaded wisdom? Cyberspace technologies will not help the millennial generation extract knowledge and wisdom from data if they are not *taught* to recognize that some ideas are more important than others and some are, in fact, true and worth emulating. Internalizing the teachings of the Bible, for example, will be far more useful for life than any number of database "hits" without context or underlying values. What is needed in the cyber-millennium, Michael Novak believes, is to

> learn again how to teach the virtues of the noble Greeks and Romans, the commandments God entrusted to the Hebrews, and the virtues that Jesus introduced into the world—even into secular consciences—such as gentleness, kindness, compassion, and the equality of all in our Father's love. We must celebrate again the heroes, great and humble, who have for centuries exemplified the virtues proper to our individual peoples. We must learn again how to speak of virtue, character, and nobility of soul.[17]

The huge sales of William Bennett's *Book of Virtues* show that many people agree.

While the early cyber-millennium on-line culture is heavily tilted toward the frontier free-speech model, the control concept may ultimately win out—to our dismay. That is because the Net and future interactive-TV networks are forecast to become home to a multibillion-dollar cybermall—once enough people are enticed to peel off crisp new, digital e-dollars*[18] for products hawked on-line. Behind all the buying, selling, and market research hides an inescapable reality: *datamining.* Commercial on-line services regularly vacuum data on customers' on-line habits; software companies are feverishly developing programs to direct sophisticated metering of

---

*Electronic dollars.

"hits" at corporate Web sites. And do not forget all your ATM visits and credit card purchases—those are stored in cyber-space, too. Urban planner Michael Sorkin notes,

> It is an irony . . . that in many ways the most enfranchised members of the electronic city are those willing to submit to the most draconian forms of observation. To fully partici-pate in the electronic city is to have virtually all of one's activities recorded, correlated and made available to an enormous invisible government of credit agencies, back office computer banks and endless media connections. To exist in the public realm means to be wired in. The ultimate consequence is that the body, the person, no longer simply exists in public space but actually becomes it. . . . The media system—the electronic city—is all about the disappearance of privacy, about the surrender of all aspects of personhood to visibility and manipulation.[19]

Knowing Revelation 13 by heart is not necessary for Sorkin's insight to generate a primal, fight-or-flight response. How ironic that the frontier model, with its exciting lure of freedom and privacy, migrates the masses not to empty cyber-space vistas, but to data-crowded virtual cities where—as urban cyber-consumers—we willingly submit to ever-greater surveillance and control.

Data Kills, But the Spirit Gives Life

"Data kills, but the Spirit gives life."

That is what Vancouver School of Theology professor, David Lochhead, says. He explains:

> Information that is given its value and purpose by enabling the exploitation, the manipulation, the alienation of human beings is demonic. Information technology does have the power to exploit and oppress. But it also has the power to heal. . . . The technology of bits and bytes can become a medium of the Spirit. It can be a means by which

we reach out and touch our neighbor and, in that touch, a word of faith, of reconciliation, of hope, is spoken.[20]

I quote Lochhead because, like him, I am ultimately hopeful about the church's potential to spread the knowledge and grace of God in the city of bits. I have written above on the two dominant models of cyberspace because techno-hype obscures the reality: cyberspace is becoming a high-value, high-stakes battleground in an amoral, postmodern society. Many of us are already working and playing in cyberspace, without thinking much about the hidden political and economic dynamics influencing the space behind our screens. The millennial generation will have little choice—from childhood, they will log-on, jack-in, and Net-surf. Unless we wish to join the Amish in principled cultural irrelevancy, we will stop fearing cyberspace, and learn where it is going in the cyber-millennium.

Then we will go there, too. We will teach our kids the value of books over video, the Bible over Beavis, and F2F ("face to face") over virtual relationships. We will also ask God to guide us in:

- making sure our kids are computer-savvy, while not becoming addicted;

- monitoring their use of software and their on-line friendships;

- making positive contributions to selected conference forums, newsgroups, and mailing lists;

- developing personal e-mail relationships with selected Christians and unbelievers;

- contributing to on-line e-journals* and archives, or starting our own;

---

*Electronic journals.

- helping create "Mars Hill" situations for gospel presentations in live forums on America Online, CompuServe, and other commercial services;

- creating Web pages with either heavy (evangelistic) or light (pre-evangelistic) Christian content;

- providing hypertext links on our Web pages to good-quality Christian and secular Web sites;

- encouraging our churches and parachurch ministries to set up their own Web sites;

- joining the privacy advocates in negotiating privacy guarantees for on-line purchases and other personal data;

- contributing letters to the editors of *Wired* and other influential cyber-culture journals.

Those of faith will need to navigate the city of bits with dexterity and caution that Christians have had to show down the ages during hostile times—from ancient Rome to modern New York—remaining in but not always "of" the world. The digital environment offers perils and temptations that a modern-day John Bunyan might well describe in a digital *Pilgrim's Progress Through Cyberspace*. Yet it is also a time of acute need, when wanderers on the electronic plane become easily lost since they have no ultimate road-map of meaning. Such people can—and must—be reached.

3

VIRTUAL
MAN

John Moore

— OVERVIEW —

Will human nature take a much anticipated "evolutionary leap" through cyberspace technology? Some futurists speculate that an anticipated quantum leap will come through untapped potentials unleashed deep in the recesses of the human mind. Others are looking into the potentials of cyber-technology as a passage to a kind of virtual immortality. They ponder the question of whether it is possible to download a human mind into a big enough computer to store it forever with personality intact. Of course, such humanists never question whether a spirit or soul could ever be part of the human makeup. Could all of these attempts at techno-enhancement backfire, creating a kind of cyber-Frankenstein? John Moore explores some of these frontline issues.

The process . . . [of "downloading" a human mind into a computer] involves precise mapping, copying, and simulating in a neural net computer every structure and pattern in the human brain. The consciousness those biological structures and patterns supported should then reboot, reanimate as a separate, evolving cyberspace intelligence . . . I propose that this moment be known as your bootday.

—Professor Mel Seesholtz,
Pennsylvania State University[1]

I read the article in which the above quotation appears. Then I reread it. Then I went back to read it through for a third time. My sense of amazement grew with each reading. The ideas were not new to me. My background in cognitive psychology had exposed me to the possibility of human intelligence being transferred to computers via future developments in the field of artificial intelligence (AI). No, what surprised me was where the ideas were found, and from whom they were coming.

This was a paper written not by some underemployed computer science graduate student, but, according to his one-paragraph bio, by a professor of English at Penn State University. It appeared not as a posting to some science fiction newsgroup on the Internet, but in the background essays prepared for a program presented at the 1992 American Libraries Association (ALA) summer conference. In this scholarly, respectable context the transfer of human intelligence into the digital realm was being presented not as a conjectural possibility, but as a virtual certainty, just waiting for the necessary technological puzzle pieces to fall into place.

Professor Seesholtz's paper was just one of many prepared for a presentation that featured Hans Moravec (roboticist and author of "Mind Children: The Future of Robot and Human Intelligence"), David Brin (author of "Earth"), and Bruce Sterling (science fiction writer in the "cyberpunk" tradition). The presentation was targeted at librarians and other information science professionals who would be attending the ALA conference. Most of the papers had been written by professionals in those fields.

Reading through these papers, I was struck by the number of times I kept running across the same ideas, written by different people from various backgrounds and locales. Paper after paper echoed the same eerie certainty about the future of the man-machine interface: computers would think; they would think *for* us, they would think *through* us. "What do these people know that I do not?" I wondered. "Who and/or what has been selling them this vision of the future?"

Virtual Reality

When Jaron Lanier coined the term "virtual reality" in the early 1980s, he was trying to describe his vision of the future of the man-machine interface. It would be an immersive three-dimensional world, a shared digital realm, where man could interact with man and machine—creating, exploring, searching the vast storehouses of man's collective knowledge base. By Lanier's estimates, the ultimate realization of this technological vision could take hundreds of years—perhaps a millennium—of technological and cultural innovation and adaptation. The dream is a virtual world where man can interact seamlessly with the information storage capabilities and computational miracle of the digital computer. Ultimately, it is a world where man can express his creative power unhindered by the constraints of our sorry material existence, unhindered even by the constraints of language into which we are now forced to compress and mold our thoughts. The virtual interface of the future will tap directly into the thought patterns of our minds, allowing a form of communication that Lanier called "post-symbolic communication"[2]—that is, communication unfiltered by the grid of a symbolic translation scheme such as language.

Ah, it is a wonderful dream. Meanwhile we have virtual reality of the present and near future. It involves a techno-kludge of three-dimensional displays, gloves, and suits that translate body motions into computer commands, "virtual mice," "virtual keyboards," eye-tracking schemes, voice recognition schemes, and everywhere, *virtual hype*. No matter, virtual reality-mongers from all quarters have already proclaimed the new reality the answer to everything from world peace to kitchen remodeling (it is already being used for kitchen remodeling). But what should not be missed, amid the noise and confusion of the building project just underway, is that the proposed platform for the man-machine interface has switched decisively from the realm of man to the realm of machine; from the *real*, for lack of a better adjective, to the *virtual*.

The Robot Is Waiting

The "robot" of olden days (that is, anything up until about 1984) was a machine that clanked and rattled around the house, factory, or spaceship—doing its best to pretend to be man and perform manlike tasks. Alvin Toffler, in his 1970

classic *Future Shock*, however, predicted the imminent appearance of the humanoid robot:

> At that point [the point of having created robots that are
> indistinguishable from man] we shall face the novel sensa-
> tion of trying to determine whether the smiling, assured
> humanoid behind the airline reservation counter is a pretty
> girl or a carefully wired robot. The likelihood, of course, is
> that she will be both.[3]

As it turns out, the human body is more of an engineering
feat than once imagined. While robots have grown increasingly sophisticated over the last 25 years, we now see that they
have a long, long way to go before anyone mistakes an ATM
for a bank teller. What has turned out to be more plastic is
man's ability to enter the artificial world of the computer.

If current trends are any indication, the pretty girl and the
airline reservation counter she stands behind will both have
gone "virtual" long before things ever get to the stage of
humanoid robot development that Toffler envisions (if in fact
they *ever* do). The "robot" of the virtual future is a computer
mind linked to a virtual "body," and we will probably be using
a virtual body when we interact with it. Mohammed is going
to the mountain; man is going to the machine. Pygmalion,
tired of waiting for an answer to his prayers, has decided to
become a stone. The robot has arrived, and it is sitting on
your desk.[4]

The Birth of Cyberspace

> "Coming into the Virtual World, we inhabit Information.
> Indeed, we become Information. Thought is embodied,
> and the Flesh is made Word. It's weird as hell."—John Perry
> Barlow[5]

The interlinking of computers around the world has been
going on in relative obscurity since the late 1960s. It is only
recently, with the curious glut of media attention on the "information superhighway" (super-hypeway), that the possibilities

inherent in this worldwide communication network have become the object of popular fascination. The Internet, the oldest and most important of the computer networks, began in the mid-1960s as the ARPANET (some old-time Internet residents refuse to yield to modern trends, and still refer to the network by its original name). ARPANET was a federally sponsored project to link computers by telephone to allow military scientists to exchange information. In November 1969, scientists at UCLA tested the first "node"* in the ARPANET by sending a message to San Francisco, and the network was born. By mid-December, the network had four nodes; by mid-1970 the number had grown to ten. Today there are more than three million nodes in the Internet, and the number is growing exponentially. More than a million nodes were added in the first half of 1994 alone.[6]

This Internet and other computer networks like it are the platform on which a true virtual reality will be built. But like a framework without any covering, the "Net," until recently, has been mainly devoid of images, a protean world that could be inhabited but not seen. It was a world waiting for the lights to come on.

This world has been christened "cyberspace," a name given to it by cyberpunk novelist William Gibson in his visionary book *Neuromancer* (1984). Prior to its recent explosion of popularity, cyberspace had been a rather private community, a somewhat anarchic enclave of scientists and other academics exchanging scholarly information and discussing everything under the sun in the newsgroup discussion lists. Also participating were a smattering of disaffected techno-oriented Generation-X'ers, hacking and cracking and adding their own views to the encyclopedic discussion lists.

All this is changing now, however, and rapidly. As PCs (microcomputers) become more powerful, their interface with the Internet (or Net) becomes increasingly more graphical,

---

*A "node" is any network device that has an electronic address on the network.

and the tools available to access the Net become increasingly more sophisticated. Perhaps as a result of the improved interface, and definitely as a result of the increased number of commercial networks now providing Internet access (such as America Online, Prodigy, and CompuServe), the number of new users finding their way into the Net is skyrocketing. The World Wide Web (WWW), an Internet tool that presents information in a graphical, hypertext-based format,* has become the hot ticket.

As more and more "Internauts" sign up for the ride, climb aboard a "web browser," and fire off to the far reaches of the Net, old-time residents worry that the continual influx of users threatens to fundamentally change the nature of cyberspace. Novices take up precious "bandwidth" in the discussion lists with their newbie questions and make egregious breaches in netiquette.** Worse, the economics of the net will have to change. The free ride that many netizens have enjoyed is coming to an end. As the maintenance and support of the network becomes a more substantial issue, government and the telecommunications industry will battle it out to determine who foots the bill and who maintains control. The result of any outcome will almost certainly mean the increased bureaucratization of the Net. But there is no turning back. The doors of cyberspace have been thrown open, and the world is coming to the Net, ready or not.

Beyond 3-D

The World Wide Web adds sounds and pictures to the Internet. But it does not yet qualify as a true virtual reality interface. What is still needed is the ability to provide an "immersive 3-D" visual experience: the user should experience the Net as a location, seen in three dimensions from the vantage point of an "inhabitant" of the virtual world. This type

---

*Hypertext is a means of linking information based on key words or topics.
**Net etiquette.

of interface has been pioneered in the flight simulators and other training devices used by the military and has recently found its way into mass-market gaming machines. The leap into the world of the PC (microcomputer) should not be far behind.

Even this, however, will provide only the minimum requirements for the type of experience being sought by the virtual reality visionaries. Some, for example, imagine future technological advances that will allow a machine to tap directly into the thought processes of a human brain. Imagine a database search engine coupled to a "mind-reading" interface of this sort. The users of such a system merely think about the information they would like to find, and the machine retrieves it from its own database—perhaps even inserting the retrieved information back into the user's mind at the location the user would expect to find it if it had been retrieved from his or her own memory banks. The effective outcome for the user would be as though all the information in the machine's database were actually contained in the user's own mind.

Sound far-fetched? Of course it does. So did color TV at one time. The question is, "Is it possible?" Only time will tell. But at least one leading Silicon Valley firm is doing research into developmental neurophysiology with the aim of producing structures in the brain that will allow this sort of direct linkup between humans and machines.

The ultimate goal, the Holy Grail of the virtual reality intelligentsia, however, appears to be the more or less *complete* transfer of the human intellect into the virtual realm. The end product of such a transfer would be a completely independent intellect, a "persona analog" that starts as a copy of a "biological intelligence" (a "bio-I"), but proceeds to "evolve" along its own independent path as a "cyber-intelligence" (a "cyber-I"). Whether such a being can actually be created is the question of the day. But whether or not there can ever be a complete transfer of the human to the virtual realm, what cannot be questioned is that man is in the midst of a very marked, and remarkable, entry into the realm of the machine.

Virtual Man

The trend toward the increasing "virtuality" of the man-machine interface is an important one. It may, in fact, be tangible evidence of a change in underlying assumptions about what man is, and the nature of reality itself. Or it may be a strong factor in *effecting* that change. But whatever it is—the chicken or the egg—it represents at its core the triumph of the virtual over the created reality. What man is is a question that has only two answers worth considering: he is either a created being, or a product of mindless evolution. The answer we choose reveals much about our view of the whole nature of reality.

The book of Genesis tells us that man was created: "So God created man in his own image, in the image of God he created him; male and female he created them" (Genesis 1:27 RSV). Evolution, on the other hand, tells us that man is the result of an almost impossibly long series of accidents—the collective "wisdom" of eons of mutation and selection.

Genesis tells us that man is a finished work—the consummating work of a good creation (Genesis 1:31). Evolution, in contrast, tells us that man is the expression of a process that has no known beginning, no guiding purpose other than survival, and no known destination. According to this view, any path of divergence is as good as any other, so long as it produces viable offspring.

Evolution, then, places no special importance on the human being. The only truly special thing about the human being—the only *remarkable* thing—is that he has achieved self-consciousness. If this consciousness now exists, there are no rules that preclude it from being involved in the next step of the evolutionary process. The human being, according to this view, is just a "Mr. Potatohead" with parts that we can mix and match as we please. If virtual reality, or any other reality for that matter, will serve us better than the current version, then hooray and off we go. Life will be blissful in the New World, with perhaps only an occasional return to stock up on Jolt! Cola. Imagine a world without hangnails! The stakes are, of course, potentially much higher: *omniscience, omnipresence* (or at least "telepresence"), and *immortality.*

Now hear what God has to say on the matter: "Shall the potter be regarded as the clay; that the thing made should say of its maker, 'He did not make me'; or the thing formed say of him who formed it, 'He has no understanding'?" (Isaiah 29:16).

The humanist-evolutionist paradigm that currently reigns supreme has no ultimate use for questions such as, "Is it wise to attempt to change the form of human being?" It may be a question that is pondered as an interesting problem from the standpoint of psychology, or ethics, or even sociology. The essential question, however, has already been answered. The clay has, in effect, said of the Maker, "He did not make me." The thing formed has said of Him who formed it, "He has no understanding." With the question of accountability to a Maker out of the way, there is no brake to stop the thing made from tinkering with its own form.

Descartes Revisited

All this brings us back to the original question: could a human being actually be "downloaded" into the realm of virtual reality? The possibility may not be as far-fetched as it sounds, if one necessary assumption is allowed. The necessary assumption is this: *the essential "beingness" of a human being is the mind of the individual.* The brain, then, is the organic structure that houses all of that which is truly human. Everything else— feet, legs, arms, torso, and so forth—is simply an evolutionary convenience to allow the human being to exist in one specific set of externally defined constraints (that is, physical reality).

With this assumption in place, the problem of replacing the current mode of human existence with another mode is therefore reduced to just this: *finding an alternative structure to house the mind.* Neural net research, a branch of artificial intelligence (AI), has been working on just that problem, with some success. Neural nets are complex networks of interrelated data that are able to "learn" from presented stimuli. They are modeled after the human brain, and appear to mimic its behavior in acquiring, storing, and interrelating information. Hans Moravec, in his book *Mind Children*,[7] discusses the theory that one day it will be possible to "download" a mind into a sufficiently sophisticated neural net and produce an independent, conscious cyberspace intelligence—a "Cyber-I." The intelligence thus produced will, by virtue of the assumption stated above, be equivalent to the one from which it was downloaded.

A full critique of this position is beyond the scope of this chapter.[8] However, one point must be noted: it completely ignores or denies the element of spirit in the makeup of the human being. It is a fundamentally mechanistic view of the nature of life: life is mind, and merely amounts to organized patterns of neurons colliding. In contrast, Genesis tells us that life comes from God, who is Spirit: "Then the Lord God formed man of dust from the ground, and breathed into his nostrils the breath of life; and man became a living being" (Genesis 2:7).

The Image of the Beast

Life and death are the final enigmas. Throughout the ages, man has wrestled with his inability to create life, and his powerlessness to prevent its ending. Only one man has ever experienced death and overcome it—Jesus Christ the Lord. Even in this century, with all the amazing growth of man's ability to see into the mysteries of time, space, and matter, we are still humiliated before the task of creating a life-form as simple as an ant, or even a bacterium. God seems to have reserved for Himself the power to create life and to overcome death. Maybe it is because of this obvious limit on the extent of human powers that our mythology is replete with the dangers of man creating life. In Jewish folklore, the Golem is the creature of man's creation, loosed on the earth to wreak havoc. In the 20th century, Mary Shelley's Frankenstein is the model: *the creature born of technology who turns on and destroys the creator.*

This sense of foreboding and danger is not absent in the present debate over the possibility of creating "virtual man." Roger Penrose, professor of mathematics at Oxford University and author of the best-selling *The Emperor's New Mind,* is one of those voicing an alarm. Reviewing Moravec's book *Mind Children,* in the *New York Review of Books,* Penrose uses the word "nightmare" to describe Moravec's proposed "downloading" scenario. Moravec responds:

> As the words "frightening" and "nightmare" in your review suggest, intelligent machines are an emotion stirring prospect... Our emotions were forged over eons of evolution, and are triggered by situations, like threats to life or territory, that resemble those that influenced our ancestor's reproductive success. Since there were no intelligent machines in our past, they must resemble something else to incite such a panic. . . .[8]

Maybe. Or maybe they represent something from our future. God, in His Word, has warned man about things to come in a time when the seeds of man's rebellion will have come to full flower. Consider this passage from the book of Revelation:

> Then I saw another beast which rose out of the earth. . . . It works great signs, even making fire come down from heaven to earth in the sight of men; and by the signs which it is allowed to work . . . it deceives those who dwell on earth, bidding them make an image [of] the beast . . . and it was allowed to give breath to the image of the beast so that the

image of the beast should even speak, and to cause those
who would not worship the image of the beast to be slain.
(Revelation 13:11-16)

Those on earth are deceived into making an image of the
beast, an image of a man. The second beast is "allowed" to
give breath to the image. *The image speaks!* Try as I might to
resist the temptation to interpret this notoriously difficult
book in ways that are only applicable to this point in history, I
cannot resist making the following observation: it seems to me
that what John warns of here in terms of a "talking image" is
frighteningly similar to the "Cyber-I" of virtual reality fantasy.
An image of a man, a downloaded replica of a human mind,
given the ability to speak—that is, given the ability to think
and communicate as an independent intelligence. All who
will not worship this image are to be eliminated.

The Word Became Flesh

"In the beginning was the Word, and the Word was with
God, and the Word was God. . . . And the Word became
flesh and dwelt among us . . ." (John 1:1,14a).

The Bible records several amazing aspects of the relationship between God and man, but none more amazing than
this: that the very co-eternal Word became like one of us. Man
has been created in such a way, in the image of God, that God
Himself could inhabit this flesh. The Creator entered into His
own creation, and became one of us. In His wisdom, God was
able to pull off this feat, and the result was the salvation of the
world. Maybe the record of this transaction, the Old and
(especially) the New Testaments, should have been prefaced
with the warning: "The following acts have been performed by
almighty God. Do not attempt to do this at home."

Through virtual reality, man sees perhaps an opportunity
to perform a similar act—to fashion a world of his own design,
and then to inhabit that world as one of its created beings.
The imagined gospel of the new world might say: "And the

Flesh became virtual and dwelt among us." What would the outcome be of such an event? I am afraid that what I see being voiced by the various representatives of the artificial intelligence and library-information science communities is just a techno-variation on the age-old gnostic dream—escape from the bondage of this fleshly existence into . . . what? The world of the electron?

When God came to be with us in the person of Jesus the Christ, He assumed life in the flesh *in its entirety*—conception, birth, childhood, adolescence, maturity, and death. Speaking to the Jews of His day, in language calculated to offend, Jesus said: "I am the living bread which came down from heaven; if any one eats of this bread, he will live for ever; and the bread which I shall give for the life of the world is *my flesh*" (John 6:51, emphasis added).

This is the basis of our hope—that God from the realm of spirit became a man of flesh, one like us, not that man from the realm of flesh will become a virtual god.

4

THE FAUSTIAN BARGAIN—

COMPUTERS AND HUMAN POTENTIAL

Brooks Alexander

What was the Faustian bargain? In the classic legend, Faust sold his soul to the Devil for an irresistible package of self-enhancing powers, including an extra 24 years of life. In the end, he lost his soul in what he realized too late was a futile bargain in what started out as a simple quest for knowledge.

Can we stand back from the flashy technology that has besieged us and question what is really going on? What are the real prospects for human betterment? Will we actually participate in our own conscious evolution? Or will we slip into various cocoons of pleasure, self-absorption, and quests for godlike powers—alternate realities of our own creation—that will lead us collectively down a darker path? Brooks Alexander probes these issues by looking for historical barometers that reflect on these perplexing issues—the primary barometer being the ageless wisdom of Scripture.

The so-called "computer revolution" has been underway for almost half a century now. (The term "cybernetics" was coined in 1947 by Norbert Weiner of the Massachusetts Institute of Technology.) If you take your impressions of reality from the mainstream media, however, you might think it began just a few years ago. Only recently have the subjects of cyberspace, computers, virtual reality, and the information superhighway attracted much media attention—but once the attention began, it turned to a media frenzy. To say the subject has been widely covered in recent years would be a gross understatement. The explosion of information about the information-explosion is one of the ironies of our time.

Not the *only* one, however. Here is another: we know more today than it was even possible to know a mere few years ago. There is a staggering amount of information at our disposal, just waiting for our command to come forth and display itself on our computer screens. Yet, *knowing more* than before, we *understand less* than ever. We are so preoccupied by counting trees that we cannot make sense of our local grove, much less the forest it is part of. Despite the glut of information about computers, it is becoming more difficult than ever to understand their real impact on our lives. One reason for this is that the incessant innovation in computer technology and software tends to entangle our attention in the present moment. Like other forms of information overload, relentless novelty has the effect of numbing our attention and narrowing it down to the manageable details of the ongoing process of change.

The "computer revolution," however, cannot be understood outside a context that includes both the past and the future as well as the present. Unfortunately, that kind of understanding is beyond our grasp. Our understanding of the past is sketchy at best; our understanding of the present is virtually nil; our fanciful understanding of the future amounts to little more than self-serving speculation. As Otto Zeit notes, "What some have called 'futurism' is not a science at all, but a forum for technocrats to swap fantasies of social engineering."[1]

As to the past, we do have some knowledge of our history in relation to computers. We know their military origins, their early, awkward, civilian applications, their increasing power and decreasing size, and their expanding presence in every aspect of our lives. The body of information and comment on that process is large and growing, even at the popular level. There are several literary (and video) versions of what we could call the "Chronicles of Silicon Valley." We know how the personal computer was invented, who the principal perpetrators were, how they dreamed, how they schemed, how they jockeyed among themselves, how their business grew, how it spawned other businesses, and so forth. That sort of information is available in elaborate, often gossipy detail.

Drowning in Data

The irony is that all our historical knowledge does not help us to understand what is going on today—or to foresee where we are headed. Despite our fascinating catalog of trees, the forest (*that is,* the developing influence of computers on our lives) remains uncharted and is probably unchartable.

Trying to interpret the "computer revolution" resembles a problem in quantum physics. At the subatomic level, one cannot measure a particle's position and velocity simultaneously; that is one of the little things that makes reality unpredictable to our minds. Likewise, at the macro-level of computer influence and social change, one cannot describe the current state of things and keep up with their ongoing development at the same time. Events are happening so fast that it is impossible to stay abreast of them and write about them simultaneously. By the time one has paused long enough to put thoughts into words and words onto paper, the reality one is writing about has surpassed both the facts gathered *and* one's analysis of them. Even such an experienced and knowledgeable thinker as Jacques Ellul has struggled with this problem—and acknowledged defeat in the face of it:

> My first intention was to write a book on all aspects of the impact of the computer on society . . . but I was too late. The world of computers was evolving so fast that I was always two years behind. I could never catch up. I thus abandoned . . . the whole project of clarifying the computer jungle and its relations to our world. I obviously never succeeded in mastering the material. It slipped through my fingers as soon as I thought I had grasped it.[2]

If the present we live in is too complex and slippery to describe, then the future yet to arrive is even more so. We cannot foresee the results of our computers any more than Gutenberg could foresee the results of his printing press— and for the same reasons. One reason is that we are just now at the beginning of the process that we are trying to see to the end of. The changes we are trying to grasp are still unfolding around us; we can only *perceive* them in part because they are only *present* in part.

That much is obvious to common sense. A more basic (and less obvious) reason for our difficulty is that what we are really trying to understand is our own nature. In the end, the computer, like all technology, is about empowering the human will (that is, amplifying human nature)—in all of its manifestations. In trying to understand the computer, then, we are really trying to understand ourselves, and to understand our own impact on the world.

Technology and Social Change

Unfortunately, self-understanding has eluded us ever since we were thrown out of Eden—and there is no evidence that we have gotten better at it over time. In fact, the evidence shows that in case after case we have remained either oblivious or indifferent to the dangers of increasing the potency of the errant human will. The history of technology shows that over thousands of years we have devised increasingly powerful ways of transforming the world into our own image. History also shows that we have been totally unprepared to deal with the consequences we thus set in motion, and have been taken by surprise by them every time.

In 1964 Marshall McLuhan told us that we are changed by the things we make, and we begin to resemble the things we use. "We become what we behold," he said. "We shape our tools, and thereafter our tools shape us." The list of history's culture-changing inventions begins with fire and the wheel, and runs through writing, gunpowder, printing, steam power, internal combustion, electrical power, the telephone, nuclear power, television, and now computers and high-speed information processing. All these technological advances have carried an invisible price tag: besides fulfilling their immediate promises of power and control, they created vast changes in the conditions of human life and the organization of human society. They restructured social arrangements and remolded social attitudes—often through violence and upheaval. And those changes always caught us flat-footed. We have *never* been able either to foresee or to prepare for the long-range results of our own behavior.

The invention of writing illustrates the complex relationship between technology and cultural change. Writing probably originated as a way of keeping records of material resources—that is, as an accounting device. Writing began, in effect, as a business tool. But its effects did not stop with revolutionizing business practice. In the end, writing destroyed the culture of oral tradition and the whole order of society that went with it. Basic social roles were reshuffled. The priests who memorized and recited the "tribal encyclopedia" became irrelevant. Their societies—defined by the oral transmission of knowledge—disappeared or were transformed overnight. Whole classes fell from social grace and new classes rose to replace them. Things formerly valued were now discarded, and things formerly unheard of were now esteemed. The magnitude of those social changes is almost beyond conception—and they were just the beginning.

In preliterate tribal cultures, learning was collective and relational: knowledge was passed on by speaking and hearing, from one person to another. With the advent of writing, however, knowledge could be made into a permanent record. *The transient spoken word could be frozen into a form that was available any time, not just when it was uttered. Now, learning and thinking could be individual and continuous, rather than communal and periodic.* The invention of writing made possible the very concept of individuality as we know it.

Thus, the far-reaching and entirely unforeseen effect of writing was to detribalize Western man. It broke the grip of the tribal group on the power of information. It led directly to the emergence of new and higher political entities—that is, the city-states of Mesopotamia, Egypt, and later, Greece. It also led, of course, to a new concentration of power (politically, economically, and religiously) in the hands of those who were masters of the new medium—namely, those who could read and write.

Writing brought even more changes. It is the basis of literature by definition, and so established the foundation for philosophy. By giving concrete form to revelation, it created scripture, and made possible the broad dissemination of the knowledge of God. It also made science possible. In an oral culture, knowledge is mythic, communal, and initiatory. Once information is freed from the constraints of oral transmission, individuals can seek knowledge systematically. They can record their own experience, survey their record at leisure, and interpret it for themselves—quite apart from rituals of communal indoctrination.

Looking for the Future

All those social changes were double-edged, of course, in the sense that they produced disruption and suffering as well as empowerment and happiness—even by human standards, and more or less in equal measure. By biblical standards, they produced evil as well as good. For example, writing helps to spread both the verities of revelation and the errors of human speculation. As part of that "existential ambivalence," many of the changes that writing unleashed worked their way through society in a process of conflict and turmoil.

All the results described above seem obvious in retrospect. Yet none of them were foreseen at the time (indeed, they were not even seen as such when they were happening). We are too intoxicated with the promises of our technology to see beyond the immediate (or projected) applications of its power. Unfortunately, obsessive attention to trivial detail has become a habit of thought with us. Throughout history we have signally failed to grasp the larger meaning of every technological advance we have invented so far—up to and including the computer. To date, our record of historical self-understanding has been one of unrelenting failure. Humans create their conditions and they create their times. If they do not understand themselves, they will understand nothing, including their times.

Can we hope to do any better today? Can we hope to understand the advent of computers better than our ancestors understood the advent of writing? Can we understand the information superhighway any better than our own parents understood TV? Surprisingly, the answer is—*perhaps*. It all depends on how we proceed.

One thing at least is certain—we will only add to our confusion and misunderstanding if we try to understand the cultural impact of computers by focusing *on computers themselves*. If experience teaches us anything, it teaches us that it is a fool's errand to look for the *results* of technology by studying the *instruments* of technology. We cannot understand the implications of our machines by studying the machines themselves. Technology enables us to *do* certain things. By thinking about the technology itself, we gain an idea of what we are *able* to do, and thus can decide what we *want* to do. But no amount of thinking about technology will tell us the results that will follow once we have actually *done* it. The reality always exceeds our expectations (even our most "expert" expectations), precisely because our fascinated focus on the instruments themselves is nearsighted and misleading. Thinking about our gadgets can only tell us what will happen when we use them; it can never tell us what will happen afterwards.

The limitations of instrumental analysis can be easily illustrated. Consider the impact of gunpowder on warfare and society. Military men of the fourteenth century consciously tried to adapt their strategies to the potential of their new weapon. Some thought ahead, and imagined how the cannon and other firearms could be improved, especially as to their range and rate of fire. They tried, in other words, to sense the present and future potential of their technology and exploit it. In some short-term, limited ways, they were enormously successful. Moated castles and fortified strongholds fell easily before artillery bombardment, and military tactics soon made the most of that increasingly evident fact. Few of the warrior-class, however, saw any implications of their weaponry beyond the conduct of their next battle. No one saw the vast social crisis they were stirring up with their new powers of destruction. The coming of cannons meant an end to feudalism because it meant an end to the defensive fortresses that were the center of feudal life. The castle was the tangible, architectural hub of feudalism's complex social system. Once the castle was rendered indefensible, feudalism was rendered *de facto* defunct.

No one at the time had a clue, however, that those changes were happening. They were too busy figuring out how to apply their new technology in ways that would kill people and break things more efficiently. They could not anticipate the larger results of their firearms because they were thinking about the firearms themselves, and about their immediate application. In a similar way, no one during the "age of steam" understood the social or cultural implications of the "industrial revolution" because they were too wrapped up in thinking about the machines themselves, and about how they could be used.

The same challenge faces us today in our thinking about computers. The irony is that we cannot hope to foresee the results of computers unless we back away from computers themselves. We must look beyond the instruments to the choices we make in creating and using them. And we must look to the universal human factors that shape the making of those choices to begin with. We must go back to *how* we perceive the problems that confront us, and *why* we try to solve them as we do.

We must begin, in other words, with the fundamentals of our own nature. Technology cannot change who we are, but it can and does change the impact of who we are on the world around us. If we can get a handle on our own nature, we have some hope of bringing our behavior under control. If not, we are condemned to lurch from crisis to crisis—propelled by self-will but protected from self-understanding by delusion and denial.

Square One: Ourselves

Delusion arises when we inflate the potential of technology into a fantasy of imagined outcomes, without factoring in the realities that will actually govern the outcome. At the root of delusion, therefore, lies denial. Denial makes delusion inescapable. When we suppress knowledge that would challenge our fantasies or constrain our desires, we insure that our fantasies will remain unfulfilled and our desires will remain unsatisfied. Denial itself comes from the deep self-division we all inherit as part of our human nature. Because we are self-divided (ambi-valent), all our works are ambivalent. This is especially true of technology, which magnifies our ambivalent nature in extraordinary ways.

This is not a novel observation. Many writers have addressed the so-called "ambivalence" of technology. The naive view is that technology itself is inherently neutral, and the goodness or badness of its results depends entirely on how it is used—and especially on the motives with which it is used. Jacques Ellul summarizes this view and thrusts it rather rudely aside:

> From an elementary standpoint the ambivalence of techniques has often been stressed (as in my study in 1950). Techniques can have both good and bad effects. . . . It is often added quietly that everything depends on the use one makes of technique. With a knife one can peel an apple or kill one's neighbor. I tried to show that this comparison is absurd and that technique carries with it its own effects quite apart from how it is used. . . . If we want to know what the issue is when we speak about technique, we must begin by eliminating the futile argument about its use. . . . No matter how it is used, it has of itself a number of positive and negative consequences. This is not just a matter of intention.[3]

Ellul says we must not only notice the ambivalence of technology, we must analyze it. We must see its dynamics as they really are. As a basis for doing so, Ellul advances four propositions, all more or less verified by the common experience of life:

First, all technical progress has its price.

Second, at each stage it raises more and greater problems than it solves.

Third, its harmful effects are inseparable from its beneficial effects.

Fourth, it has a great number of unforeseen effects.[4]

Technology and Humanism

Ellul's observations gain strength from the fact that others have come to similar conclusions without sharing either his starting point or his approach. In *The Arrogance of Humanism,* for example, David Ehrenfeld arrives essentially at Ellul's understanding of technological ambivalence by coming from a completely different direction. Ehrenfeld (a Rutgers biology professor) discusses humanism as a form of religious faith.

At the core of the humanist faith, according to Ehrenfeld, is

a supreme faith in human reason—its ability to confront and solve the many problems that humans face, its ability to re-arrange both the world of Nature and the affairs of men and women so that human life will prosper . . . humanism elevates our inventiveness to divine levels and celebrates it as infallible.[5]

Ehrenfeld does not start out to discuss technology as a topic, but the issue is soon raised by his critique of our faith in human reason. After all, reason always tries to "confront and solve our problems" through the application of technique and technology. Ehrenfeld's most important insight is his observation that when we try to use technology to solve any large-scale problem (such as the fouling of our environment with the "by-products" of technology), we set off a chain reaction of consequences that is depressingly predictable, plainly observable, and routinely explained away.

Ehrenfeld cites evidence to show that by choosing a techno-answer to, say, environmental problems (his example), we lock ourselves into an escalating cycle of partial solutions that are then followed by new problems—some left over from the original problem, and some generated by the technology that was sent to solve it but didn't. Following Eugene Schwartz, in his book *Overskill*, Ehrenfeld refers to this process as the cycle of "quasi-solutions" followed by "residue problems."

There is no mystery about where this cycle comes from or where it leads. Ehrenfeld describes the process in three simple, easy-to-understand stages.

1) No techno-solution to any environmental problem can ever be complete (or come close to it) because a) the complexity of the environment exceeds our knowledge and understanding to begin with; and b) our technology is a crude instrument that can only intervene awkwardly in a complex ecosystem.

2) The incomplete solution ("quasi-solution") then generates new problems, because the technology assembled to solve the initial problem causes problematic "side effects" (a euphemism for "we did not know *this* would happen") of its own. These "residue problems" are then addressed by new techno-solutions. Each new round of quasi-solutions produces, in turn, a new set of residue problems—which, of course, increases the complexity, the difficulty, and the expense of trying to deal with them. Finally, the problems proliferate faster than solutions can be found to correct them.

3) Our misguided quest for control thereby spirals ironically out of control. But in the process it produces three certain results: a) we *will not* solve the problems we set out to address; b) we *will* create many new problems along the way; and c) most ominous of all, we will also create a cumbersome, expensive, and intrusive bureaucracy to *administer* the stacked layers of corrective technology, added to partial solutions, derived from defective analysis, *and so forth, ad infinitum.* Ehrenfeld describes a pattern of arrogance and naivete that we recognize all too well. The ordained results of that combination (the two always seem to go together) are pride and

bungling, blindness and stumbling, producing disasters in the name of relief.

Ehrenfeld echoes Ellul's discourse on the ambivalence of technology. Both men clearly see and plainly say that all forms of techno-power work to produce both good *and* bad effects. That happens unavoidably because of the inherent flaws and limits of human nature.

Scripture and Understanding

Ellul is a professing Christian. Ehrenfeld is a Jew who plainly takes the biblical worldview seriously. Their converging views should encourage us to consider the *source* of their insight—that is, the Bible. Does the Bible have anything to say about the ambivalence of technology? In fact, it does. It has a great deal to say about the ambivalence of human nature in general (which is fundamental), and its language says something about the nature of technology in particular. (See Appendix A, "Technology and the Fall.")

According to the Bible, there are two relevant facts to understand about human nature: 1) we are created in the image of God; and 2) we are fallen. Because we are made in the image of God, we are creative, dynamic, and purposeful. Because we are fallen, all these qualities are routinely applied in the pursuit of ungodly ends. The net result of those two facts is that all of our thoughts and all our acts express *both* sides of our nature at once.

From a biblical standpoint, therefore, the ambivalence of technology is inevitable. It is the result of empowering the fallen will to act in a fallen world. Because of our self-division, whenever we exercise power in the world, both sides of our nature will be at work to produce their respective results. The greater the power given to the human will, the greater the blessings it will dispense, *and* the greater the damage it will leave in its wake. It is spiritually impossible to have one without the other, because the fall has made us into something we were never created to be—beings divided against ourselves and opposed to our Creator, constantly in conflict with our own created nature, and constantly in friction against God's created world.

With that insight, we come to the threshold of understanding. If we can comprehend ourselves, we may thereby understand our times. If we know *what* the fall is, and *how* it skews our purposes, we may be able to anticipate *how* our technologies amplify our double nature.

The fall has many aspects, but three are particularly important in forecasting the fruits of technology. The three salient aspects are: 1) our obsessive drive for control (and its Siamese twin, the need to dominate); 2) our general inclination toward decay and decline (and our general disinclination to resist the process); and 3) our reflexive impulse of moral evasion and denial (we never want to call it "decay," or to take responsibility for our part in it).

Even at first glance, we can see that this collection of qualities is a surefire recipe for producing a series of corrupt and tyrannical governments, enforced in the name of righteousness (which, by the way, *has* been a prevailing pattern in human affairs). If we unpack the fall even further, however, we can see that it influences every aspect of our lives individually. Each of the three fallen factors—control, corruption, and denial—is personally working in all of us. They affect our personal view of the world, and therefore determine how we react to the world. In other words, the fall warps both our motives and our behavior. What we want is to understand *how* it does so.

The Obsessive Urge to Dominate

Saint Augustine (A.D. 354–430) understood the fall more thoroughly and more biblically than anyone before him or since, with the possible exception of Adam and Eve. In his monumental *City of God*, Augustine unraveled some of the tangled dynamics of the fall.

According to Augustine, the fall locks us into a deepening cycle of defensive alienation. To get the process rolling, as the third chapter of Genesis indicates, we separate ourselves from God. As the bumper sticker puts it, "If you feel far from God— guess who moved?" By seeking *our* way rather than the ways of God, we find that we have departed from the presence of God. By relying on *our* strength rather than the strength of God, we find that the strength of God has departed from our lives. Suddenly we face an overwhelming world with *only our* strength to rely on. Without God, our strength is transparently inadequate. We are acutely aware of our helplessness and are overcome by existential panic.

Because we sense that our power is inadequate, we compulsively try to assert it, almost as a reflexive act of denial. We do not premeditate that response and cannot control it. It cannot be erased by "enlightenment," educated away, or trained not to happen. The fall has made it a part of our nature.

Our drive to dominate others is the unmistakable stain of that disorder. The one sure way we can create at least the appearance of control is in connection with those of our own kind. We cannot control nature, but we can control (or *pretend* to control) other people. So we try to assert our power first and foremost by subjecting others to our will—even as they do the same to us. Thus, all our relationships are characterized by a sense of insatiable desperation. The basic fact of our inner life is that we are infected with deficiency and fear, to which we involuntarily respond with over-assertion and obsessive self-concern.

The urge to dominate, the rule of violence, and the unjust layering of society are all just parts of that same fallen pattern. Everyone bemoans some part of the pattern, but the pattern as a whole is our own creation. It continues to exist because we continue to sustain it by behaving out of our inherited, primal anxieties—especially in relation to one another. The continual interplay of fallen motives is enough to create the entire structure of human affairs that we know as the fallen "world system." That is as close to the mechanics of original sin as Augustine can bring us, and it is close enough to expose the inner workings of the global system of sin that Augustine called the "Earthly City" (as distinguished from the "City of God").

Computers and the Domination Impulse

What does all this have to do with the impact of computers? Quite a bit. Some implications of Augustine's insight are visible right away. First, it means that the potential of computers for controlling, manipulating, and monitoring people will be explored enthusiastically, and the exploration will be well-funded. All the "Big Brother" features of a computerized society will be eagerly investigated, and many of them will be eagerly implemented—at every level. From the heavens, invisible spy satellites already peer into the open trunk of a car, or through an unshuttered window; they can see in the dark and probe beneath the ground with radar and infrared. Somewhat more down to earth, the city-state of Singapore provides a chilling example of the way sophisticated technocrats can use computers to create a totally managed and monitored society. Government, however, is not the only place the "Big Brother temptation" is at work; the gadgetry of snooping is already well-developed for use in businesses that rely on computers extensively. As Clifford Stoll observes,

> Computers lend themselves to being used as management tools. They can keep track of idle time, number of words typed, number of errors made. Telephone operators must handle a certain number of calls per minute. Secretarial staff face a quota of typing a certain number of insurance claims every hour. A digital dungeon.[6]

Augustine's insight also means that the power of computers in our society will be unequally and unfairly distributed. The more complex computer technology becomes, the wider the gap will become between those who can afford real computing power (mainly governments and large corporations) and those who can only afford to play with the trickle-down of lesser toys. Society always divides into *haves* and *have-nots*—based on the obsession to exercise control and the struggle to dominate. The raw fact is that in any struggle for control, some will prevail and some will not.

In an information society, the basic division will occur between the info-rich and the info-poor, between those with wide access to information and those with limited access, between the cyber-illuminati and the cyber-ignorati. The power shift that is currently underway will give the techno-elite the power to remold society in *their* image, and to shape our social arrangements to fit *their* vision of the ideal polity. It goes without saying that the ideal polity, in the view of the techno-elite, is one that is organized to service the needs of *their* technology and to promote *their own* happiness and general welfare. It should surprise no one but the incurably naive that such an agenda has the "side effect" of creating a new underclass of info-serfs that will toil in the so-called "service industries" to support the technical needs of the information hierarchy and to cater to its personal desires.

Myth Meets Reality

Cyber-enthusiasts protest that this is a jaundiced view. In fact, many of them are confidently expecting the exact opposite to happen. The real impact of the computer revolution, they tell us, will be to "democratize" access to information, and actually *undermine* the power of any presumed "information elite." This optimistic view is based on the potential of computers to provide nearly universal access to their resources, and the *assumption* that this potential will be fulfilled. Techno-optimists envision the new information society as a kind of happy anarchy—a state of benign, unstructured social chaos—in which every individual is empowered to control the circumstances of his life through the medium of his multi-functional computer terminal (or "communications center" in cyber-speak).

Unfortunately, this view ignores all the thorny questions about how the technology will *actually* be used. How much of the potential will be realized, and how much will remain a wistful dream—or even become a destructive delusion? Techno-optimism barely recognizes the question. In addition, techno-optimism seems blind to the very real biases and exclusions that are built into the technology itself. *At its best,* the information superhighway will be as universally accessible as the interstate highway system—that is, anyone with a car can use it. The unstated side of that equation is that those without cars cannot and will not use it. Any technology requires the ability to use its instruments; the opportunity to use them is a *prerequisite* to enjoying the benefits of that technology. "Universal access" is a myth.

The problem is inherent. Every technological advance reshuffles social priorities and rearranges the social hierarchy, rewarding some people and disenfranchising others. Computers simply speed up that process, and they do so because of the nature of their technology, completely apart from the conscious intentions of anyone who uses them. Clifford Stoll describes the exclusionary nature of technocratic culture:

> For all the talk of friendly, open systems, there's no warm welcome for novices. It's up to the user to figure out which system is best, up to the user to install and maintain the software.
>
> In the same way, the networked community is an exclusive club for the initiated. Too often, there's an established hazing ritual to get online.
>
> Result: the computing elite claim that theirs is an open, accessible world, while barring outsiders through a liturgy of technology. It's the culture of exclusion . . . engineers

routinely use cryptic labels that mystify the technology and
deny access to ordinary people.[7]

Techno-optimists claim that with dedication and good
intentions, all these problems can be overcome. The biblical
realist responds that *yes*, many things *might* happen, in an
imaginary world of consistently sane and compassionate
choices. In the real world, however, our choices are made in a
state of existential panic, and they most often are made in
pursuit of our blind urge to control and dominate. The exclusionary nature of the technology is thus reinforced by our
own fundamental motivations—and vice versa—because the
technology is a product of our fundamental motivations to
begin with.

Will the information society become a stratified world of
social perks and power, with whole classes of people relegated
to techno-serfdom? Today, that is a redundant question.
Never seriously in doubt, the results of our technology are
already evident. No forecasting is required, only observation.
The unskilled, the undereducated, the poor, the homeless,
African-Americans, Hispanics, and women are already being
left in the dust of the accelerating revolution. Some writers
have noted and lamented that problem, but no one has proposed a viable solution to it. Everything we know suggests that
such social gaps tend to widen rather than to shrink.

A Disturbing Look at Our Real Future

David Noble is a vocal critic of "computerism" and the
information society. His comments are notable because he
bears an impressive set of credentials. He taught at Massachusetts Institute of Technology for nearly a decade and was the
curator of industrial automation at the Smithsonian Institution in Washington, D.C. He is considered something of a
techno-apostate in the academic community, and it is not difficult to see why. In the passage below, he enumerates the
observable socioeconomic results of computerization so far,
and the list alone is unnerving. Noble looks at the world with

unblinking realism and expresses his vision with devastating clarity.

To see where we are headed requires no voodoo forecasting or futuristic speculation, much less federally funded research. We just need to take a look at where we've been and where we are. The returns are already in on the information age, and the information highway promises merely more of the same, at an accelerated pace.

In the wake of the information revolution (now four decades old), people are working harder and longer (with compulsory overtime), under worsening working conditions with greater anxiety, stress and accidents, with less skills, less security, less autonomy, less power (individually and collectively), less benefits and less pay. Without question the technology has been developed and used to de-skill and discipline the workforce in a global speed-up of unprecedented proportions. And those still working are the lucky ones. For the technology has been designed above all to displace.

Today we are in the midst of what is called a "jobless recovery," symptomatic and symbolic of the new age. Outputs and profits rise without the jobs that used to go with them. Moreover, one fifth of those employed are only part time or temporary employees, with little or no benefits beyond bare-subsistence wages, and no security whatever.

None of this has happened by accident. The technology was developed, typically at public expense, with precisely these ends in mind by government (notably military), finance, and business elites—to shorten the chain of command and extend communications and control (the military origins of the Internet), to allow for instantaneous monitoring of money markets and funds transfer, and to enable manufacturers to extend the range of their operations in pursuit of cheaper and more compliant labor.

For decades we have silently subsidized the development of the very technologies that have been used to destroy our lives and livelihoods, and we are about to do it again, without debate,

without any safeguards, without any guarantees. The calamity
we now confront, as a consequence, rivals the upheavals of the
first industrial revolution two centuries ago, with its untold
human suffering. We are in for a struggle unlike anything any of
us have ever seen before. . . .[8]

In Noble's view, it is needless to wonder and redundant to
ask *how* computers will affect our society. The answers are
already before us, and the news is not good. The only question left is whether we can deal with that news or whether we
will try to rationalize it—continuing to scratch our heads in
bemusement and confusion, and continuing to search for
new answers to displace the answers we do not want to hear.

The Effects of Decay and Decline

The second salient aspect of the fall that determines the
real impact of computers is our general tendency toward
moral and spiritual corruption, and our general disinclination to resist it. In a fallen world, corruption is a natural,
almost mechanical process. We are all familiar with it through
the phenomena of nature. The cycle of death and decay as we
know it is a product of the fall, which distorts a natural, God-
given process of self-renewing change and transformation
into a process of self-destroying breakdown and dissolution.

What is true on the physical level also has its analog in the
higher realms of personality, relationships, collective morality,
and society in general. All these are subject to degradation
over time, through the repeated making of choices that cater
to our own lower tendencies—especially that of seeking our
satisfaction regardless of the consequences. That primal
fallen motivation, multiplied millions of times a day, acts as a
slow corrosive on the bonds of culture and the sinews of
society. Here again, we have a self-reinforcing process, as radical selfishness promotes social breakdown, which encourages
more—*and more extreme*—forms of radical selfishness.

The process, though vast, is not totally impersonal. The
fallen world has its own fallen "ecology," and there are always

those who promote the process of cultural decay because they expect to gain from it. The very nature of decay is to break down existing structures, releasing energy in the process, which the agents of decay then feed on. Biologically, energy is locked up in units of living cells. A piece of meat left in the open air will soon begin to rot, as decay bacteria break down the structure of its tissues. The bacteria flourish, feeding on the energies of life released by the dissolving cells.

Culturally, energies are stored in various institutions such as marriage, the family, the neighborhood, the tribe, the race, the nation, a shared morality, and the like. When the structures of society break down, that locked-up energy is released at large. Much of it manifests immediately in the form of commercial profits generated by merchandising our decline (MTV is a good example). Some of the energy turns into the passion and zeal (and the money) to pump up our culturally radical movements and ideologies. And some of it goes to advance the agendas of those who are cynical enough and skilled enough to work the process of social decay to their personal advantage (this is the "earthly, demonic wisdom" referred to in James 3:15).

What does this have to do with the information superhighway? It has to do with the kind of information that travels on it. We can confidently predict that pornography on the Internet will increase in volume and depravity, as will destructive, violent, hateful, dangerous, and dehumanizing information of every other kind.

The development of television provides an exact analogy of what we can expect from the development of an electronically networked society. In 1939 David Sarnoff of RCA expansively declared, "It is probable that television drama of high caliber and produced by first-rate artists will materially raise the level of dramatic taste of the nation." Fifty-six years later we can see for ourselves the river of repugnant sludge that television entertainment has become—insulting to aesthetics and toxic to the soul.

We are entitled to laugh, therefore, when the cyber-enthusiasts boast that the information superhighway will open up a
spontaneous cultural renaissance and lead to a literary revival.
It will not happen. It is already not happening. Clifford Stoll
comments that the great preponderance of messages on the
Internet are badly written and sloppily organized renditions
of half-baked ideas. He says that much of the "information"
available on-line is a waste of time to read, not to mention the
time wasted in "accessing" it. (Sounds like TV—"500 channels, and nothing on.") Stoll says he will tune into the on-line
discussion groups "the next time I have to spend a week in
traction . . . one of the joys of computers is how they are great
at wasting time that might otherwise be difficult to waste."[9]

Stoll's skepticism is that of an initiate, not an outsider. His
expertise in navigating the networks is unquestioned. (His
first book, *The Cuckoo's Egg*, is the story of how he tracked
down and eventually trapped a German spy ring operating
through the Internet.) Like David Noble, Clifford Stoll simply
tells us what he knows to be the case from watching it
happen—or in this case, *not* happen.

> One of the more pernicious myths of the online world is
> that of a literary revival. . . . Since the networks rely on the
> written word, you'd expect a rebirth of reading and writing.
> The Internet should be a garden for literate, well-trained
> users to take advantage of a new mode of communications.
> . . . The result should be the honing of literary skills and a
> new wave of creative literature.

> But instead of an Internet-inspired renaissance, mediocre
> writing and poorly thought-out arguments pour into my
> modem. E-mail and postings to network newsgroups are fre-
> quently ungrammatical, misspelled, and poorly organized.
> After trolling up and down the Usenet . . . I rarely find prose
> that's articulate and creative.[10]

This flood of the banal, the bombastic, and the irrelevant
clutters the information superhighway like junk mail clutters

the postal system. But you can't simply sort it and discard it the way you do with the junk mail that clogs your mailbox. You have to scroll through all of it to get to the good stuff—if *there is* any good stuff, and *if* you can find it. It is irritating and inconvenient, but at least it does not precipitate an immediate social crisis.

The human potential for perversity and degradation, on the other hand, will certainly trap us in an impossible dilemma very soon. This is our inescapable quandary: given the power and scope of the information superhighway, there is no way to avoid toxic levels of information-sewage in society without resorting to totalitarian methods of information monitoring and control.

Neither of those alternatives are acceptable, but before long we will have to actually make the choices that are just facing us today. Issues of free speech versus censorship are already being raised with an urgency that is bound to increase. Of course, this is nothing new. The conflict of free self-expression with the forces of social constraint is as ancient as society itself. The advent of computers, however, intensifies the conflict and magnifies its outcome in ways we are poorly equipped to understand or respond to.

Divided human nature drives the dialectic between personal license and external restraint. Excessive freedom always leads to corrupt and corrupting behavior, because of our fallen center of gravity. Eventually the socially destructive results of such behavior become clear. Society reacts defensively to expunge the decay by fiat and force. We become a society of repression and intrusion to avoid becoming a society of corruption and debility.

The cycle is basically simple. As the process of social decay advances, social institutions lose their power to restrain behavior and to bind people together. Society increasingly atomizes into self-seeking ego units. Depravity and criminality explode, anarchy prevails, disorder descends, and tyranny rises to replace it.

What part will computers play in the currently unfolding
version of that cycle? We have already seen how readily computers can be used as instruments of personal surveillance
and social control. *Thus computer technology not only brings our
social crisis to a head, it also becomes our means of coping with the
crisis—a neat package of self-contained historical cause and effect.*
That is the closed, reinforcing cycle of fallen human nature
expressing itself through the medium of a fallen world. Our
fallenness reverberates in a feedback loop. The outcome of
that process is gruesomely depicted in St. John's *Revelation.*
Apart from the Second Coming, this scenario has no happy
ending.

Instincts of Evasion, Philosophies of Denial

"Denial" is the third fallen factor that distorts our technology. G. K. Chesterton said that the fallenness of man is the
only Christian doctrine that is empirically verifiable. One persistent and verifiable *result* of our fall is a deep inner compulsion to deny our own fallen nature. Common experience
confirms this to us on a daily basis. It usually takes the form of
avoiding personal responsibility for our behavior. Psycholo-
gists call it "projection." Most people just call it "passing the
buck." The Bible describes the first case of it in Genesis 3:11-
13. Whatever you call it, the gist of it is to say "the problem is
not in here, it's out there."

Plainly, though, if the problem *really is* "in here" (as Scripture insists), then to deny that fact creates a major reality gap.
If we cannot begin at the personal level by dealing honestly
with our condition, then all our clever efforts at understanding the larger world will only come to naught—or worse,
will build delusions that turn against us and create confusion
and suffering.

Our fallenness is part of the real world in which we live. If
we try to understand the world while avoiding the fall, we will
only build an architecture of evasion and denial. Our basic
moral avoidance regarding ourselves unavoidably distorts our

understanding of everything else—including the rest of creation.

The logic of that process is simple and straightforward: if we insist on asking "why?" but refuse to acknowledge the real "because," we are bound to end up with a bogus "because." Once we embrace the bogus answer, bogus action follows. We develop misguided strategies for dealing with misunderstood problems, while our real problems go unattended. If we cannot admit the truth about ourselves, we can never find the truth about anything else. In the words of de Rougemont,

> One of the reasons confusion is spreading in the world is that we are afraid to face its real causes. We believe in a thousand evils, fear a thousand dangers, but have ceased to believe in Evil and to fear the true Danger. . . . We are never in greater danger than when we deceive ourselves as to the real nature of a threat, and when we summon our energies for a defense against the void, while the enemy approaches from behind.[11]

In the long run, all such systems of denial fail, as do the misguided strategies and deluded expectations based upon them. Some false systems simply lose their credibility over time; others collapse and fall in spectacular fashion. Freudianism and communism come to mind as recent examples—both of them, by the way, crafted explicitly to contradict the biblical view of man. Those particular false ideologies have failed in a publicly visible way. Privately, however, all of us are philosophers of denial. Eventually, our personal systems of moral evasion will collapse as well. Human fallenness is the uncharted reef that will ultimately shipwreck the humanist fantasy—and the reef is not on the chart precisely because of our primary moral denial.

Denial and Idealism

What does our pattern of moral evasion have to do with computers? Some implications are obvious; others are more subtle. In the realm of the obvious, our evasion means we will always embrace our technology by reaching for its "positive potential," blissfully blind to its inevitable fallen consequences. It means, in other words, that mere idealism will always lead us astray, because we cannot factor our own defects into our dreams and ambitions. Specifically, it means that the worst consequences of "computerization" are going to sneak up on us because we are in denial about their source—that is, *ourselves.*

It is folly to believe we can understand ahead of time the problems computers will present; it is a greater and compounding folly to believe we can forestall those problems by means of preventive public policy. By trying to regulate the *symptoms* of human fallenness, we insure that the underlying *cause* of the problem remains untouched. So long as the cause remains untouched, it can generate an infinite variety of symptoms. Even if we succeed in suppressing one set of symptoms, another set will arise to replace it. Trying to cope with the symptoms of the fall from our condition of fallenness is like a classic "Three Stooges" comedy: no sooner do we finally get the top drawer of the dresser shut (after much struggle) than the bottom drawer pops out and bangs our shins. We kneel down to struggle with the bottom drawer, and finally wrestle it shut, only to be banged in the face by the middle drawer—*and so forth,* apparently *ad infinitum.*

The spread of computer technology brings us to another crest in a repeating cycle—a cycle of techno-solutions that turn themselves into problems. Computers are currently undergoing that same cycle—but enormously speeded up. The results of that cycle still remain a matter of uncertainty, but they will not stay that way for long. We will soon find out firsthand how computers can be used to manage and monitor our lives. We can confidently predict this general outcome because our historical pattern of false optimism is both obvious and unbroken—and the pattern will continue unbroken for as long as we continue in our primary denial.

Denial and Gnosticism

In the realm of the not-so-obvious, the impulse of denial has religious implications, as well. The spirit of denial lies at the bottom of Gnosticism, that perennial spiritual counterfeit.

Gnosticism says, in effect, that the problems of this world are built into the material nature of the world. Our wrongness, in other words, comes from the wrongness of what we are made of. We are really pure spirits who are tragically trapped in physical bodies. The gnostic goal is to free the spirit from the fleshly bonds that tangle it in ignorance and delusion.

In the end, the gnostic temptation is another example of the quest to escape the realities of our own condition. It is a classic case of moral and spiritual buck-shuffling: "The problem is not in here, it's out there, in those pesky atoms and molecules."

Today the gnostic dream takes shape as the quest to become a disembodied mind—existing as pure digital intelligence—infinitely free in cyberspace to know, do, or *be* anything the mind can imagine. If you think that sounds like the same vaulting ambition that brought us the Tower of Babel, you are right: "This is what they began to do, and now nothing which they purpose to do will be impossible for them" (Genesis 11:6 NASB). In cyberspace an entity can be anything it wants—male or female, stern or seductive, brilliant or stupid. It can be a complete fantasy—a persona that has no real world counterpart. Does such a "cyber-person" really exist? Can the human self duplicate its identity in the form of an infinitely complex digital code, then manipulate the code—and thus the identity—at will?

Vaporizing the Body

Do these ideas seem outrageous and far-fetched to you? Then you have not tuned into the cyber-culture recently. If you listen to what some of our cyber-poets, cyberpunks, and cyber-pundits are saying, you will begin to sense how thoroughly the fallen impulse of denial drives the gnostic quest to escape the constraints of bodily existence into a virtual world where reality is malleable and freedom is unlimited.

> Virtual Reality is the dream of pure telematic experience. . . . In virtual reality, flesh vaporizes into virtuality as twentieth-century bodies are repackaged with twenty-first-century cybernetic systems for speeding across the electronic frontier.

> The wired body is perfect. Travelling like an electronic nomad through the circulatory flows of the mediascape, it possesses only the virtual form of a multi-layer scanner image. Abandoning the heavy referential history of a central nervous system, the wired body actually grows a telematic nervous system that is freely distributed across the electronic mirror of the Internet. A product of neural tapping and image processing, the wired body is the (technoid) life-form that finally cracks its way out of the dead shell of human culture.

> Technotopia is about disappearances: the vanishing of the body into a relational data base, the nervous system into "distributive processing," and the skin into wetware. As technology comes alive as a distinctive species, we finally encounter the end of (human) history and the beginning of virtual history.[12]

Computers amplify the gnostic option. The association of computers with a gnostic worldview is perfectly natural, even inevitable. Cyberspace provides what seems to be an actual, technically feasible medium in which to realize our ancient gnostic dream—that is, to escape from dependence on the physical world and ascend to the limitless freedom of pure, disembodied intelligence. Through computers, the prospect of practical omniscience beckons, as does the promise of virtual omnipresence, as the mind extends its presence at will across the reaches of the global network.

The cyber-world fits the gnostic mind-set like a glove. Some of the connections between the two virtually call attention to themselves. Original Gnosticism was an elitist religion, based on spiritual technology, and above all on spiritual *knowledge*—the "gnosis" from which the gnostics got their name. Computers store and manipulate "knowledge" *par excellence.* Therefore, as the gnostic impulse seeks technological expression, the technology naturally tends to generate tech-gnosis ("cybernetically mediated enlightenment").

The techno-gnostic connection is not just an abstract historical possibility. It exists already and *has existed* from the earliest days of the cyber-culture. The hippie counterculture, especially in its New Age version, has always influenced the thinking of the cyber-pioneers. By now, gnostic spirituality has been thoroughly woven into the way most of the people in Silicon Valley think about computers—and about the world and their place in it. Partly because of its historical association with computers and the computing-elite, neo-Gnosticism has already established itself as an influence in our process of cultural change.

> New Age elements are rife throughout the post-1960's Bay Area culture that laid the groundwork for much of what we call cyberculture. A psychedelic, do-it-yourself spirituality directly feeds the more utopian elements of this Northern California subculture of Virtual Reality designers, computer artists, and computer programmers. . . . For many of these folks, computers are the latest and among the greatest tools available for the achievement of the Aquarian goal: the expansion of consciousness by whatever means necessary.

> But the influence of the New Age movement on cyberculture extends beyond that of the psychedelic fringe. . . . For the more futuristic New Agers, the self is an information-processing entity that changes nature, depending on the information-flows it receives and the various media to which it connects. This emphasis on information-flows stems in part from the New Age role as the religion of the Information Age. It also explains the crucial role played by one particular occult technique: channeling.[13]

Balancing the Discussion

If anyone protests that this has been a one-sided look at the computer revolution, I say, "exactly so." The side I have emphasized is the side being ignored. The optimists, idealists, and gnostic dreamers already have their voice. Our ears are filled to overflowing with their promises. If we need anything, we need a corrective vision. We need someone to say, "Wait a minute—it isn't going to happen this way. We are overlooking something real, and despised reality will take its revenge. Just because we want to fly doesn't mean that gravity has been abolished. Just because we want to escape the pains and constraints of our fallen human condition doesn't mean we can."

Yes, the computer revolution has its positive aspects. Yes, I personally use a computer for word processing (it makes the text wonderfully malleable). For the moment, at least, our technology has given us remarkable ways of turning up the volume on our message and general commentary.

We should not ignore, however, the fact that our double nature means that all our behavior has effects in *both* directions. Because we are made in the image of God, even our evil intentions routinely produce good results as a "side effect." But the fallen will operating in a fallen world has a double advantage in that balance. We are faced with a kind of "Gresham's Law" of the spirit—the effect of our bad intentions seems to drive out the effect of our good ones. The fallen factors tend to reinforce one another, while the godly influences have to establish themselves against the tide.

In the long run, therefore, our fallen center of gravity tends to set the compass for the course of history. In this fallen age, the "image of God" side of our double nature acts mostly as a brake on our worst tendencies and a barrier to realizing our worst possibilities, rather than as an active reforming and cleansing force (cleansing and reformation mostly result from God's direct intervention). That conclusion commends itself to our intelligence not only because it is found in Scripture, but because its proof is found in our everyday lives.

Unfortunately, this clear-eyed vision of reality leads directly to an existential dilemma: if we ignore the fallen factor, we are doubly at its mercy; but if we attend to it, we are quickly brought to despair. What is the answer?

Slouching Toward Dystopia

The bad news is that within the self-contained world of fallen human motives and means, there *is no* real answer. As history progresses, the fallen side of human nature gradually solidifies its hold on human affairs, abetted by technology—a metaphysical metastasis that is occasionally interrupted by episodes of divine judgment, but is never in remission. Nor can we defer the impact of a given technology by refusing to use it ("just say no to computers"). In the larger pattern, the "Amish option" is simply a part of the dialectic by which technology extends its influence.

We try to pretend there are answers, that things are getting better, and that we can yet solve our problems with the wise use of technical means. We disguise our unbroken record of failure in that regard with ideologies of "progress" and "evolution." But they are transparent disguises. Otto Zeit defines progress as "the monotonous repetition of the same human errors at ever higher levels of technical skill."

Our double nature locks us into a downward spiral. There is nothing we can "do" to stop the process, because our "doing" is what the process consists of in the first place. As Jacques Ellul put it,

> In the face of technique, and of our inability to confront it,
> I would say then, with Livy, that we can endure neither our
> evils nor their cures, and with Tacitus, that the weakness of
> human nature means that cures always lag behind evils.[14]

The Bible concludes with the Apocalypse because *that* is the end that fallen human nature inexorably descends to. Human fallenness means denial; denial produces delusion; and delusion leads to disaster. *Welcome to reality.*

The Real Balance

Yet there is an answer after all. From *beyond* the fallen cycle of human cause and effect, providence does intrude. The book of Revelation shows how the force of denial collapses in upon itself to produce an escalating series of judgments. It also shows us that behind those judgments lies God's redemptive purpose.

If any of us have the power to affect events, it will not be by what we *do*, but by who and what we *become*. In our own strength, we can never control our compulsion to assert control. We can never address our fallen condition from within our fallen condition. It takes something *from outside* the world to redeem the world. *We* cannot make that happen, but we *can* link ourselves to the One who already made it happen, the One who already broke into our closed system. The first stage in creating that link is to position ourselves appropriately in relation to our Creator. We are created; He is not. That "gnosis" is the beginning of wisdom—and the beginning of the end for denial and delusion.

PART TWO

Virtual Reality and the
Quest for Digital Godhood

5

VIRTUAL GODS, DESIGNER UNIVERSES

Tal Brooke

———————— OVERVIEW ————————

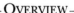

Only in its infancy, crude forms of virtual reality have just begun to appear in video arcades, movies, and virtual entertainment theaters. The technological wonder of virtual reality—"the Holy Grail of cyberspace"—has appeared just in the nick of time to enter the next millennium. This computer-generated marvel promises to fully duplicate the real world to such an extent that the human mind and senses will not know the difference. Its effects will surpass movies of today to the same degree that digital cinerama surpassed the turn-of-the-century silent screen with its halting motion and grainy film. If virtual reality can provide a breathtaking array of lifelike experiences—with no limits on how surreal or exotic—this same electronic genie might also penetrate the mind in unforeseen ways. It could even introduce a level of human surveillance—indeed governance—that will end cherished freedoms with the suddenness of an earthquake. Beyond entertainment and human enhancement, we need to contemplate what might happen once the switch is engaged and the vast turbines of this technology are turned on.

Virtual reality is not just the upper story of cyberspace, it is considered its Holy Grail, for it promises to be a new gateway to unlimited experience—*without apparent consequences.* This makes it a kind of cosmic Rubic's cube of entertainment and pleasure that men have sought throughout the ages. What the mind imagines can be thrust up instantly into existence. And this is surely a godlike power. For magic will have arrived—coming at just the right time to a generation that venerates experience over almost everything else.

When the technology fully comes of age, you will be able to bring any fantasy to life and actually don some superhero's body and dive off the World Trade Center, swooping by windows and waving at astounded onlookers. Or you might bungee-jump from an airplane over the jungles of Sumatra, whooshing toward a smoking volcano till you hover inches above the boiling lava, feeling the adrenaline rush of a lifetime. It will not kill you and you do not have to spend exorbitant amounts of money for the real experience. A child might decide to appear on someone's coffee table the size of an ant, or even wander across the Martian desert in some alien tribal gear.

More sedate folks can have tea at Buckingham Palace with the Queen, feasting with gold cutlery and precious china. Or they might take the Grand Orient Express to Budapest as old Europe passes by. Those who long for youth can be young again . . . for a while. Women in their 20s and 30s can live out some long-cherished dream, such as standing in the place of Greta Garbo while clutching onto Clark Gable and watching the spray of the Victoria Falls—and holding on to this pregnant moment in time that never happened in the real world. Virtual reality intersects human vulnerability, perhaps on some level where desires and longings meet the imagination. And that makes it a formidable mind-machine.

Virtual reality is a kind of scientific magic. It promises to create seamless synthetic illusions that can bend and shape perceived reality like the powerful spells of the great sorcerers of medieval legend. Broomsticks can splinter, clone themselves, and carry pails of water down the spiraling stairs forever in this version of the *Sorcerer's Apprentice.*

The genie that provides the engine for this magical illusion is the computer. As computers grow in power, the spell becomes more convincing and overpowering. Some feel the illusion will eventually surpass reality once there is sufficient power.

The computer has outgrown itself time and again since the halfway point of this century when it was first called *ENIAC* and spread across several giant warehouses of vacuum tubes and electronic components. Yet this giant 1940s monster is barely a glowing ember when compared to today's simplest handheld calculators.

"Deep Blue," the latest computer prototype—a hungry intelligence that can speed through 200 million decisions per second while "seeing" billions of moves ahead—almost beat the world's top chess player, Gary Kasparov, tying him three times and beating him once in a match. Previous computer chess matches were almost no contest for human grand masters. The next prototype to come will be significantly more powerful while the present human victor will feel his waning powers. At some point soon, the creation will be greater than its creator in yet another domain where human intelligence previously reigned uncontested.

Computer visionaries conceived of the computer with far more ambitious purposes in mind than simply playing chess, or keeping track of things like cyberspace, geosynchronous satellites, or the New York Stock Exchange. One long-range purpose has been the mind-machine interface that would provide a means of creating a sense-experience realm so palpable, so immediate and convincing, that it could be called "virtual reality." Part of the vision was the sheer entertainment it would provide. Another was the quest for mind expansion. Other darker visionaries might have seen in it a certain potential for social engineering and mind control—the totalitarian downside.

Aldous Huxley foresaw virtual reality. He also predicted a correspondence between virtual entertainment and mind control in his futuristic novel, *Brave New World*. This novel described "talkie-feelies"—interactive movies that totally immersed audiences in lifelike experiences so intense that they lost themselves in the experience. In Huxley's futuristic world, the masses were gradually being domesticated through entertainment, a kind of mind control that made them livestock in the hands of the "world controllers," a techno-dictatorship. These passive human cattle looked to pleasure as their supreme goal in life, their *raison d'etre*, and they auctioned away their freedoms to the social engineers in exchange for welfare and pleasure. Too intellectually dim to ever see any cause and effect, they had been herded in a slow campaign of gradualism from democracy to technocracy.

Luxor, Las Vegas

An audience is screaming and it sounds like a roller coaster ride as a scene out of *Indiana Jones* fills the television screen on another prime-time documentary about an explosive new technology. A mining train barrels through an underground mine shaft at incredible speed. It is a pure cinerama

roller coaster ride. Surround-sound effects jump out at you—
from metallic braking sounds to crashes and rumbles deep in
the mine. The camera then backs up. What you thought were
riders on the train behind you are a balcony audience in a virtual reality theater. They have been watching the same scene in
3-D cinerama while pitching and rocking on a moving floor.
Clearly the experience is riveting, and it is happening at the
brand-new Luxor Casino, a huge 2,500-room supercasino in
Las Vegas. This towering pyramid has the ultimate entertainment theater at the very top, with virtual reality effects that are
pure state-of-the-art. The audience is giddy by the end of it.

Howard Rheingold, a virtual reality visionary who wrote
Virtual Communities, reports that the three-theater "Secrets of
the Luxor Pyramid" is the biggest thing Douglas Trumbull has
done since he revolutionized the special effects business in
1968 with *2001: A Space Odyssey*. As the wizard credited for special effects in *Close Encounters of the Third Kind* and other blockbusters, Trumbull is one of the few artists capable of creating
virtual reality-based attractions that can transport an audience
of 350 to another reality. Trumbull regards Luxor as "an
experiment in finally going over the edge of a belief barrier
through careful control of photography and projection, to
the point where a motion picture can be seen to be a real live
event."[1] In the words of Rheingold, "Trumbull is consciously
experimenting at the edge of the envelope of human ability
to assimilate media."[2]

Trumbull, says Rheingold, has had a long-standing desire
to go beyond the photo-realistic ideal of today's computer
artists and create perceptions that are even more fine-grained
than reality. If reality is 50 million polygons per second, as
computer graphics whiz Alvy Ray Smith has been quoted as
estimating, Trumbull wants 500 million.

Photo-real graphics are soon to come. And computer
visionaries other than Trumbull (Steve Jobs of Pixar, for
instance) boast they will make their virtual realms with more

pixel-depth than the actual surfaces our eyes see in the real world.

In the end, as described in the blockbuster futuristic movie *Total Recall*, where virtual reality has become fully state-of-the-art, "your brain won't know the difference."[3] At that point, seamless illusion will be as tangible and real as outward reality. Then people can really get lost in the maze of experience. It can be used to alter consciousness. Boundaries can be broken like never before. As God said in Genesis, "and now nothing will be restrained from them, which they have imagined to do" (Genesis 11:6 KJV). *What men imagine, they will be able to do.*

The Hardware

There are a variety of virtual reality systems currently in use, and new techniques are being devised all the time. The most basic system uses a conventional computer as a window through which a person can view the virtual world. More convincing systems use specialized hardware to create an "immersive" experience. A simple version of the immersive technology uses several large display screens to build the experience around the user. Glove interface devices also fit into this environment, though they tend to limit the freedom that is built in this atmosphere.

"Telepresence" is a form of virtual reality that connects the user of the system to remote sensors in some part of the real world. Surgeons who use tiny cameras to see inside patients for the most nonintrusive kinds of surgery are a current model for this kind of activity. So are on-the-street cameras that allow users to see, talk to, and eventually even touch real people in another location. But full-bore immersive systems are far more complex and will be described below. They are the classic virtual reality outfit.

A spate of new movies such as *Virtuosity* and *Lawnmower Man* have portrayed the full outfit—a computer and wires attached to someone wearing a full-body outfit that resembles a space suit in something like an operating theater. Participants can stand or sit. In most cases, the virtual reality outfit consists of a head-mounted display (usually a helmet with goggles), data gloves, and sometimes force-feedback armatures.

At present, there are problems with immersive body gear. It is still cumbersome and distracting. The real trouble is that present helmets with viewing screens do not work the way the real world does. Two video displays (one for each eye) with parallax are not exactly what your eyes are used to seeing. At the least, they cause eyestrain (imagine being a few inches from a TV set for several hours). Even more ominously, they can cause "binocular dysphoria," a defect in depth perception, for several hours after removing the head mount. Undoubtedly, bioengineering will overcome these obstacles.

Even considering the cumbersome body gear, current immersive virtual reality systems provide a realistic enough environment so that people training for high-risk jobs can use this technology to gain crucial experience without danger, such as the flight simulator. Nicholas Negroponte, director of Massachusetts Institute of Technology (M.I.T.) Media Lab, remarks that pilots can take the controls of fully loaded passenger planes for their first flights because they have learned more in the flight simulator than they could in a real plane. In the simulator, a pilot can be subjected to rare situations that, in the real world, could be deadly—for example, going into a spin, a stall, or a free fall. Thus he learns how to react in a situation where a wrong reaction could be lethal. Both a human life and an expensive plane are saved.

David Kupelian, of Chancellor Broadcasting, reports that the U.S. Defense Department is now using a virtual reality training program called SIMNET to train helicopter pilots. In use at military installations nationwide, it simulates a variety of battles including the Persian Gulf War. In other applications, architects can walk clients through a virtual building. Architectural modeling systems allow new home buyers to see what their as-yet-unbuilt houses will look like from the inside. Surgeons can practice operations on virtual bodies from a distance. The Boston Computer Museum has a virtual reality exhibit on cellular biology. And there is now a high school math program that uses virtual reality for visual representation of calculus equations. By the year 2001 virtual reality is projected to be a $4.5 billion industry.[4]

Digital Engines and Simulated Realities

The stunning and lifelike dinosaurs in *Jurassic Park* were created by computer animation at George Lucas's Industrial Light and Magic studios in Marin County, California. By contrast, Walt Disney's *Fantasia*, the greatest of all animated films of yesteryear, was completely composed by teams of human artists and shot frame-by-frame on film. None of it took place inside a computer. In the most spectacular digitally enhanced movies such as *Total Recall, Terminator 2, Apollo 13, Casper,* and *Jurassic Park*, the computer illusions ranged from six minutes in *Jurassic Park* to 40 minutes in *Casper*. But what put a 1996 film entitled *Toy Story* in a whole new league is that *all of it is virtual.*[5]

A computer animation company near Berkeley called Pixar Productions has shown audiences exactly how effectively computers can generate alternate realities. Pixar's *Toy Story* is the first major film ever made *without* human actors, props, cameras, or physical locations of any kind. The film was born in cyberspace as Pixar's bank of 300 Sun processors rendered the movie into its final form as massive amounts of digital information determined the animation, shifting perspective, shading, and lighting. The only human element present was the human voices dubbed into the talking animations. Even those could have been synthesized by computer, except the effect would have been too alien to appeal to the sentiments of present audiences.

Toy Story won over audiences with a certain mechanical charm through the "personalities" of its computer-generated talking toys. Perhaps that is more scary than it sounds. Audiences were able to participate in a movie fantasy of sounds and sights coming directly from the digital realm in a seamless computer-generated fantasy world.

If you want to picture what fully operational virtual reality is like—which is not quite here yet—just think of yourself thrust interactively into *Toy Story* as one of the characters. You are the size of the other toys and you can now talk to the space ranger, Buzz Lightyear, or Cowboy Woody while you "see" on their three-dimensional plane. You can see, hear, smell, and feel things within the perspectives and confines of that world. You also have the ability to act, and your actions create direct cause and effect, rippling out to ten million permutations, like a stone skipping in a giant pond. If you scream at the various talking toys from the bed, they will all respond in individual ways. Some might grimace, some might choose to ignore you. You can even push the space ranger out the window, as Cowboy Woody did, and hear him scream as you watch him fall in three-dimensional simulated space and then bounce near the drainpipe and into the bushes. As you push him through the window, you can feel it with your hands and body. You are fully there in the virtual realm. To pull this off takes immense computer power and a man-machine interface that we do not have yet. Digital technology is still working on the visual gateway. And that aspect of virtual reality is creeping into more and more movies, replacing expensive sets.

As things stand, computer-generated virtual-reality landscapes in live interactive sessions still have a cartoonish and ghostly appearance. Silicon Graphics in Mountain View, California offers a graphics supercomputer—called the RealityEngine2—that can render two million polygons per second under ideal conditions, which is less than two percent of the speed needed for verisimilitude.* We perceive the real world at more than 50 million polygons per second. "If you want photorealism, then for many environments, a RealityEngine2 is

---

*The quality or state of being realistic.

woefully inadequate," states Joshua Larson-Mogal of the Advanced Graphics Division at Silicon Graphics. "But while realism may have something to do with virtual reality, it is not a necessary condition by any means."[6]

There are other limitations as well. As Wayt Gibb reports in the *Scientific American*,

> Fooling a human brain into believing it is somewhere it is not is a tricky task. So far most research has focused on deceiving the eyes. High-resolution, wide-angle, three-dimensional displays are one obvious prerequisite; devices that track the direction of your gaze are another. Yet current virtual reality helmets that place a miniature liquid-crystal screen in front of each eye are grainy and expensive. The military spends up to $1 million each for the best, which offer the resolution of a typical desktop computer monitor—viewed at a distance of about four inches.[7]

A World of 20,000 Polygons

When I attended a worldwide premier of virtual reality at Club DV8 for a selected audience, put on by Spectrum HoloByte in San Francisco in a state-of-the-art exhibit for December 1991, what I experienced was a virtual landscape that was disappointingly wispy and crude. It was a world with objects made out of transparent tissue paper, atoms and pixels of far less density than the actual world.

My guess is that I was seeing less than 20,000 polygons per second—a mere fraction of what a RealityEngine2 computer produces, which itself is less than two percent of perceived visual reality. I found the cartoonesque landscape far too simple to be fully engaging. The primary colors and simple geometrical structures were not really what I had expected. And physically pivoting, with a heavy helmet on, attached to wires and hoses, was awkward and constraining.

Each attendee was invited to participate in a four-player game called "Dactyl Nightmare." Players stood on an elevated platform, blind to onlookers, with helmets on, virtual gloves, and holding cable-gun joysticks. Each participant would pivot in various directions while squeezing buttons and spasmodically pointing cable-gun joysticks. They were, in fact, shooting at each other and trying to escape flying pteredactyls. To me the first irony was that the theme of the debut of virtual reality was a death game in an imaginary realm of horrors. I sensed this would set the tenor for things to come. This was the first among what would be the next generation of video arcade games—*virtual* arcade games.

If I had to choose a metaphor, I would say the participants looked like *insect* pupae, each standing in the darkness with a full-fitting arachnid helmet and body gear attached to various black hoses and wires coming out of the elevated cages. On the surface, the whole thing looked antinatural and alien. At the time, I noted to myself, and later repeated in a radio interview about the future of virtual reality, "Say little Johnny is at a video arcade some years hence and feeds into a scanner the yearbook picture of his fifth-grade teacher who just reprimanded him. What he does with her in the fields of virtual reality is up to him. He might start by shooting her. Later he might put her in the middle of the Tower of London or a voodoo ceremony, and so on. Johnny—immune from cause and effect on this virtual plane—could slowly grow strange new tastes along the lines of serial killer James Bundy." It is a perfect doorway to dehumanizing others.

If taste in video arcade games is any indication, virtual games, such as the ever popular "Mortal Kombat" or "Doom," will be just as dark. They could propel the minds of new generations of youth to strange new places. The moral ceiling of these games will be no higher than the cyber-mind-set of those who put together most of the world's network and entertainment technology in the San Francisco Bay Area—from Silicon Valley, Palo Alto, Menlo Park, San Francisco, Marin County, to Berkeley. By default, they are the youth's tutors through their sophisticated games. These games do much more than just entertain as they explore the occult, sex, and violence above all. If you need to be convinced, go out and buy some of the top-selling video games like "Doom." One CD-ROM game even involves hunt and rape. What is the moral level of the cyber-culture that is setting the cutting-edge pace of video—and soon virtual reality—games?

Wired editor Eric Davis wrote an article about technopagans, citing Bay area cyber-whiz Mark Pesce as a case in point. Pesce is an M.I.T. dropout who practices witchcraft and coordinates a Bay area coven of fellow software and hardware cutting-edge innovators. He describes himself as a "gay witch." He does not write games per se, but is doing much more. He is creating a major cyberspace doorway that would have the power to allow global game-playing in three dimensions among international participants—games of all varieties, such as cyber-Dungeons and Dragons. Davis comments,

> Sure, he spends his time practicing kundalini yoga, boning up on Aleister Crowley's Thelemic magic, and tapping away at his book *Understanding Media: The End of Man*, which argues that magic will play a key role in combating the virulent information memes and pathological virtual worlds that will plague the coming cyberworld. But he's also the creator of VRML, a technical standard for creating navigable, hyperlinked 3-D spaces on the World Wide Web. . . . As Pesce's technomagical children, WorldView and VRML may well end up catalyzing the next phase of online mutation: the construction of a true, straight-out-of-*Neuromancer* cyberspace on the Internet.[8]

Davis then makes a telling remark about the technopagan cyber-culture in general:

> If you hang around the San Francisco Bay area or the Internet fringe for long, you'll hear loads of loopy talk about computers and consciousness. Because the issues of interface design, network psychology, and virtual reality are so open-ended and novel, the people who hack this conceptual edge often sound as much like science fiction acidheads as they do sober programmers. In this vague realm of

gurus and visionaries, technopagan ideas about "myth" and "magic" often signify dangerously murky waters.[9]

"Your Brain Will Not Know the Difference"

In the futuristic blockbuster about virtual reality, *Total Recall,* starring Arnold Schwarzenegger, the science of virtual reality has evolved from all the burdensome external body gear to a direct computer hookup at the neurological gateway of the five senses—right inside the brain. Instead of a crude electrode interface to nerve endings, an enormously powerful computer chip—a *bio* chip—is implanted. Now the visual, auditory, and tactile centers are reached directly and respond at their full range. It produces a level of virtual reality that equals, if not surpasses, reality.

In *Total Recall,* virtual reality has become a commercial enterprise among competing high-tech corporations who guarantee the ultimate vacation or thrill of a lifetime, cheaply. It all happens inside the brain and the brain cannot tell the difference. The virtual package also custom-tailors the experience for individual personal tastes—in this case, Doug Quaid's tastes, played by Schwarzenegger:

> "Now let me see. The basic Mars package will run you 899 credits," said the salesman for RECALL Inc. "Now that's for two full weeks of memories, complete in every detail. If you want a longer trip that'll cost you a little more, because it's a deeper implant."

> "What's in the two-week package?" asks Quaid.

> RECALL salesman: "First of all, Doug, let me tell you. When you go RECALL you get nothing but first class memories. Private cabin on the Shuttle, Deluxe suite at the Hilton, plus all the major sights—Mount Pyramid, the Grand Canals, and of course, Venusville!"

> Quaid: "But how real does it seem?"

> RECALL salesman: "As real as any memory in your head."

Quaid: "Come on, don't BS me."

RECALL salesman: "No, I'm telling you, Doug, your brain will not know the difference. . . . When you travel with RECALL, everything is perfect. So what do you say?"

Quaid even has the option of customizing a virtual woman for his individual tastes:

RECALL doctor: "How do you like your women? Blonde, brunette, redhead?"

Quaid: "Brunette."

RECALL doctor: "Slim, athletic, voluptuous?"

Quaid: "Athletic."

RECALL doctor: "Demure, aggressive, sleazy?"

Quaid: "Sleazy . . . and demure."

RECALL doctor to technician: "41A, Ernie."

Ernie: "Oh boy, is he going to have a wild time. He's not gonna want to come back!"[10]

Entertainment and mind control have less than two degrees of separation in *Total Recall*. They are virtually the same thing. The film engrosses the audience in a massive plot of intrigue revolving around a corporate colony on Mars. *Recall*'s entertainment package lives up to its billing . . . or, *was it all real?* Did Quaid's force of will overcome the implant, or did the implant uncover hidden areas of his brain blocked out by a CIA-level program going back to a prior identity of Quaid as a high-level agent? Or . . . is that memory part of the virtual chip? You get the point. We are on a balance beam trying to interpret what is going on as the movie rockets along from intrigue to violent encounter.

The point of the film is that they have balanced things down to the last detail. Evidence is divided down the middle for either interpretation. Either the whole incredible drama was a virtual reality experience, or it all really happened. To quote RECALL, Inc., "Your mind does not know the difference." And this goes for the audience looking at the film as well as Quaid.

What this virtual reality fiction brings up is the question of what happens to a mind once invaded with an alternate reality as real as the outward world. Or can this technology be used as a weapon for mind control? Or, in the Huxley sense, can it finally bring entertainment and mind control together?

What lures people to go through these doors of experience is the constant quest for knowledge, power, and expansion of abilities. At the seat of the quest for mind expansion is the seeming capacity, in altered consciousness, to find heightened abilities, godlike powers, and universal knowledge.

Altered Consciousness

Cyber-culture has pondered the following combination.

The first stage: Take the human mind and hook it up to what will someday become fully functional virtual reality, the seamless illusion at full thrust invading all the doors of perception—visually at more than 50 million polygons per second, audibly by holographic surround-sound, plus full-body sensing and tactile gear, and maybe even smells thrown in as well.

Now, the booster rocket: Take the subject's mind while hooked up to virtual reality and manipulate it directly, either with a range of powerful psychochemicals, such as LSD, or by hypnosis. Keep in mind that under LSD alone just gazing at a flower can rocket the subject off to other worlds. What happens if that same person on LSD were to enter fully charged virtual reality? Could it amplify the psychedelic experience an entire order of magnitude—the very catalyst the 60s generation has longed for—to a new kind of critical mass of consciousness? These are questions the cyber-culture—already into designer and smart drugs—has been asking for a long time.

If someone under deep hypnosis were hooked up to full-bore virtual reality, could that person enter a doorway opening up psychic powers? If the virtual reality program itself fully simulated psychic or occult experience, such as astral projection, remote viewing, or contact with spirit beings, could that catalyze a genuine mediumistic experience? And would this not especially apply to someone who had a mediumistic family history? As David Kupelian remarks, "To be totally immersed in a computer-generated 3-D environment that results in the suspension of one's normal sensibilities is perhaps *the* technological two-edged sword of the future."[11]

In *The Other Side of Death*, I reported that the hypnotic trance state was the critical factor that opened up most psychics and mediums in the first place. Suddenly they had various powers and could sense familiar spirits. After Edgar Cayce learned to self-induce a trance, he became much more psychic than when he was simply lucid dreaming. Cayce travelled out of the body, met spirit guides or "entities," and gave life readings. The breakthrough happened when a famous Jewish theosophist in Chicago paid Cayce to be hypnotized and asked him ultimate questions about reincarnation and soul evolution. Suddenly the man who looked like a Baptist school teacher became a New Ager. When Cayce went under, it was as though something else took over. After that, his notoriety grew quickly and he was able to go from "medical readings" to "life readings."

It is a fact that most mediums *became* mediums in the first place by undergoing hypnosis and then accessing realms that the Bible plainly warns against. Mediums usually learn to self-induce trances as part of their craft. In the same way, subjects under today's modern hypnotherapists increasingly report past-life recall or UFO encounters. *The key thing is the trance.*

How deeply can the mind be penetrated when it is not only hooked up to computer-generated virtual reality but when it is further opened up by hypnosis or psychotropic drugs? Sense-experience fanatics of this generation will no doubt combine drugs to enhance their virtual reality trips. It will be the next great thing, the thing to surpass LSD in the same way that acid broke the ceiling of experience in the 1960s, if you will, occultizing the mind. It will also be perhaps another quantum leap in occultizing American culture, perhaps as much as acid did in the 1960s.

Virtual Gods

Like all powers, there is a dark side to this quest for mind expansion and virtual entertainment. "Virtual lab" is a dead giveaway. It is also a metaphor. To enter virtual reality, people must first abandon the real world, like ghosts, and descend into a darkened chamber to stare into a realm created out of artificial light. It will never be as bright as the noonday sun. And the tastes it feeds will never rise to those aesthetic levels of sheer beauty that nature can satisfy in the middle of spring in myriad settings across the globe. Virtual tastes will rise to no greater level than that provided by those who feed the machine, both the thrill-seekers and software and cyber engineers. Its moral ceiling will go no higher than the dim light of an underground world.

As man creates his own book of Genesis, his creation will ultimately grow dark and turn on him, much like Frankenstein turned on its own master in that famous novel written in the last century. Whether or not there is a "ghost in the machine" with some kind of supernatural interface, the entertainment aspect alone can turn ghosts out of its viewers as they escape to simulated worlds, leaving family and friends behind. Then more baseball gloves will hang in the basement along with picnics, walks in the park, drives through the country, and a thousand other activities in the real world, activities that make life rich and bring people together in real intimacy. In virtual worlds, other hungers are fed and exchanged for activities in the real world. You can read about some of these hungers in the ancient accounts of Sodom and

Gomorrah. They were real then and they are becoming real again now. *Sin recruits through corruption.*

When the doorway to seduction goes from being a trap-door to a city gate, offering a full flood of experiences, then recruitment grows small numbers to hoards. That is how cultures change. It happened in Rome and it happened in Sodom and Gomorrah. Another way to describe change is *decay* and *corruption.* When that happens, cultures are destroyed through the momentum of their folly when their actions bring back thunderous consequences. That is the human side of the momentum of God's judgment.

Let's discuss corruption within the human soul by looking at the slag heap of recent history. Part of the delusion of our time is to minimize evil and deny that people can be so evil. What kind of thoughts do you think serial murderer and pedophile John Wayne Gayce had? Thirty decomposed bodies were buried under and around his house. Most had been tortured. What kind of thoughts do you think homosexual serial killer Jeffrey Dahmer had? In his case, some of the decomposing bodies were in his icebox—bodies sexually assaulted, murdered, some of them even eaten. I will spare you the horrific details of both cases. For most of us, this terrain is far too alien to plumb. It is mean stuff. My point is, though, that when the Bible uses the word *vile* or *abomination* it does so for a purpose. Such things exist in our culture and they exist in our history books and *God warns about it.* Evil has a way of spreading. That was the point of recounting the example of Sodom and Gomorrah.

How much more quickly would today's youth corruption increase if, somewhere in the middle of the technopagan culture of software geniuses, several came along with the inner landscape of a Jeffrey Dahmer or a John Wayne Gayce? They would have the power to create the software entertainment for millions of youth. That is quite a pipeline into a culture. They could push the envelope of accepted thinking here and bend it there. They would be playing their own private video game with a whole live culture. And the moguls of Hollywood, seeing a profit, would not stand in their way, but in defense would cry "censorship" to narrow-minded protestations from the "religious right." And adults who were oblivious to the high-tech youth culture would not have a clue what was going on. Of course, this is a hypothetical example.

Will virtual reality be any more virtuous as entertainment than its predecessors in the movie, television, cable TV, and interactive CD-ROM industries? Will it raise us to new heights of moral purity and virtue, restoring our lost national innocence? Only someone very naive and dull, I think, would answer yes at this point in history. Virtual entertainment will continue to steer us—apart from an act of God—toward the spiritual landscape that existed before the last great judgment when imaginations before the great deluge dwelt only on evil day in and day out. The doorway is the imagination. To repeat an earlier observation, virtual reality intersects human vulnerability where desires and longings meet the imagination. And that makes it a formidable mind-machine. With it, man will spin new webs.

As man creates his universe with no other gods in it but himself, his creation will ultimately grow dark. The human creator who himself is long estranged from his Creator, the Living God, will now try to play God as he creates alternative realities. Virtual realities can never be more than either a poor mirror of the actual reality that God created, thus borrowing from whatever is already in existence, or they will simply be mutations and perversions of these previously created things.

> And they said, Go to, let us build us a city and a tower, whose top may reach unto heaven; and let us make us a name, lest we be scattered abroad upon the face of the whole earth.
>
> And the Lord came down to see the city and the tower, which the children of men builded.

And the LORD said, Behold, the people is one, and they have all one language; and this they begin to do: and now nothing will be restrained from them, which they have imagined to do (Genesis 11:4-6 KJV).

6

VIRTUAL BODIES
IN THE CITY OF BITS

Donald L. Baker

──────────── OVERVIEW ────────────

Donald Baker takes us into the digital sea of cyberspace to help us understand the forces shaping and bending this emerging electronic society that hovers over the earth and its national boundaries. It swims with all sorts of beliefs. There are hybrids of political correctness tied to neopagan notions forming new norms. There is the infestation of postmodern beliefs in endless invisible (electronic) conference rooms. For the millions entering this unchartered sea, especially cyber-youth, their minds and beliefs are out there for the picking, to be gathered and trimmed by those controlling the predominant modes of belief. There are black holes and eddies lying deep within the folds of cyberspace poised to attract straying net-surfers. Some open the gateway to witch-craft and others into gender-bending experiments. At the same time, there are endless legitimate sites that can tell you almost anything— from the price of a four-year-old Mercedes Benz in Bonn, to the weather in Cairo, to how to get discount tickets for theaters around Shaftesbury Avenue in London. How do we navigate this maze? is the oft-asked question.

Cyberspace, we are often told, is a disembodied medium. Testimonies to this effect are everywhere. . . . In a sense, these testimonies are correct; the body remains in front of the screen rather than within it. In another sense, however, they are deeply misleading, for they obscure the crucial role that the body plays in constructing cyberspace. In fact, we are never disembodied.

—N. Katherine Hayle
Immersed in Technology: Art and
Virtual Environments[1]

I n chapter 2, I discussed two hidden building blocks of cyberspace—two mythic concepts whose proponents are currently engaged in a Darwinian struggle for cyber-cultural dominance. The first posits an electronic frontier, a wide-open digital vista in which cyber-citizens are allowed total freedom to communicate and share files without "real-life" government control or community-imposed restrictions. The second model imagines cyberspace as a place of control, a place where massive quantities of data are manipulated and made useful through helpful software programs (including virtual reality), and where children are protected from obscene on-line material through similarly helpful software filters. The telecommunications reform bill enacted in 1996 leans to this second model, assigning Internet service providers the task of policing their networks to prevent the availability of obscene content.

Commenting on this model, Michael Sorkin notes that in cyberspace, "the body, the person, no longer simply exists in public space but actually becomes it. . . . "[2] And virtual reality only exacerbates the potential loss of privacy, according to art and robotics professor, Simon Penny:

> The prospect of real-time surveillance is so much more simply facilitated in virtual reality: not only will the computer know where you are, but what kind of information you are accessing and where your various body parts are at the time. As digital media become ever-more encapsulating, so the possibility of permanent real-time surveillance becomes real.[3]

Our growing fear of physical monitoring and surveillance in cyberspace is but one aspect of cyber-millennial anxieties relating to our physical bodies. What are the sources of this anxiety?

The Body in Question

The adoption (in Europe and America) of the 18th-century Enlightenment belief in reason over faith, and the similarly man-imposed cleft between materiality and spirituality, are at the root of the problem. Loss of faith in a transcendent God and, by extension, belief in the inherent dignity of the human body are the result.

God created man in His image, and we are intended to fulfill that function in our whole being. Brian J. Walsh and J. Richard Middleton comment:

> Human beings are God's ambassadors, his representatives, to the rest of creation. We are the stewards he has set in

authority over the earth to manifest his presence and to reflect his glory in all our cultural doings.

But note that the image consists in our bodily representation of God. The whole person, and not some inner spiritual part, is created in God's image. We reflect God's glory and represent him on earth by our total, physical presence. Indeed, visibility is of the essence, for we are to make the invisible God visible by our lives.[4]

In losing faith in the God of the Bible, Western culture kicked out the support for understanding man (*in the body*) as God's representation on earth. Also lost was the truth that the body of every redeemed believer is a temple of the Holy Spirit (1 Corinthians 6:19). A corresponding desire for a secular utopia romanticized the role of machines, notably in artists' movements prior to the mechanized slaughter of World War I:

The Futurists, such as Marinetti and Malevich, saw in the machine the energy and strength sufficient for the construction of utopian societies. For cubist painters, human beings began to resemble complex mechanisms. Artists such as Leger, Feininger, Kandinsky, and Picasso began to fill the visual landscape with robotlike creatures.[5]

Beginning with the Great War, the experiences of the 20th century have provided one body blow after another to the culture. More humans have been killed and mutilated in our century—in more various and horrific ways—than ever before. Marxism-Leninism and Fascism in particular—the most utopian of modern philosophies—seem to have held the greatest hatred for the body, even as they denied an otherworldly existence.

Advanced technology has been deployed for much of this century's grim-reaping. Then, too, first machinery and now computers have been responsible for the loss of millions of jobs in the name of efficiency, even as many more jobs have been created by the new technologies. Industrialization—and now computerization (also known by its euphemism, postindustrialization)—has occurred so rapidly that we have had insufficient time to adapt to the existence of machines in our landscape, and to their effects on our lives. (In the U.S. only the Amish, who I mentioned in chapter 2 as living in "principled cultural irrelevancy," have made the decision to accept new technology at their own pace, and in their own ways.)

Pop culture has repeatedly mirrored our anxiety over our relationship with machines—from Charlie Chaplin's struggle with ruthless metal gears in *Modern Times,* to the unstoppable man-machine hybrids, the Borg, in "Star Trek—The Next Generation." Cultural critics Arthur and Marilouise Kroker contend that the media are offering us images they call "panic bodies" that reflect all the grisly symptoms of culture burnout:

> The hysteria around physical fitness, civil liberties, AIDS treatment, the right to life, the right to death, eating disorders, the war on drugs, surveillance in the workplace, steroids in pro sports, and the sexual exploits of public figures are all symptoms [of panic bodies].[6]

Multimedia artist and writer Nell Tenhaaf draws on Freudian psychoanalytic theory to suggest that our current fixation with cyberspace may be "a 'hysterical' fantasy of the late twentieth century . . . expressing an inutterable [sic] desire for a more fluid subjectivity and a body that knows itself better, and this by a simulation through technologies of enhanced organic behavior [that is, a wired-up body]."[7]

According to the postmodern philosophy popular in the current cyber-millennial period, the body is tainted by its inescapable connection with sex-based gender, and thereby with sexual politics—particularly the perceived white-male domination of women and the non-Western world. The following statement, from a Canadian (male) professor, is typical:

> Men's fascination with technology is linked to the masculine need to be in control of the material world, to know how to extend that control, to be able to act, and to be

independent of reliance on others. In this respect science and technology are dominantly male in nature and have been forged from the development of capitalism, materialism, and individualism in western culture since the Renaissance. Reason is the supporting structure of the masculine fascination with technology and its products.[8]

Postmodern philosophy views the body as the locus of a continuing battleground for political and sexual power. Kathy Acker, a feminist author, was asked: "Your books always return to the site of the body: as a source of power, a center of struggle for power, as the place we finally exist in, as opposed to our thoughts. Why generally are you so interested in the body?" Her answer is enlightening:

> When reality—the meanings associated with reality—is up for grabs—which is certainly . . . one of the central problems in philosophy and art ever since the end of the 19th century—then the body itself becomes the only thing you can return to. . . . It's the body which finally can't be touched by all our skepticism and ambiguous systems of belief. The body is the only place where any basis for real values exists anymore.[9]

The Body Inadequate?

Kathy Acker, Neil Tenhaaf, and Arthur and Marilouise Kroker are responding, in their own ways, to the relentless assault of science, technology, and postmodern culture upon our self-concept. Our society is rendering the body obsolete through the technologies of communication and calculation, which mock our physical limitations. At the same time, the processes of postindustrialization and urbanization, and the breakdown in morality derived from the "death" of God, have alienated us from each other, increasing the natural fear and distrust we have of those we perceive as outsiders.

Postmodernism teaches that reality is socially constructed—not objectively factual—and that language is a tool used by the powerful to control others. "According to the postmodernists," notes Gene Edward Veith, "all reality is virtual reality. We are all wearing helmets that project our own separate little worlds. We can experience these worlds and lose ourselves in them, but they are not real, nor is one person's world exactly the same as someone else's. We are not creating our own reality, however. Rather, we accept a reality made by someone else."[10] Therefore, it seems logical that our bodies are the only refuge left to us. Yet, even the body is not a safe haven, for we are all subject to detection, surveillance, and penetration by an increasing number of technological devices.

As a result, many today seem to harbor a secret inner wish to leave the flesh behind, to project their consciousness into the cyberspace of TV, computer networks, and virtual reality. Rejecting transcendence through traditional Western religious practices, many in our culture are desperately seeking a gnostic release from the body. They seek this release in a number of ways—through orgiastic sensory experience, Eastern religious experiences, and escape into cyberspace.

There are some, however, who are desperate, not because they hate the body, or seek safety in it, but because they see it as inadequate to participate in the possibilities available to the mind in the cyber-millennium: the comprehension and manipulation of electronic data directly through the brain; the augmentation or substitution of body parts with manufactured replacements or prosthetic devices; the possibility of life extension—even "immortality"—through the transfer of consciousness to computers. The body is imagined, to be blunt, *as obsolete*—no longer worthy of the psalmist's praise (Psalm 139:13-14).

The Australian performance artist, Stelarc, makes his living by demonstrating the body's need for technological augmentation. He fabricates and straps on a variety of electro-mechanical devices to his body, manipulating them for his audience. He has even inserted a camera into his stomach to videotape his interior. Though Stelarc asserts he is only an artist, not a scientist, NASA engineers have been impressed enough with his skills to examine his robotic "third arm." Here are some of Stelarc's ruminations on obsolescence:

> It is time to question whether a bipedal, breathing, beating body with binocular vision and a 1400cc brain is now an adequate biological form. The human species has created a technological and information environment it can no longer cope with. . . . Distraught and disconnected, the body can only resort to interface and symbiosis. The body may not yet surrender its autonomy, but certainly its mobility. Plugged into a machine network, the body needs to be pacified. In fact, to function in the future and to truly achieve a HYBRID SYMBIOSIS, the body will need to become increasingly anesthetized.[11]

The perceived need for a "hybrid symbiosis" has permeated academia. Carnegie Mellon robotics professor Hans Moravec is perhaps the best-known supporter. In his book *Mind Children*, Moravec advocates the development of technology that, one day in the not-too-distant future, will be capable of "downloading" one's very consciousness from the physical brain into a computer, thence becoming a silicon-based life-form. As Katherine Hayles points out, "it is apparent that Moravec equates subjectivity with the mind. The body is treated as a flawed and unwieldy vehicle, necessary in the early stages of human evolution but now become more trouble than it is worth . . . a superfluous accessory."[12]

This attitude has been graphically developed in the cyberpunk science fiction novels of the 1980s and early 1990s. In William Gibson's *Neuromancer* series, freelance "deck cowboys" named Case and Count Zero project themselves into a worldwide virtual-reality cyberspace called the Matrix, from which they steal computer data for corporate clients. While not "jacked-in," the hackers suffer the indignity of entrapment in the flesh, or "meat," and prowl an international street-culture where designer-drug addiction and bionic implants are commonplace.

What makes reading cyberpunk so unsettling—besides the characters' foul mouths—is realizing that Gibson and his colleagues have simply extrapolated current technology trends into the future. In the cyber-millennium, it will soon become easy to connect all sorts of personal electronic devices—cell phone, Walkman, medical monitoring system, global positioning system, pacemaker, and so forth—into an integrated body-net linked wirelessly to the Internet. As we age or encounter disease and accidents, more microelectronic and inorganic replacement parts will become available to repair—*even augment*—our failing bodies. More surgery will be performed by computer-guided, robotic surgeons whose "hands" will prove far steadier than the finest surgeon's (who will be relegated to operating the keyboard or joystick). At what point in the 21st century will we—or our children—admit we have actually become cyborgs, experiencing what postmoderns call "boundary problems"?[13]

Polymorphous Perversity and Cyberspace

Virtual reality and other cyberspace experiences have, especially in cyberpunk fiction, been regarded hopefully as the means of collapsing boundaries between the body and the overwhelming amount of data generated by advanced information systems. But the prospect and reality of cyberspace-induced boundary-collapse excites many academics, and not because they want to demystify the datacloud. Rather, they are looking to cyberspace as a laboratory for advancing theories of gender-based sexuality.

I noted earlier that the body has become a battleground for neo-Marxist, postmodern proponents eager to bring to an end what they see as the power-mongering patriarchy inherited from Western ("Christian") culture. This patriarchy, woven into our concepts of reality and language, is considered responsible for continuing oppression of minority groups in general and women in particular. Overthrowing

Western cultural institutions, beliefs, and legal structures will, they believe, eliminate oppression.

So where does cyberspace (virtual reality) fit in? It is the malleability of cyberspace that is exciting to radical postmodernism fans, in that persons interacting in cyberspace can adopt their own personas, and have the freedom (except on company time, of course) to change anything about themselves they want: name, age, sex, personality—in short, they can lie without suffering face-to-face consequences. Cyberspace appears to allow one to escape the controls imposed by the patriarchal culture—to collapse the boundaries between *the actual* and *the desirable*. Future multimedia and virtual reality software will permit even more radical alterations in reality's perception to the point where one may be able to adopt any appearance desired, and to interact not only with other persons, but even with programmed ideas and concepts that may exhibit more interesting behavior than real people express in real life.[14]

The guiding postmodern principle here is that personality is not fixed, but is—like reality—a social construct. Neo-Marxist, radical feminists take this idea one step further, and decouple the concept of gender from physical sexuality. Thus, gender is not a given, they claim, but "polymorphous perversity"—a performance or learned behavior that need not be linked to physical sexuality.[15]

The technical term for this belief is gender feminism. It is an attempt to force society to accept not only the total equality of women with men, but also the total normality of homosexuality in all its variations, including transsexuality (the physical transformation, through surgery, of a person from one sex to the other) and transgenderism (to my understanding, the conscious choice of one's sexual identity, unrelated to one's possessing either male or female sex organs).

Gender feminists mounted a major international campaign for acceptance of their agenda at the Fourth World Conference on Women, held in Beijing in September 1995. In their pursuit of a radical restructuring of power between men and women on a global basis, gender feminists from the United States, Canada, and Europe largely ignored important developing-world women's issues, such as protecting the status of stay-at-home mothers and protecting families from religious persecution. Instead, the developed-world representatives, including former congresswoman Bella Abzug, pushed for 50-50 male-female quotas for all elected and appointed government positions, and called for abortion and sexual rights for lesbians and adolescents to be declared fundamental human rights.

A similar agenda was advanced in a smaller, but nonetheless influential, venue a year prior to the Beijing conference. Attenders at the Fourth International Conference on Cyberspace and the Art and Virtual Environment Symposium, held at Canada's Banff Centre for the Arts in May 1994, heard a number of speakers interpret cyberspace and virtual reality in overtly gender-feminist terms.[16] The most influential among these was conference organizer and self-styled "Goddess of Cyberspace," Allucquere Rosanne "Sandy" Stone, director of the Advanced Communication Technologies Laboratory at the University of Texas at Austin. Stone described Habitat, a Japanese virtual world with 1.5 million subscribers, which has since been brought to the United States as WorldsAway. A graphics-based on-line network, Habitat permits participants to choose male or female bodies (and human or animal heads) to represent themselves in the Habitat environment. Stone claimed that in Habitat, as well as in many other areas of cyberspace, the incidence of on-line "cross-dressing" is high. Men pose as women to attract attention, while women pretend to be men in order to avoid on-line creeps.[17]

Stone declared that her conscious goal is "getting at the power structures that maintain [gender bipolarity]" in a very real way. She performs this by deliberately placing the audience—*her students*—in a state of shock in order to introduce destabilizing ideas. Stone does this by showing slides of hermaphrodites, of people with mutilated bodies, such as war veterans with terrible wounds, and fakirs suspended by hooks through their flesh. After showing these slides to the attenders, she commented:

> When I show images like these to my students who are not sophisticated in the ways of art, I find that frequently they gasp. Their gasping tells me that a process has happened inside, some internal disruption. Something has interfered with their normal, seamless way of viewing the world. . . . And in that moment of interruption, when for just an instant the fabric of normality is ripped open a little bit, and they can see the nuts and bolts of the way reality is put together—if that moment can be encouraged and that rip teased further open, not just for them but for all of us, then perhaps we can get a handle on the nuts and bolts of reality and find ways to unscrew some of them. . . .
>
> These slides demonstrate aspects of the human form that we don't ordinarily see. Things that don't fit our accustomed structures of visual knowledge, our ways of perceiving shape or gender. When we think about the way that we normally see humans in the age of electronic communication, i.e. through some representational medium, they're being represented to us in terms of text, as strings of numbers or words turned into images. That is, they are not only visible, but legible, in the same way that texts are legible. And for that reason I refer to these kinds of disruptive images as being nearly legible, but not quite. There are different degrees of the legibility of the human body, and it's the boundary status of these images—shapes and genders that inhabit the boundaries between the accustomed and the utterly strange, the territory of the near-legible—that gives them their disruptive power. And the power of disruption is the power of change, the opportunity to see with new vision.[18]

One rarely hears such a radical agenda stated so plainly. Stone admits that her intent in showing images of bizarre behavior and extremely rare and unfortunate physical conditions is to disrupt her students' foundational beliefs about what is real, what is normative. Her goal is to influence others with gender-feminist ideas concerning self-concept and sexuality. Since most college students are in their late teens and early 20s—barely out of adolescence—Stone's strategy could be quite successful in destabilizing her students' deeply held, but unarticulated, beliefs about the nature and practice of sexual identity. More important, Stone is hardly a lone academic when she states, "The fact of the body changing is something I'm interested in promoting."[19]

Stone's description of her goals and methodology makes clear that the new world of digital cyberspace is not merely a place where people are trading files and searching for reference information. Cyberspace, like outer space, has become a new battleground in the sociopolitical struggles underway in the cyber-millennium. It is a place where the twin forces of technology and ideology chip away at the human frame, created by God with a glory and dignity that our society has largely forgotten.

It is crucial that we understand cyberspace as a place where we will spend increasing amounts of time, and get much useful work done. Since God created us as physical beings, however, *cyberspace can never be our home*. It will never be a place of escape from our body and its limitations, or from God. I agree with linguist George Lakoff when he muses:

> I could imagine some interesting and fun things to do with virtual reality and some important ones. . . . On the other hand, . . . the more you interact not with something natural and alive, but with something electronic, it takes the sense of the earth away from you, . . . robs you of more and more embodied experiences. That is a deep impoverishment of the human soul.[20]

7

EMBODY
THE AVATAR

John Moore

OVERVIEW

One of the hottest rages among the youth for more than a decade—interactive role-playing—has come on the Internet and it is creating an intoxicating cyber-world. At the moment, millions of net-surfers are speeding down the largest superhighway on the Internet to participate in this newly arrived imaginary realm constructed from virtual reality and various interactive games.

Fifteen years ago Dungeons and Dragons, the game that started this rage, took the nation by storm. It contained complex rules and long-term strategies seen in war-game theory used by the Pentagon. Instead of modern weapons being used, however, the players had magical powers and cast spells. Experience-hungry youth looking for an escape have become increasingly addicted to the alternate realms of these games.

Now with the advent of such games on the Internet—forming a kind of electronic astral plane—the population there will most likely soar. We need to ask in what direction the countless travelers who are choosing to live on the Internet will be taken as these realms become ever more exotic and powerful.

At first the scene is static: a featureless green plain stretches off into the distance, ending where it eventually meets a range of medium-sized mountains. These look a lot like the coastal range one might see driving down Highway 1 in California from the coastal area off Palo Alto to Santa Cruz. The scene is the same no matter which direction I face, except for the changing features of the mountains in the hazy distance. Now, suddenly, the green surface of the ground is beginning to roil—form and feature are beginning to appear.

I am "parachuting in" to AlphaWorld, a 140,000-square-mile tract of virtual landscape that recently appeared on the Internet. Now I can see that I am standing on the actual surface of AlphaWorld, at a spot designated "ground zero." This is the beginning of an AlphaWorld adventure.

In front of me I can see the "avatars" of several other recent arrivals. The other avatars—and this is an interesting term the software creators have used because it comes from only one source in the world, Hinduism, and has only one meaning, "incarnation of God"—are beginning to stumble across the virtual landscape. Each one responds to the movements of a "mouse" on a desktop somewhere, perhaps thousands of miles away from the computer that actually houses the bits and bytes of the plain upon which we are all standing. (To be fair, there are other labels in use, such as "agents," and "bots," but "avatar" is the reigning favorite and will likely drive the rest out.)

One avatar is communicating something to the other inhabitants of the world—a typed message above its head reads, "Help me ... the teleport to the left of me is not working." It is a silent cry in a strange new world, and my avatar moves silently by, looking for clues in a land of unknowns. The irony of the situation is striking: the helpless cry of the "avatar"—this manifestation of a "god," over-whelmed and impotent—without a voice and without a friend on the plains of the new frontier.

Cyberspace is the new frontier of the imagination. And avatars are our first stumbling steps into the new world, the first pass at inhabiting this land of the mind and the machine. These avatars, however, are not just alter egos in a new techno-social matrix, they are also idols that exist on a virtual plane. Not formed of wood or stone—though grounded in silicon—they occupy a seamless digital plane. They are images of our-selves, of what we would like to be. And as the technology of virtual reality improves, they will increasingly become the images of what we dream we might become—the supermen, the avatars if you will, of the virtual world.

Virtual Dungeons and Dragons

AlphaWorld, and the various other avatar-based worlds that exist in cyberspace, represent the latest wave in man-machine interface. These worlds, also known as "habitats," allow a kind of social interaction to develop between the occu-pants. The roots of these worlds go back to the "MUD" (multi-user dungeon), which is the on-line version of multiplayer fantasy/role-playing adventure games such as Dungeons and Dragons. MUDs, which go back at least to the 1970s, have flourished on the Net, with player communities growing up around college and university computing networks.

Essentially, MUDs and their variants (MUSHs, MOOs, Tiny MUDs, and so forth) are text-based neighborhoods of cyberspace. For those unfamiliar with these Internet-based games, a MUD (multiuser dungeon) is a combat-oriented environment and the goal is often to build up your character by combating monsters. A MOO (multiuser object-oriented environment) is typically more socially oriented, allowing you to create your own rooms and objects. There are also MUSHs (multiuser shared hallucinations) and MUCKs (no meaning known) that are more difficult to define and tend toward the bizarre. Users interact with the multiuser dungeon environment and with each other by typing and receiving messages. Consider the following interaction between a player (P) and a MUD:

P: Turn left.

MUD: You are looking at a closed door.

P: Open door.

MUD: The door will not open.

P: Use key.

MUD: The door swings open, revealing a long passageway lit by torches mounted on the wall every 30 feet.

The cyberspace here, such as it is, has been created by the designer of the multiuser dungeon; the actual images, smells, sounds, and textures of this landscape are left to the imagination of the player. To paraphrase Snow Crash author Neal Stephenson, in some ways text may be the most effective virtual reality that will ever be developed. Multiuser dungeons have been created almost completely from textual descriptions of characters, spells, weapons, monsters, wizards, enchantresses, villages, wilderness areas, and, of course, dungeons. The power of these fantasy/role-playing games to capture the imagination of participants is well documented—even to the point that the "reality" of the fantasy world can sometimes wash over into the player's real life, creating bizarre episodes.

In AlphaWorld, on the other hand, the backgrounds, buildings, trees, ground, sky, and so forth, of the virtual world are stored as graphics in the computer, and displayed in three dimensions on a user's display. The computer is also in charge of maintaining the visual representation of the player's avatar for the benefit of the other players on the system. The movement of an avatar is under the control of the player's mouse or keyboard. A player can change the way he appears to others by choosing from a gallery of prefabricated, but slightly less generic, avatars. Advanced players can import their own custom avatar images, enabling players to become, essentially, whatever they want to be. Of course, restrictions apply: when transferred to the virtual realm the creator (man) must assume the form of his virtual creation in order to interact with it; he must therefore become the "avatar."

LucasFilm Habitat

This graphical type of interface was first introduced in the 1980s in a virtual world known as LucasFilm Habitat—or simply "Habitat" (also known as "Club Caribe").[1] Habitat ran on an early on-line service known as QuantumLink (the parent company, Quantum Computer Services, later went on to create a highly visible and immensely successful on-line service—America Online). Since QuantumLink was primarily targeted at Commodore 64 computers—now vastly outdated—there were severe restrictions on the computing horsepower that could be used to create the interface to the Habitat world.[2] Consequently, the images and avatars of Habitat were two-dimensional and cartoonish. Nevertheless, in its prime Habitat hosted several thousand on-line gamers. Habitat succeeded in becoming what was generally agreed to be the first of its kind—an avatar-based virtual world (a "habitat," according to the creators of the original Habitat).

Habitat was no kid's toy. Underneath the simplistic exterior, a serious experiment in "social computing" interface was underway. It was an experiment in creating a "very large scale commercial multi-user virtual environment."[3] Habitat eventually migrated to Japan as the "Fujitsu Habitat," then returned to the United States in an upgraded form as WorldsAway—now available on CompuServe. WorldsAway and AlphaWorld are just two of the many avatar-based worlds currently open for business on the Net. The creators of the original Habitat project, Chip Morningstar, and F. Randall Farmer have gone on to become key players in a new venture called "Electric Communities" (see Appendix B).

Ground Zero

While widespread distributed computing continues to revolutionize both business and personal life, the full benefits of this communications revolution will not be realized without a system that encompasses the *full richness of human interaction.*[4] (From the Electric Communities Web site, emphasis added)

Every technological advance must start somewhere. Powered flight began at Kitty Hawk, and today we have space shuttles and fleets of commercial jets ready to take travelers to destinations anywhere in the world. We are now witnessing the infancy of avatar-based virtual reality, but already the shape of the future is taking form. In AlphaWorld's less ambitious but more developed predecessor, WorldsChat, users browse through the avatar gallery, searching for that appropriate on-line alter ego. The avatars are presented as a series of framed pictures, hung in a gallery somewhere in cyberspace. As you stroll through the gallery, if you find an avatar that looks interesting, you can simply click on the picture for a demonstration of what the avatar looks like in action. The avatar springs to life; now it is out of the frame and resident in three-dimensional cyberspace. It turns around so you can see it from all sides: *Is this the cyber-body you would like to use to present yourself to others?* If so, click the "Embody Me" button; congratulations, you have a new persona. If not, simply click "Keep Looking"; the avatar returns to its framed position on the wall.

AlphaWorld and its kin—such as WorldsAway, Moondo from Intel, and PointWorld from Black Sun and and Point Communications—represent not just the next stage of the MUD, or multiuser dungeon. They represent the jump from the old technology of the imagination, *text*, to the new technology of the imagination, *virtual reality*. This is truly "ground zero" of something new: the birth of global cyberspace. The baseline goals of immersive virtual reality have been met, which is to present the virtual world as a three-dimensional space inhabited by the viewer. It is a primitive sort of virtual reality that is currently being offered, to be sure. By the standards of military simulators, or even virtual reality game machines, this stuff is crude, it is buggy, and it is balky. But it is on the Net, and you can go there now.

The goal of cyberspace is to create a medium where it is not just the message, but the messengers themselves, who are transported. As Paul Saffo of the Institute of the Future in Palo Alto put it, "the essence of cyberspace is that communication is no longer just a conduit we pass through, but a destination in its own right."[5] Or, as the creators of AlphaWorld boast, "Cyberspace is now a place."

This is the purpose of the avatar—*to take you there.* Your avatar shares a set of defining constructs—rules, laws, constraints, abilities—with the other avatar-actors. You are pioneers in the new "new world." Eventually, these images come to represent for you the people behind the digital masks—you begin to know their habits and hangouts, their likes and dislikes; you know the ones you can trust and the ones to avoid, who is an old hand and who is a newbie. And someday, in the not-too-distant future, you will have to decide who is a person and who is a machine.[6] While all this is going on, you yourself are "embodying the avatar"—you are becoming the symbol. This is the point, after all, of the design: to create an inhabitable world that supports the "full richness of human interaction."

Fluid Identities

A virtual place populated by real people, AlphaWorld takes social computing to the next level. By immigrating to AlphaWorld you become one of its citizens and help to shape it. . . . This is not some preprogrammed simulation—it is as unpredictable and unique as the individuals who help create it. Including you.[7] (From the AlphaWorld Home Page)

To Jaron Lanier (who first coined the term "virtual reality") and other cyberspace seers, the final destination of cyberspace is a world without limits, a place of infinite creative possibilities. Gone are the constraints of material bodies, of the material world, even of language. The idealized virtual reality of the future is a seamless interface between our deepest, most inexpressible wishes and desires, and the effectors in the virtual world. "Your wish is my command" becomes the operative experience of all mankind (all of "wired" mankind anyway), as the genie of magic technology does our every bidding.

The fulfillment of every technological dream begins with a single step. Interestingly, that first step in AlphaWorld is the creation of fluid identities. The avatar can be whatever one wants it to be—man, woman, child, butterfly, penguin, whatever. Even going back to the LucasFilm Habitat, whatever other capabilities may have been lacking, each avatar had at his disposal a command to change sex—from male to female or vice versa—at will. It is an important aspect of these virtual worlds, seemingly, that sexual identity (and all other forms of identity) are up for grabs. Beyond the control of personal identity, virtual world designers are now also beginning to offer inhabitants the ability to shape their surroundings.

Building Worlds

In AlphaWorld, for example, avatars are given a taste of the plastic world of the future by being able to build their own "houses." Each avatar can stake out a plot in the AlphaWorld terrain and choose from an assortment of prefabricated building materials to build the virtual dwelling of their dreams. Hurry, all the best lots are getting snatched up even as you read this!

This dream of the ideal world of the future is fueled by the notion that the imagination is the magic wand that will save us from our circumstances, the force that will free us from the decaying forms of the past, and from the constraints of sorry material existence. It is an idea that is spoon-fed to anyone who comes into contact with the pervasive organs of the mass media, which increasingly means the whole world. It seems that everyone from John Lennon to Barney (the purple dinosaur) has one message for us: "Just imagine." And this, ultimately, is the carrot of cyberspace—the place where everything will be just what we have always imagined.

In the plans for global cyberspace, there are more than faint echoes of another grand project from man's past:

> And they said, "Come, let us build ourselves a city, and a tower whose top is in the heavens; let us make a name for ourselves, lest we be scattered abroad over the face of the whole earth." And the Lord said, "Indeed the people are one and they all have one language, and this is what they begin to do; now nothing that they propose to do will be withheld from them" (Genesis 11:4-6 NKJV).

The purpose of that building project on the plains of Shinar was to create a unifying achievement that would somehow elevate man to the heavens, the level of "the gods." God, looking down upon this effort, observed that if this were to happen, "nothing they propose to do will be withheld from them." Nothing that came into the imagination of man would be impossible to achieve. This was not an outcome God was willing to allow. The tower was also a kind of idolatry of self and of what man could become; its intended result was to be security, cohesion, and uniformity. How ironic, then, that its actual result was babel.

As Santayana observed, "Those who ignore the past are destined to repeat its mistakes." Perhaps, then, it would be worthwhile, in this look at what is to come, to pause for a second to reflect on that which has already taken place.

Gods of Silicon

"Then the people bowed and prayed
To the neon god they made . . ."

> — Simon & Garfunkle
> "The Sound of Silence"

The subject of idolatry seems foreign to the modern mind. After all, we do not sacrifice to bronze statues, or consult the kitchen god in this day and age, do we? Nevertheless, one cannot help but be struck by the number of times believers are admonished in the pages of the Old and New Testaments to guard themselves against idolatry. The first of the Ten Commandments is this: "You shall have no other gods before me" (Exodus 20:3). *Every* writer of the New Testament warns against idolatry. Have we, then, somehow become immune to this ancient defilement?

Webster's Dictionary defines worship as "reverence offered a divine being or supernatural power; extravagant respect or admiration for or adoration to an object of esteem." Worship involves our priorities—that to which we ascribe the highest importance, or worth. That is why, for example, greed is a form of idolatry; it involves replacing God with something else, money.

Interestingly, the proscription against having "other gods" is directly tied to the prohibition against the creation of images. In Exodus 20:4, the commandment continues: "You shall not make for yourself an idol, or any likeness of what is in heaven above or on the earth beneath or in the water under the earth."

Avatars and Images

I am back in AlphaWorld. The "parachuting in" process is more or less complete. The avatar is responding to my mouse movements as I turn to survey the landscape in all directions. A little ways off, I see what appears to be a virtual newspaper stand, no doubt stocked with copies of the *AlphaWorld Times,* and I move in that direction. Maybe I will try to read one. Suddenly, my display is frozen. I try to move, but the avatar has stopped responding to the mouse. The scene in front of me is fixed. And then, after a few seconds, the screen goes blank. Suddenly I am looking at that most elemental of PC icons: "C:\" and a blinking cursor, white characters on a black background. I am out of AlphaWorld, out of Windows, and all the way back out to DOS. Strangely, I am comforted. I have gone from the cutting edge to the nothing edge in less than a minute; my 486 computer with 8 megabytes of RAM is clearly overmatched by the challenge of AlphaWorld's real-time 3-D rendering. As I sit looking at the useless screen, it occurs to me that if I cannot get into AlphaWorld, then neither can a lot of other folks. There is still a little time . . .

I have been on the plane where the superhuman abilities of the computer combine with the creative power of the human mind. It is the place where man can *be* what he wants to be, *where* he wants to be, *when* he wants to be. Rising out of this possibilities-milieu is—*the avatar,* the person we always imagined we could be. Worship of the avatar allows man to make an idol of both himself and his creation in one fell swoop. Here, then, we catch a glimpse of the new god, the god that will finally displace that angry, patriarchal god of the ancestor's imagination, the god that will finally lead us into the promised land of techno-security and multicultural uniformity.

Cyberspace is a world of images. There is nothing in cyberspace that has not been borrowed or captured from the real world of sights and sounds. The world around us is a world of living things; a place where the sea roars, the rivers clap their hands, the mountains sing together for joy before the Lord (Psalm 98). Cyberspace, on the other hand, is a world of lifeless images created by an apprentice who has not been given the secret of life. There, nothing speaks the Creator's praise; only a faint, sad echo, a paean to the dabblers, the created creators.

8

VIRTUALITY AND THEOPHOBIA

Brooks Alexander

OVERVIEW

In man's constant quest for a place to hide—all to escape an infinite God whom he cannot control or manipulate—he has perhaps found a supreme haven in his most recent creation, cyberspace. Brooks Alexander explores how this digital garden of delights promises to offer what other sanctuaries down through the centuries—from shamanism to neognosticism—could offer only in part. Now man can temporarily remake the very outward reality with which he has been at enmity since time immemorial. In cyberspace the human creator can form the laws of his own domain. He can finally become the god of his own creation.

Of course, this is true only as long as he is joined to the machines of his own creation, machines which themselves are mutable. When they fail, he is faced once again with the age-old dilemma of a universe and a God that he did not fashion. And that is the terrible conundrum of cyberspace, a digital reality that can be turned off with the mere flip of a switch. Not so with the other reality—the one that was fashioned ex nihilo *and conceived long before the world was made.*

C hristianity has been called "a form of sanctified cynicism." Biblical faith means we cannot be skeptics about the supernatural, but we must be cynics about human nature.

Most people are not accustomed to thinking of cynicism as a quality of Christian thought. But the Gospel—like Christ Himself—is utterly without illusion in assessing human motive and behavior. Christianity is thoroughly cynical in recognizing human fallenness and everything it entails. It understands fully that fallen human beings are relentlessly self-seeking and grotesquely shortsighted about it; that they are born buckpassers, quick to blame and slow to accept responsibility. It understands that they obsessively seek to manipulate others (and reality in general) to their own advantage, regardless of the consequences. Most of all, it understands that fallen humans instinctively recoil from God's presence and reflexively reject His purposes—all the while concealing their real agenda from themselves and others by invoking high-minded excuses for their behavior (see Appendix C: The Other Half).

Theophobia: Hiding from God

Christian cynicism particularly knows that fallen human beings shrink from the presence of God. That evasive impulse was the first of the new characteristics Adam and Eve exhibited after their fall (Genesis 3:8). First the couple draped themselves with the foliage of the forest. Then they tried to disappear into the forest itself. They literally tried to hide from God by blending in with the rest of nature: "Nobody here but us plants and animals!"

Their offspring have continued to do the same thing, from the beginning of history down to the present day. Our strategies of concealment are more complex than those of Adam and Eve, but we still hide from God for the same simple reason they did—namely, because we are all out of harmony with Him.

Being at odds with God means that we find ourselves in conflict with a power we cannot even resist, much less overcome. Our so-called "contest" with God is a gross mismatch. It is like the "contest" between a thatched hut and the force of a hydrogen bomb.

Because of that imbalance, when we encounter the living God, we feel not only confronted but overpowered. To put it clinically, we feel "spiritual discomfort" of an urgent and threatening intensity. We recoil from God's presence by spiritual reflex, just as we recoil reflexively from physical pain. It is a visceral reaction that bypasses the thinking mind. We react to the presence of God like an amoeba reacts to an acid solution—we freeze in shock, shrink in pain, and flee in fear and trembling.

One of the things we do in our spiritual flight is to seek spiritual "cover"—that is, to preemptively engage the part of us that God wants to be connected with. We tune God out most effectively by making sure that the spiritual part of our nature is fully occupied with something else. Thus, we hide from God in substitute spiritual relations—with spirits, totems, gremlins, gods, ghosts, *devas*, demons, angels, ancestors, fairies, leprechauns, UFOs, or whatever. The void created by our estrangement from God does not stay empty for long. As G. K. Chesterton famously remarked, "When a man ceases to believe in God, he doesn't believe in nothing, he believes in anything."

Technology and Tech-Gnosis

Today our compulsion to flee from God is sending us into strange new hiding places that technology is opening up. Now we go looking for our preemptive spiritual connections in the labyrinths of our own computer networks. Contemporary theophobes are too sophisticated to believe in the biblical God, of course, but not too sophisticated to believe in a kind of cyber-supernaturalism that includes almost everything else. They are even ready to believe in ghosts—or at least in an up-to-date version of the "ghost in the machine." Some cyber-enthusiasts speak of the Internet as a "global mind"—created and operated by human beings, but animated by a higher, collective consciousness. Others claim that virtual reality opens a "portal to transcendence," creating a new, nonspatial world of infinite freedom that exists in and through our interactions in cyberspace—a kind of "collective hallucination" given "virtual flesh" in the patterns of digital bits and bytes that pulse through the World Wide Web.

In this way, we ourselves become the elusive presence that haunts the recesses of our own hardware and software creations. We become the animating "soul" of the works of our own hands. The prophet Isaiah derided the primitive idolator for making an object of wood or metal by his own effort and then expecting the thing to be inhabited by a "god." Today we have pressed the envelope of idolatry far beyond that primitive presumption by building artifacts for *our* divine inhabitation. *We* become the god who lives in our new techno-totem—*we are the ghost in our own machine.*

Such rarefied levels of idolatry require a hubris that has more in common with Gnosticism and self-deification than it does with idol worship in the normal sense of the term. Self-deification is the ultimate hiding place from God, and ancient

Gnosticism turned the pursuit of "the god within" into a spiritual system.

In the almost two thousand years since Gnosticism's first advent, its so-called "gnosis" has proved to be a highly effective means of hiding from God. Presently, resurgent (neo) Gnosticism is having a field day in popular culture.[1] One reason for the appeal of Gnosticism today is that our inborn tendency to gnostic thinking has been reinforced by our technology. Modern techno-culture is itself a form of "instrumental Gnosticism"—a kind of delusionary "knowledge" about reality that is mediated to us through the instruments of mass communication.

The spiritual world and the techno-world intersect in the media. Today's mass media encourage our gnostic tendencies by making the world of shared imagination seem real to begin with. Aberrant spiritual ideas flourish readily in that realm of collective fantasy. As the media reduce all events to info-tainment, the line between interpreting reality and inventing it starts to blur in the popular mind.

The cyber-revolution gives us new tools with which to take that confusion to even higher levels. Finally, we start to blur the boundaries between the personal self and ultimate reality. Gnosticism merges with technology to become tech-gnosis— that is, technologically mediated enlightenment. In cyberspace, our flight from God acquires new wings.

Gnosticism—Ancient and Modern

Original Gnosticism turned theophobia into a religion. Gnosticism created an elaborate system of distancing us from God by means of an angelic hierarchy. According to the most developed forms of gnostic theology, "God" is too pure, too spiritual, too high and holy to have any hands-on contact with the crude material world. He (or rather *It*) did not create physical reality, a lesser, flawed deity did. The pure, noncreating God is therefore separated from the impurity of the physical world by an array of angel-like beings, called *aeons,* arranged in a descending order—away from pure God, and toward gross matter.

Gnosticism offered its believers a "salvation" that committed them to a lengthy, difficult, and dangerous climb up the angelic ladder toward the goal of union with their "God." At the end of that climb lay the promise of enlightenment— the "knowledge" (*gnosis*) that gave Gnosticism its name.

Now, as then, the gnostic's all-consuming quest for enlightenment becomes a form of spiritual flight in itself. But the *purpose* of flight is safety and refuge (that is, an *end* to flight), and the state of mind called "gnosis" is therefore a final, defensive lock and seal against God. Like other forms of enlightenment, "gnosis" is a way of folding human subjectivity in upon itself, so that the unregenerate mind reflects its nature back to itself in an infinite feedback loop. It is almost impossible to penetrate that self-contained spiritual world. The false infinity of self-reflecting solipsism is a perfect refuge from the impending presence of God.

Today, neo-Gnosticism is setting up that same delusionary house of mirrors. The process of construction, however, has been streamlined, thanks to computer technology. Original Gnosticism required dedication and hard work to condition the mind for enlightenment. But computers promise to make that kind of mental discipline obsolete. Some scientists believe that with the aid of computers and neurophysiology, enlightenment can be produced without any effort—or even any intent—on the part of the enlightenee.

David Porush is a professor at Renssalear Polytechnic Institute, where he conducts research on artificial intelligence (AI). Porush envisions cyberspace as a kind of electronic designer drug:

> Neurophysiologists suspect that lurking somewhere in the brain—most likely in a formation at the base of the brain stem called the dorsal raphe nucleus—lies a facility that makes us feel, under the right conditions, like we're in communication with gods or that we have voyaged out to meet

some Higher Presence. Certain configurations of data delivered to the brain by electronic stimulation could flood this
region of the brain with serotonin, a neurotransmitter
involved in many functions, including hallucination. In this
way, the right software might evoke that oceanic, world-
embracing feeling known so well to mystics and psycho-
tropical beachcombers.[2]

Porush's final pronouncement is not exactly what you
would call a modest proposal. Cyberspace, he says, "could be
our civilization's burning bush."

Occult Traffic on the Info-Bahn

Even Porush's ambitious approach to cyberspace seems
mundane to many pagans and occultists. One of the real surprises of the 1980s was the emergence of a strong relationship
between the magical worldview and the cybernetic mentality.
The connection came to light in 1985 with the publication of
Drawing Down the Moon, by Margot Adler (National Public
Radio commentator, daughter of philosopher Mortimer Adler,
and a self-identified witch). Adler's groundbreaking book was a
survey of the social and spiritual history of neopaganism and
modern witchcraft, with particular emphasis on current developments in North America. As part of her research, she sur-
veyed the pagan community and discovered that

> an "amazingly high" percentage of folks drew their pay-
> checks from technical fields and from the computer
> industry. Respondents gave many reasons for this curious
> affinity—everything from "computers are elementals in dis-
> guise" to the simple fact that the computer industry pro-
> vided jobs for the kind of smart, iconoclastic and experi-
> mental folk that paganism attracts. . . . But if you dig deep
> enough, you find more intimate correspondences between
> computer culture and paganism's religion of the imagina-
> tion.[3]

Such connections may seem odd to the secular mind. However, they come as no surprise to anyone who understands what a biblical worldview means. The Bible depicts occultism in general and self-deifying occultism in particular as the ultimate rejection of God (see Genesis 3:5, Isaiah 47, and Revelation 17:1-5). Biblically speaking, occultism is the last refuge of the theophobe; magic, sorcery, and spirit contact are a last barricade thrown up against the sensed approach of the presence of God. Occultism always manifests itself as a terminal form of self-will, culturally as well as personally.

As we have already noted, computer technology does the same thing all technology does—that is, it amplifies human will and purpose. It does so, however, at a staggering rate, and with universal application. Whereas earlier machines only amplified our power for *specific* purposes (for example, steam locomotives gave us power to haul loads on rails), the cyber-machine amplifies our power for literally *anything* we want to do—from manipulating genes to visualizing weather systems. And it takes weeks, not years, for the impact of its improvements to be felt.

Computers therefore empower every aspect of human nature without exception, and they do so with breathtaking speed and breadth of effect. Given what we know about human nature, that is a sobering prospect. Because theophobia has become a built-in part of human nature since the fall, we can unerringly predict that the computer revolution will greatly increase the number and power of available ways to flee from the presence of God—with particular emphasis on the more radical ways, such as techno-magic and digital spiritism.

Weaving Pagan Webs in Cyberspace

It is redundant to even speak of "prediction" at this stage—simple observation makes the point. On a sociological level alone, the neopagan movement is highly networked in cyberspace, as pagans communicate with one another through a number of occult-oriented chat rooms on the Internet. One author speaks pointedly of the Internet as "the clearinghouse of contemporary heresy."[4] Much of the neo-pagan movement's growth and a lot of its evolving practices are generated through interaction on the Net.

Cyber-savvy pagans also incorporate both computer hardware and software directly into their magical operations. Individual variations on that theme are as numerous as the individuals involved. But two examples will serve to illustrate how computers are being used as tools of magic in the quest for occult power and enlightenment.

The first example involves Tyagi (an adopted name), a 33-year-old Californian from San Jose who calls himself a practitioner of "chaos magic."

> After reading and deeply researching philosophy, mysticism and the occult, Tyagi began cobbling together his own mythic structures, divination systems and rituals—an eclectic spirituality well suited to the Net's culture of complex interconnections...."Using popular media is an important aspect of chaos magic," Tyagi says . . . "Most pagans would get online and say, 'Let's get together somewhere and do a ritual.' Chaos magicians would say, 'Let's do the ritual online.'"[5]

Tyagi is a solitary chip-monk in a silicon monastery. He spends four to six hours daily on the Internet, weaving his cyber-spells and occult Web connections. "Being online is part of my practice. It's kind of a hermit-like existence, like going into a cave. I'm not really connected to people, I'm just sending out messages and receiving them back."[6]

Computers as Magical Implements

Mark Pesce of San Francisco is a different breed of techno-pagan. He is nothing if not "connected"—being part of the gay scene, the pagan scene, and the computer scene all at once. Pesce is an ex-Catholic, ex-Pentecostal, M.I.T. dropout who is currently an author, software creator, homosexual, and witch. Pesce claims that the Craft is "nothing less than applied cybernetics." Computers and computer programs can be magical objects or even sacred objects, he says, because they "embody our communication with each other *and with the entities—the divine parts of ourselves—that we invoke in that space.*"[7]

Pesce uses physical computers to help frame the metaphysical space that ceremonial magic seeks to create. For example, he recently celebrated a "Cyber-Samhain"—his own

> digitally enhanced version of the ancient Celtic celebration of the dead known to the rest of us as Halloween. Of all of paganism's seasonal festivals, Samhain (pronounced "saw-when") is the ripest time for magic. As most pagans will tell you, it's the time when the veils between the worlds of the living and the dead are thinnest. For Pesce, Samhain is a perfect time to ritually bless *Worldview* [his new computer program] as a passageway between the meat world and the electronic shadow land of the Net.[8]

Pesce's cyber-ceremony is typically neopagan in that it follows the traditional occult practice of "casting a circle," within which the ritual is to be performed and the magic is to occur. In most traditions of ceremonial magic, the circle is seen as a zone of protection from the dangerous forces the magician is calling forth. But neopagans see the circle as a way of creating a special place with room for spirits to be and magic to happen—a metaphysical enclave set up in the midst of a mundane world that has no room for metaphysics.

Pesce's ritual updates the casting of the magical circle by using computers to mark both its physical and metaphysical boundaries.

> Pagans carve out tightly bounded zones in both physical and psychic space . . . the stage is often set by invoking the four elements that the ancients believed composed all

matter. Often symbolized by colored candles or statues, these four "Watchtowers" stand like imaginary sentinels in the four cardinal directions of the circle.

But tonight's Watchtowers are four PCs networked through an ethernet and linked to a SPARCstation with an Internet connection . . . The four monitors face into the circle, glowing patiently in the subdued light. Each machine is running *Worldview,* and each screen shows a different angle on a virtual space . . . a ritual circle that mirrors the one Pesce will create in the room. . . .

A roomful of geeks, techno-yuppies and multimedia converts circle around in the monitor glow, chanting and laughing. . . . I join in with pleasure. . . . We are woven into a world without which we are nothing, and our glittering electronic nets are not separate from that ancient webwork.[9]

The End of Theophobia

Magic and technology are two versions of the same impulse—*the impulse to self-will*—and it is inevitable that they reconverge. It is no accident that our feats of computer technology are rising to the level of virtual magic at the same time that we are embracing computers as instruments of actual magic.

The result of that partnership will be a new and improved refuge from God, a uniquely enthralling and widespread delusion not seen before in the history of the world. Computers have empowered our God-avoidance reflex along with everything else. In cyberspace we are constructing not just a spiritual hiding place, but a spiritual bomb-shelter. In the end, of course, our shelter will prove completely useless. In His own timing, God blows through our most well-prepared defenses as though they are not even there.

In the meantime, however, we should expect the theophobic delusions that flourish in cyberspace to intensify. They will also become increasingly influential socially and politically—at least within the context of collective consent that sustains them. Those who do not consent to the delusion will be marginalized at best, since computers will increasingly dominate human life, and tech-gnostic delusion will increasingly dominate the computer elite.

No matter how strong the power of collective consent may be in human terms, however, in God's terms it remains a closed circle of denial and self-deceit. Its *reality* remains *virtual*—and therefore impotent in the face of *actual* reality. We should not forget that through His sovereignty over nature, God has some serious options available for upsetting our theophobic schemes. We may be the ghost in our own machine, but our machine is more fragile than we imagine. What happens to the "collective hallucination" when the power-grid goes down? Does its "virtual flesh" moulder in a virtual grave, awaiting virtual resurrection?

Science fiction writer Philip K. Dick said, "reality is that which doesn't go away when you stop believing in it." Today we could add ". . . or cut off the electricity." In the face of God's actual reality, theophobia—even computer-enhanced, virtually realized theophobia—has all the prospects of the proverbial snowball in hell. The fallen delusions that haunt cyberspace may be impenetrable to us, but they are utterly transparent to God.

A Final Word

LOST IN THE GARDEN OF DIGITAL DELIGHTS

Tal Brooke

The present dawn of cyberspace is still barely a land of shadow figures compared to what it will become when the current technology is fully powered up. The combination of factors needed for this to happen is obvious—faster, sleeker technology with leaps in memory capacity, transmission speed, and central processor power. Computers alone have increased in power more than 100,000-fold in the past 50 years, and the other components of cyberspace will not remain far behind.

When the present trickle of data that animates cyberspace with crude motion and sound effects at 28,800-baud jumps up to millions of baud (which is already starting to happen in some instances, as in Pacific Bell's Asymmetric Digital Subscriber Line)—when the interactive gear becomes affordable and downsized—when virtual reality enters in full-bodied form, *then* some of our projections in this book will become realities. A very powerful beast will be standing in the town square of history probably at the start of the next millennium.

Commerce is positioned to explode over this new medium according to international business consultant, Harvard professor, and best-selling author Peter F. Drucker.

Throughout his latest book, *Managing in a Time of Great Change*, Drucker boldly asserts that cyberspace will be the new conduit for global commerce, revolutionizing international business and finance in a way that comes only every other century. Meanwhile, governments and their agencies, the military, universities, media conglomerates, communications giants, and practically every other major entity is preparing for this quantum shift. Books by the score will be coming out that explore the practical domains of cyberspace.

Our interest in this book has been in the human interface of a technology that seems destined to reach every population and age-group in the world—one that has serious spiritual and moral dimensions. From the spiritual summit, our interest is even more finely tuned, for we see a new theater of operations for what has been an ageless war over the human soul.

Technology in and of itself is a neutral medium available for good or evil purposes. The most primitive tool such as the axe can be used for killing (a preferred weapon in medieval times) or for cutting down trees. Sophisticated instruments such as the television can equally be used for good or evil, but with a broader spectrum of gradations. As the forerunner of cyberspace, the television offers us an index of how cyberspace will be used. Out of 100 cable channels, five might be truly "good," constructive, and educational; 25 are less so; and the remaining channels contain shows that not only *are not* edifying, they seduce audiences and constantly push the envelope by broadening the terrain of incest, homosexuality, and the like. This trend has been obvious for years. If the range in public taste in cable TV is any indication, cyberspace will take the same course, and that is not good.

In reality, the entire bell-shaped curve of television programming has been incrementally shifting to the left for 40 years. Howard Sterne on the Entertainment network, Beavis and Butthead on MTV, among many others, could not have existed in the 1950s. The atmosphere of our culture could not have absorbed such programming then. This is obviously true with dedicated adult channels such as Penthouse that specialize in porn and violence. The advent of such entertainment has produced a certain moral tenderizing of the masses over decades. How far this slide continues, and what happens when it switches to the much more powerful instrument of cyberspace (where these experiences can be explored *interactively*), remains a key concern.

The Digital Game Room

For countless young cyber-enthusiasts, the fully powered technology of cyberspace will bring today's most sophisticated role-playing and arcade games right into their homes. Except these games will be much more engaging than anything that exists today. Even virtual reality games that cost eight dollars a pop at such progressive venues as club DV8 in San Francisco will seem grainy and cartoonlike compared to what is up ahead.

It will be a temptation for any youth to spend time in this realm, especially the growing hoard of disaffected youth from families that are barely limping through life. They will have every reason to escape into cyberspace. Each home will have an escape hatch, but it will not be the comparatively benign attic portal into the land of Narnia that we read about in C. S. Lewis's "Chronicles of Narnia."

Twenty years ago when kids wanted to steal off for a private meeting, they often resorted to playing hooky from school or climbing out the upstairs window at night. But soon they can just lock their rooms, put on a helmet with panoramic viewing, log in, enter the digital plane, pick the designer body fitting their mood, grab some digital surfboards, and go blazing down some three-dimensional tunnel while laughing and joking with their friends. They will also have easy access to new realms of experience beyond their years in this garden of digital delights.

It will be the same thing for adults who learn they can so easily meet on the sly—the old story of the bored husband or wife who wants a quick and safe fling without any dirty footprints leading back to the bedroom. Of course, it may lead to the real thing very quickly. But the anonymous meeting in a cyber-room will always remain an inviting temptation for illicit liaisons. No bars or hotel rooms; just a tete-a-tete somewhere in cyberspace. But that is only the starting point for the infinitely variegated human imagination. The garden of digital delights will offer many more diversions. Some, of course, will be unspeakably dark.

A unique problem could surface when it comes time for the cyber-generation to take off its gear and face the workaday world with its responsibilities and drudgery. Some users will never want to log off. Others will prefer their own domain of alternate worlds above the rough ride of life, especially teens who face the inevitable trials unique to adolescence—trials that are so necessary for healthy character formation.

Cyber-dependency is inevitable. We have already seen what constant indulgence in television and drugs has done to stunt succeeding generations of youth who have emerged—each a little slower, duller, less motivated, and less equipped to resist life's pressures than preceding waves. Cyberspace will offer more kicks. So far we have seen that those who become really hooked—with drugs and alcohol at the moment—readily collapse in the face of temptation only to seek further escape, fueling their inability to deal with the demands of life in the real world. A cyber-dependent generation could become what George Orwell, Aldous Huxley, and Aleksandr Isayevich Solzhenitsyn have each described in varying ways—weakened characters controlled by pleasure and pain who can so easily become putty in the hands of the all-powerful State. Put another way, what better way of domesticating a generation is there than loosing it in the garden of digital delights where it will lose the will to resist and the inner character to fight.

The dangers of cyberspace are very real. After its unique and "beneficial" offerings of unlimited information, mind expansion, full-body interaction, instant commerce, long-distance medical diagnosis, global home offices, and a whole cornucopia of other services, older deeper hungers could awaken. So could an increasing dependency arise on the mechanical genie itself in virtually every area of life. The final Devil's bargain would become evident: Seeking the illusion of unlimited freedom, people will become hooked to a machine that will hold them in a tighter grip than any prison before it, capturing the very soul.

The beast that is able to enter the human mind like an open door can also invade history with a strength unrivaled in the past—appearing first as a servant, then becoming a terrible weapon over a people, over a population.

Man's Perennial Dilemma

Ever since the terrible event in Eden, when man chose the false promise of godhood and immortality over the *Viseo Dei*—the ineffable splendor of God's presence—he has been allowed to suffer the folly of his choice. In a mere instant what had been an innocent and pellucid consciousness was flooded with an expanding darkness that stained the conscience and forever changed the human soul. Innocence and purity fled like the vanishing light of dusk.

With the sudden knowledge of evil came loneliness and alienation. Down the dark centuries that followed, depravities of all varieties cascaded from human experience: wars, murder, and all manner of cruelty—"man's inhumanity to man"— spread through history. The self-will of human nature was in a constant hunt for acquisition, pleasure, and conquest, despite the outcome. A troubled conscience became man's constant companion, forever haunted by the evils it had done and would continue to do.

To escape this troubled conscience, man has tried again and again to find sanctuary, to remake reality by blotting God out of his awareness. One such sanctuary has been those religions and beliefs that assuaged his conscience and assured him that there is no holy God to judge his life; that there are no real and permanent consequences for evil; and that his true inner nature is divinity itself. Those beliefs reached full development in ancient Babylon and India. The same beliefs have now come back as the New Age movement. The synchronicity of such beliefs arriving with the birth of cyberspace promises to fulfill man's desperate quest for an alternative reality, a place to hide.

A place to hide. The final seamless sanctuary from reality is indeed something that cyberspace—the beast that now stands in the town square of history—could offer in bounty, this garden of digital delights. The imagination can run free in the planes of cyberspace where digital reality is plastic and can be altered and reinvented at whim. The self can be endlessly redefined. It can appear as its own electronic "avatar" and descend godlike into worlds that it invents—until it runs into its own trap and becomes enslaved. The consequence is to be endlessly frozen within a universe of one's own making by playing God. Suddenly the patient has entered the darkest ward of the madhouse only to lock himself permanently in the inner chamber.

Delusion is the consequence of fleeing reality. It is the outcome of rejecting God and all He has created. It is the worst kind of alienation—from reality and from God. Should such delusion finally descend upon the world, as the apostle John indicates in the book of Revelation, then time will come full circle and the folly of Eden will have reaped its terrible harvest at the end of history.

The only remedy to a world lost in delusion will be when the eschaton arrives and God intervenes. The Son of Man, as is recorded, will appear with an effulgence that tears apart the fabric of any manmade pretense in a thunderous awaking for the world. Not even the most powerful delusion will be able to withstand the light of His coming. Nor can it spare the multitudes from seeing the reality of what they have become. The full magnitude of choice will be revealed and no one will be able to turn away from this reckoning—both an end and a new beginning.

Appendix A

TECHNOLOGY AND THE FALL

The fall did not create technology, but it set the direction for our pursuit of it. The fall determines our reasons for inventing technology, it determines how we use technology, and it determines the results that will flow from that use. Indeed, it is not overstating the case to say that the serpent's temptation to Adam and Eve implicitly promised a certain kind of "godlike" technological prowess.

Remember that the serpent first slandered God by insinuating that He is a selfish and mean-spirited deceiver. He then made three baited promises to Eve from his repertoire of deception:

> And the serpent said unto the woman, "Ye shall not surely die! For God doth know that in the day ye eat thereof, then your eyes shall be opened, and ye shall be as gods, knowing good and evil" (Genesis 3:4-5 KJV).

The opening of the eyes to good and evil is basic to the promise of godlikeness. It is not clear in the English translation, but in the original Hebrew the concept of good and evil carries a clear implication of technological power. In the Hebrew mind-set, good and evil are more than just moral categories. The words also signify "useful" and "useless." Echoes of that meaning still exist in English today. We say that a hammer is "good" (that is, "useful") for driving nails, but it is "not good" (that is, "useless") for turning screws.

The ability to make that distinction is the foundation of all technology. And the useful and useless are only distinguishable on the basis of some purpose that one has in mind. In an unfallen world our primal parents might have graduated to an anointed form of technology that served the purposes of God for our self-expression and our growth in harmony with Him and His creation. But that is not the world we live in. In the real world, the fall has distorted the development of our technology by distorting the purposes that define how we think about the issue of useful versus useless to begin with.

How do we arrive at the purposes that define our technologies? The fall involves, above everything else, the turning away from God and toward self for all our reference points. Now our own self-perceived requirements dominate our attention. Cut loose from God's purposes, we devise our own purposes, and those purposes determine what we consider "useful" and what we discard as "useless."

Technology and Hiding

How did the fruits of that new technological power first appear to Adam and Eve? The first new purpose they acquired was that of seeking concealment, and the first thing they did was to stitch some concealment together.

> And the eyes of them both were opened, and they knew that they were naked; and they sewed fig leaves together, and made themselves aprons (Genesis 3:7 KJV).

Recall what the serpent had promised. He had said that their eyes would be opened, and they would know good and evil. Here we are told that their eyes *were* in fact opened. And what did they know? They knew they were naked—and they knew what to do about it.

It is significant that this is the first form taken by their new "godlike" knowledge. They could only know their "nakedness" in relation to a standard of self-concern. But Adam and Eve did not acquire their new self-standard in one stroke.

When Eve took the fruit in order to be "wise," she was already looking for self-initiated change apart from any reference to God. Eve had gone that far in her own heart before eating anything. In the act of eating, her desire turned into behavior. And behavior produced its results. In their knowledge of nakedness, Adam and Eve's newly acquired "knowledge of good and evil" came to its pragmatic conclusion.

Through the fall, the world becomes alien and threatening, and we react to that fact with self-centered anxiety. Adam and Eve's perception of their own nakedness is based on a standard of self-need, and their response is an act of self-help—the first recorded act of technology, if you will. This is the pivotal point at which the "knowledge of good and evil" comes into play—including the knowledge of the "useful" and the "useless"—and it turns out to be something of a letdown. Adam and Eve have indeed become "like God"—just not *very much* like Him.

The fig leaves were essentially an effort to "conceal" the responsible selves. The fig leaves had less to do with concealing the sexual parts than most people think. More fundamentally, they had to do with concealing guilt by blending the human identity into the background pattern of nature as a whole. After draping themselves with the products of nature, Adam and Eve further hid themselves from the presence of God "among the trees of the garden" ("Nobody here but us plants and animals!").

That basic evasive impulse to hide by blending into the background accounts for a great deal of mysticism, especially "nature mysticism." As the natural self dissolves back into nature, so does the spiritual burden it bears. To a self under the judgment of God, self-dissolution seems like a reprieve. Thus the appeal of Buddhistic enlightenment: the world dissolves into process—and the self is part of that dissolving world. *There is no one to be judged if there is no one at all!*

Such dedicated self-concealment is a form of self-confession and, paradoxically, a form of self-retribution. Denis de Rougemont speaks of the dilemma of guilt and denial, as the conscience faces an overwhelming reality it can neither acknowledge nor avoid.

> Here we find set into motion the complicated mechanisms of the perversion, of the self-punishment of a torn conscience, and of the desire to destroy oneself at last, to destroy oneself in order to make oneself innocent!—in order still to escape the consequences of what the evil one has done; to chastise oneself without making reparations. It is the mystery of suicide and the logic of Judas; the last temptation, the supreme utopia.[1]

Of course, it does not work any better than Adam and Eve's effort to vanish into the greenery of the garden. God called them forth by name and confronted them with His presence, which they were hiding from in the first place. Once the two guilty selves were in the presence of God, the squirming commenced. When the pressure of reality began to hurt, then the sorry parade of excuses and blaming began. We have no reason to believe that our hiding will be any more successful—or that our response to being found out will be any more honorable. Even if we destroy our body with fire, ravage our personality with drugs, or dissolve our identity with mystical mental tricks, we will still be called forth by name in the resurrection. Then what?

The "Wisdom" of Self

It is clear that the "wisdom" that Adam and Eve's eyes were opened to depends on acquiring a purpose that proceeded from themselves alone. The whole concept of the knowledge of good and evil in this sense involves a decision on the part of human beings to replace God with self as the ultimate standard of reference. It involves a decision to replace God's self-disclosure with the finite needs and desires of the human self, as understood by that self. That is the fundamental turning of the will.

The immediate result of that turning is a radical contraction of consciousness. This, strictly speaking, is what is known as the "fall." Before, both Adam and Eve were resonating with the purposes of God, and were conscious of their relationship with Him. Now they are focused on themselves, drawing their awareness away from God and bringing it inward. Now everything springs from their own perception of their own needs. They have invented humanism—*and it does not work.*

It does not work any better today than it did on day one. Nor will it work any better tomorrow. Perhaps Thoreau said it best: "Our inventions are wont to be pretty toys, which distract our attention from serious things. They are but improved means to an unimproved end."

Thereby hangs the tale of human technology. It promises solutions and delivers new versions of the problem. It does so because it empowers fallen human nature, and fallen human nature is problematic to begin with.

Appendix B
ELECTRIC COMMUNITIES

The creation of a complex virtual world such as Alpha-World represents great sums of money in development and maintenance costs. Is there really that much interest in creating on-line fantasy/adventure games and cyber-chat areas? What is behind all of this development of cyberspace anyway?

As usual, the dictum "follow the money trail" yields results. Or, in this case, the "e-money trail," because the answer appears to be that cyberspace is being made ready for global commerce. As many observers have noted, no one is making money on the Net—at least not yet. But the commercial promise of the worldwide Net is fabulous, and many entities are quietly, or not so quietly, working to make the Net safe for buying and selling in the near future. Visa International, for one, is working seriously, in conjunction with Microsoft and MasterCard, on the problem of making the Net safe for bankcards.

Visa's vision goes beyond just making the Net safe for credit card transactions as we know them. Visa wants to expand the role of the card from simply storing information about your bank account to storing *all* your personal information—driver's license, medical history, *everything*. These so-called "smart cards" figure strongly in Visa's picture of the future. To quote Daniel Akst of the *Los Angeles Times*:

Visa's plan is for these know-it-all cards to be issued by your bank. Since a microchip on the card would have plenty of room for other kinds of data, it seems inevitable that such cards would soon be indispensable, almost like a driver's license, and might similarly devolve into a de facto identity card—at least until a better technology comes along. "In 15 years, it may not be a card at all," says Carl F. Pascarella, president of Visa USA. "It could be your palm."[1]

Where else is Visa putting its money? Into AlphaWorld. Visa International is one of three major investors in San Francisco-based Worlds Inc. (creators of AlphaWorld), along with UB Networks and Pearson PLC. The creators of the original Habitat, Chip Morningstar and F. Randall Farmer of Lucas-Film, reached the conclusion, based on their observations of this early virtual world, that true commerce on the Net could only take place in a virtual world that afforded the "entire range of human interaction." This virtual world would be a place where people could meet, form opinions about one another, reasonably expect to find each other again, and so forth. In other words, they concluded that cyber-commerce could only be conducted in the context of a "habitat." It is a conclusion that has not been lost on the developers of cyberspace who have followed. This accounts for the increasing interest in avatars. This is why Visa International is sinking money into AlphaWorld, why Microsoft is sinking money into virtual chat areas on its own network, and so forth. And this is why Morningstar, Farmer, and another collaborator from the LucasFilm Habitat days, Douglas Crockford, founded an outfit called "Electric Communities."

Electric Communities is a player in the giant sweepstakes of trying to turn the Net into a global commerce vehicle, and their vision may be the most comprehensive of all those currently in the game. The goal of Electric Communities is nothing less than the establishment of the basic protocols of all global commerce, embodied in something they call the Global Cyberspace Protocols (GCP). To this end, Electric

Communities recently released a new programming language, "E," which is a superset of the popular "Java" language created by Sun Microsystems. What Hypertext Markup Language (HTML) is to the web, and what Virtual Reality Modeling Language (VRML) is to 3-D cyber-worlds, Electric Communities hopes "E" will become to global commerce applications: *the de facto standard programming language.* They plan to follow this up shortly with the release of something called the "Cyberspace Operating System" (COS), which they hope will become the DOS of the Net of the future—that is, the operating system upon which all other applications are built.

Whether they succeed remains to be seen. But one thing is certain: the avatar they helped create is coming on strong as a contender to be your personal agent in cyberspace. From the virtual chat areas of the Microsoft Network, to the strange lunar worlds of Intel's Moondo, to the vast expanses of Alpha-World and beyond, the avatars have landed—and they are waiting for you.

Appendix C

THE
OTHER HALF

In the absence of redemption, cynicism is simply despair. In the light of redemption, however, cynicism is truly the ground of hope, as the universal failings of our fallen race are met and overcome in the universal Savior.

The Gospel asserts both sides of that redemptive paradox. Christ converts the works of evil to the purposes of God, yet He still affirms the wickedness of sin. Christ does not excuse the wrongness of the evil He confronts, but neither is He content to merely punish it in retaliatory judgment. Instead, through His crucifixion, He achieves a much deeper and more far-reaching victory. In His sacrifice, Christ turns evil inside out by reversing its meaning: from bad to good, from wrong to right, from defeat to victory—and above all, from death to life. He purges wrong of its wrongness by making it serve His love: "You meant evil . . . but God meant it for good" (Genesis 50:20).

God's modus operandi reverses evil from within, as the works of evil are turned (in the end) to the service of God. God's ability to weave the artifacts of evil into the pattern of His goodness is the heart of the Good News and the meaning of the Incarnation. It is also the delightful irony of the Gospel: Christ (the innocent one) submits to His death, and to the "triumph of injustice" that it represents, and His submission gives rise to the Resurrection, which overthrows injustice as well as death. As the Russian Orthodox liturgy puts it,

"Christ has risen from the dead, trampling down death by death."

That ironic paradox of the Gospel means that "sanctified cynicism" is more than an oxymoron. It means that Christians can have a realistic, clear-eyed view of the fallen world without succumbing to the bleak despair that normally accompanies such knowledge.

ABOUT THE EDITORS AND CONTRIBUTORS

BROOKS ALEXANDER

Brooks Alexander is the founder of SCP (Spiritual Counterfeits Project) and currently acts as its research director. He earned a degree in political science from Texas Christian University and did five years of graduate work in international politics (at Texas Christian) and law (at the University of Texas) before he "turned on, tuned in, and dropped out" in 1963 to become part of the emerging drug and occult counterculture. He migrated to New York City, then to California, arriving in Los Angeles the day the Watts riots started. He later became part of the Haight-Ashbury scene in 1967. Alexander became a Christian in 1969 in Berkeley and founded SCP in 1973 to help Christians and others understand the changes that our culture is undergoing.

DONALD L. BAKER

Donald L. Baker is a telecommunications analyst and writer interested in the intersection of technology with culture and the arts. He has contributed to *World, The World & I,* and other publications. He lives near Washington, D.C., with his wife and three children, and in cyberspace at HyperReal@aol.com.

TAL BROOKE

Tal Brooke, president and chairman of SCP, Inc., is author of the bestseller *When the World Will Be As One* and four other books, including *Lord of the Air*, which chronicles his years in India as the top Western disciple of the famed "god-man" of signs and wonders Sai Baba. He has degrees from the University of Virginia and Princeton and has spoken at Oxford and Cambridge numerous times as well as other prominent universities.

JOHN MOORE

John Moore works at SCP part-time while he writes a book and helps raise two daughters. John recently participated in U.C. Berkeley's Boalt Hall Law School, one of the few doctoral students admitted into this prized and highly specialized program. Feeling called by God to other work, he left the program. His wife, Bettina, also attended Boalt Hall.

NOTES

Introduction

1. George Santayana, *The Life of Reason,* 5 vols. (New York: Dover Publications, 1905-06).

Chapter 1—Cyberspace: Storming Digital Heaven

1. Philip Elmer-Dewitt, "Welcome to Cyberspace," *Time,* Special Issue, Spring 1995.

2. Philip Elmer-Dewitt, "Cyberpunk!" *Time,* 15 October 1993.

3. Ibid.

4. George Gilder, "Scoping Out the Data Highway," interviewed by Mary Eisenhart, *Microtimes,* 25 July 1994.

5. Ibid.

6. Elmer-Dewitt, "Welcome to Cyberspace."

7. Philip Elmer-Dewitt, "Battle for the Soul of the Internet," *Time,* 25 July 1994.

8. James Fallows, "Not Yet Net," *The Atlantic Monthly,* May 1995.

9. Elmer-Dewitt, "Battle for the Soul."

10. Elmer-Dewitt, "Cyberpunk!"

11. Hannah Bloch, Wendy Cole, and Sharon E. Epperson, "Cyberporn," *Time,* 26 June 1995.

12. Prodigy Interactive News Services, 22 November 1994.

13. Elmer-Dewitt, "Battle for the Soul."

14. Jerry Carroll, "The Spoiler in Cyberspace," *The San Francisco Chronicle*, 25 April 1995.

15. Victor Keegan, "The Guardian," *London*, 12 December 1994.

16. Note: I report a different visionary/dream in the last chapter of *When the World Will Be As One*. (Harvest House Publishers felt it would inundate the reader to add this as well.)

17. Robert Wright and Mitch Kapor, "Data Highway Guru. The New Democrat from Cyberspace," *Wired*, 7 May 1993.

18. Thomas Molnar, "Oh, Benares," quoted in *SCP Newsletter*, Summer 1985, p. 22.

Chapter 2—Welcome to the Cyber-millennium

1. William J. Mitchell, *City of Bits: Space, Place, and the Infobahn* (Cambridge, MA: The M.I.T. Press, 1995), p. 167.

2. John Perry Barlow, "The Great Work," *Communications of the ACM,* January 1992. Text available at the Electronic Frontier Foundation's World Wide Web site (http://www.eff.org).

3. John Lukacs begins his book, *The End of the Twentieth Century and the End of the Modern Age* (New York: Ticknor & Fields, 1993), this way: "The twentieth century is now over. It was a short century. It lasted seventy-five years—from 1914 to 1989. Its two main events were the two world wars." He goes on to discuss in depth his concept of centuries as eras, rather than 100-year blocks.

4. This was the explicit message delivered at the G7 Information Society Conference in Brussels, February 1995, which focused on encouraging the worldwide implementation of advanced information technologies.

5. Gene Edward Veith, *Postmodern Times: A Christian Guide to Contemporary Thought and Culture* (Wheaton, IL: Crossway Books, 1994), pp. 28-29.

6. See *SCP Journal*, vol. 16:4 (1992), "Education: Capturing Hearts and Minds for a New World."

7. Michael Thompson, "Kids of the Future," *Ministries Today*, March/April 1994. Thompson's six other "sociological shapers" are: demographic polarity, the breakdown of the family, stress, moral relativism, ethnic diversity, and ecological greening.

8. John Perry Barlow, "Crime and Puzzlement," 1990. Available at the Electronic Frontier Foundation's World Wide Web site (http://www.eff.org).

9. John Perry Barlow and Mitchell Kapor, "Across the Electronic Frontier," 1990. Available at the Electronic Frontier Foundation's World Wide Web site (http://www.eff.org).

10. Page Smith, "The Expansion of New England," *American Urban History*, 2d ed., ed. Alexander B. Callow, Jr. (New York: Oxford University Press, 1973), pp. 98, 102.

11. I have liberated the forward- and backward-looking motifs from their Marxist context in: Dale Bradley, "Situating Cyberspace," Public 11: Throughput, p. 11 (Toronto: Public Access, 1995).

12. For a good history of the Internet, see chapter 3 in Howard Rheingold, *The Virtual Community: Homesteading on the Electronic Frontier* (Reading, MA: Addison Wesley Publishing Company, 1993).

13. Barlow made this remark in a 4-way, 12-page debate published as "What Are We Doing On-Line?" in the August 1995 *Harper's* magazine: "I don't say that these changes are good. I certainly don't claim we're creating a utopia. I mean, I love the physical world. I spent seventeen years as a cattle rancher in Pinedale, Wyoming. I was basically living in the nineteenth century. If I could still make a living there, I would. But the fact is, there is little economic room in the physical world these days" (p. 36).

14. S. Boxx, "Re: electracy," uploaded to Internet newsgroup alt.politics.datahighway, 16 June 1994.

15. Derrick de Kerckhove, *The Skin of Culture: Investigating the New Electronic Reality* (Toronto: Somerville House Publishing, 1995), p. 62.

16. Langdon Winner, "Mythinformation," in John Zerzan and Alice Carnes, eds., *Questioning Technology: Tool, Toy or Tyrant?* (Philadelphia: New Society Publishers, 1991), pp. 166-67.

17. Michael Novak, "Awakening from Nihilism: The Templeton Prize Address," *First Things*, August/September 1994, pp. 21-22.

18. Laurie Flynn, "The Serious Money Hits the Superhighway," *The New York Times*, 26 June 1995, p. D5.

19. Michael Sorkin, "Scenes from the Electronic City," *I.D. Magazine*, May–June 1992, pp. 73, 75.

20. David Lochhead, *Theology in a Digital World* (Canada: The United Church Publishing House, 1988), pp. 93, 94.

Chapter 3—Virtual Man

1. Mel Seesholtz, "Exotechnology: Human Efforts to Evolve Beyond Human Being," in "Thinking Robots, an Aware Internet, and Cyberpunk Librarians," a collection of background essays prepared for the 1992 LITA (Library and Information Technology Program) President's Program at the 1992 ALA annual conference.

2. Interview: Jaron Lanier, chief scientist of VPL research, *Computer Graphics World*, April 1992, vol. 15, no. 4, p. 61.

3. Alvin Toffler, *Future Shock* (New York: Random House, 1970), p. 187.

4. In fairness, it must be pointed out that Toffler also noted the potential for development in the other direction. In *Future Shock*, Toffler theorizes that robot research could ultimately lead to "the direct link-up of the human brain—stripped of its supporting physical structures—with the computer. Indeed, it may be that the biological component of the super-computers of the future may be massed human brains" (p. 189).

Toffler then goes on to cite experimental evidence from the day that the brain could be sustained, at least for limited periods, as a separate biological unit. The implications of this line of thought are truly frightening. More on this later.

5. John Perry Barlow, "Crime and Puzzlement: In Advance of the Law on the Electronic Frontier," *Whole Earth Review*, 22 September 1990, no. 68, p. 44.

6. These numbers are taken from an article, "Pre-Wired," by Michelle Vranizan in *UCLA Magazine*, Fall 1994. With the rapid growth the Internet is experiencing, it is difficult to get accurate figures on the total number of nodes and users now on the network.

7. See Hans Moravec, *Mind Children: The Future of Robot and Human Intelligence* (Cambridge: Harvard University Press, 1988), and "Letter from Moravec to Pembrose," in "Thinking Robots, an Aware Internet, and Cyberpunk Librarians."

8. "Open letter from Moravec to Penrose," 9 February 1990, posted to sci.nanotech (Internet Usenet newsgroup).

Chapter 4—The Faustian Bargain

1. An anonymous Berkeley Coffee House saga.

2. Jacques Ellul, *The Technological Bluff* (Grand Rapids: Eerdmans, 1990), p. xiv.

3. Ibid., p. 35.

4. Ibid., p. 39, emphasis in the original.

5. David Ehrenfeld, *The Arrogance of Humanism* (New York: Oxford University Press, 1978), pp. 5, 10.

6. Clifford Stoll, *Silicon Snake Oil: Second Thoughts on the Information Highway* (New York: Doubleday, 1995), pp. 95-96.

7. Ibid., pp. 60-63.

8. David Noble, "The Truth About the Information Super Highway," *Loompanics*, Spring 1995, pp. 9, 10.

9. Stoll, *Silicon Snake Oil*, p. 26.

10. Ibid., n.p.

11. Denis de Rougemont, *The Devil's Share* (New York: Meridian Books, 1944; reprint ed. 1956), p. 13.

12. Arthur Kroker and Michael Weinstein, *Data Trash: The Theory of the Virtual Class* (New York: St.Martin's Press, 1994), pp. 1-2.

13. Erik Davis, "Technosis, Magic, Memory, and the Angels of Information," *The South Atlantic Quarterly*, Fall 1993; vol. 92, no. 4, pp. 610-11.

14. Ellul, *Technological Bluff*, p. 72.

Chapter 6— Virtual Gods, Designer Universes

1. Howard Rheingold, "Douglas Trumball's Big Budget VR," *Wired*, 1.5.

2. Ibid.

3. Ibid.

4. David Kupelian, "Virtual Reality: The Drug of the Year 2000," Chancellor Broadcasting Company.

5. Burr Snider, "The Toy Story," *Wired*, 3.12.

6. W. Wayt Gibb, *Scientific American*, December 1994, vol. 271, no. 6, p. 40.

7. Ibid.

8. Eric Davis, "Technopagans," *Wired*, 3.07, July 1995.

9. Ibid.

10. Dialogue from the movie *Total Recall*.

11. Snider, "Toy Story."

Chapter 7—Virtual Bodies in the City of Bits

1. N. Katherine Hayles, "Embodied Virtuality," in Mary Anne Moser with Douglas MacLeod, eds., *Immersed in Technology: Art and Virtual Environments* (Cambridge: The MIT Press, 1996), p. 1. Hayles is a professor of English at UCLA.

2. Michael Sorkin, "Scenes from the Electronic City," *I.D. Magazine*, May–June 1992.

3. Simon Penny, "Virtual Reality as the Completion of the Enlightenment Project," in Gretchen Bender and Timothy Rucker, eds., *Culture on the Brink: Ideologies of Technology* (Seattle: Bay Press, 1994), p. 247. Penny is an associate professor of art and robotics at Carnegie Mellon University.

4. Brian J.Walsh and J.Richard Middleton, *The Transforming Vision: Shaping a Christian World View* (Downers Grove, IL: InterVarsity Press, 1984), p. 64.

5. Kenneth J. Gergen, *The Saturated Self: Dilemmas of Identity in Contemporary Life* (New York: Basic Books, 1992), p. 36.

6. Scott Bukatman, *Terminal Identity: The Virtual Subject in Postmodern Science Fiction* (Durham, NC: Duke University Press, 1993), p. 245.

7. Nell Tenhaaf, "Mysteries of the Bioapparatus," in Moser and MacLeod, *Immersed in Technology*, pp. 67-68.

8. Rob Milthorp, "Fascination, Masculinity, and Cyberspace," in Moser and MacLeod, *Immersed in Technology*, p. 137. Milthorp is an interdisciplinary artist, writer, and academic dean at the Alberta College of Art and Design in Calgary.

9. Kathy Acker, interviewed by Larry McCaffery, "Reading the Body," *Mondo 2000*, #4 (1991).

10. Gene Edward Veith, Jr., *Postmodern Times: A Christian Guide to Contemporary Thought and Culture* (Wheaton, IL: Crossway Books, 1994), p. 61. This is an excellent overview of the postmodern scene by an astute and trustworthy observer.

11. Stelarc, "Redesigning the Body—Redefining What Is Human," *Whole Earth Review*, Summer 1989, p. 18ff. Further information is available at Stelarc's World Wide Web site: (www.merlin.com.au/stelarc/).

12. Moser and MacLeod, *Immersed in Technology*, p. 2.

13. See chapter 3, "Cyborg Citizens," in William J. Mitchell, *City of Bits: Space, Place, and the Infobahn* (Cambridge: The M.I.T. Press, 1995), for an extended discussion of this likely near-future scenario.

14. Richard V. Kelly, Jr., "Abundant Worlds and Virtual Personas," *Virtual Reality* Special Report, November/December 1995, pp. 35-43.

15. My discussion of gender feminism is based on Dale O'Leary's informative paper, "Gender: The Deconstruction of Women; Analysis of the Gender Perspective in Preparation for the Fourth World Conference on Women, Beijing, China, September, 1995." Copies are available for $4.00 from Dale O'Leary, P.O. Box 41294, Providence, RI 02940.

16. The papers presented at the Art and Virtual Environments Symposium—held to demonstrate most of the VR art projects sponsored by the Banff Centre 1992–94—are gathered in Moser and MacLeod's *Immersed in Technology*.

17. The quotes in this and the following paragraph are taken from my notes made at the time of presentation.

18. Stone's presentation at 4Cyberconf was a truncated version of the one from which this text has been taken. That presentation, entitled "What Vampires Know: Transsubjection and Transgender in Cyberspace," is available at Stone's World Wide Web site: www.actlab.utexas.edu:80/~sandy/).

19. Ibid.

20. George Lakoff, interviewed by Iain A. Boal, "Body, Brain, and Communication," in James Brook and Iain A. Boal, eds., *Resisting the Virtual Life: The Culture and Politics of Information* (San Francisco: City Light Books, 1995), p. 126.

Chapter 7— Embody the Avatar

1. As the name implies, the creation and development of Habitat was funded by LucasFilm Games, a division of George Lucas's LucasArts Entertainment Company.

2. The Commodore 64 was one of the earliest home computers to sell in any kind of numbers. The "64" in its name referred to the amount of RAM it held, 64K (64,000 bytes)! By comparison, a modern PC typically has 4MB minimum (4 million bytes, or

roughly 60 times the amount of memory in a Commodore 64) with some machines having four, or even eight times that much.

3. See "The Lessons of LucasFilm Habitat," Chip Morningstar and F. Randall Farmer, 1990, a paper presented at The First Annual International Conference on Cyberspace in 1990. It was published in *Cyberspace: First Steps*, Michael Benedikt, ed. (Cambridge: M.I.T. Press, 1990). Available on the Electric Communities World Wide Web site (http://www.communities.com).

4. From "Commerce and Society in Cyberspace, an Electric Communities 'White Paper,' " © 1995 by Electric Communities. Available on the Electric Communities World Wide Web site (http://www.communities.com).

5. Paul Saffo, analyst at the Institute for the Future in Menlo Park, California. As quoted in Tim Clark, "Putting People in Interactive Computing," *Inter@ctive Week*, 27 November 1995, © 1995 Interactive Enterprises, LLC.

6. Actually cases of mistaken identity—people mistaking computer avatars for human avatars—have already been reported.

7. AlphaWorld home page, 1995 Worlds Inc. (http://www.worlds.net/aworld.html).

Chapter 8—Virtuality and Theophobia

1. See, for example, Carl Raschke, *The Interruption of Eternity: Modern Gnosticism and the Origins of the New Religious Consciousness* (Chicago: Nelson-Hall, 1980); Harold Bloom, *The American Religion: The Emergence of the Post-Christian Nation* (New York: Simon and Schuster, 1992); and Peter Jones, *The Gnostic Empire Strikes Back* (Philipsburg, NJ: Puritan and Reformed Publishing, 1992).

2. David Porush, "Cyberspace: Portal to Transcendence?" *Omni*, April 1993.

3. Eric Davis, "Technopagans" *Wired*, July 1995.

4. Ibid.

5. Ibid.

6. Ibid.

7. Ibid., emphasis added.

8. Ibid.

9. Ibid.

Appendix A

1. Denis De Rougemont, *The Devil's Share*, (New York: Meridian Books, 1944), p. 37.

Appendix B

1. Daniel Akst, "In Cyberspace, Nobody Can Hear You Write a Check," *Los Angeles Times*.

CYBER-GLOSSARY

accelerator—Specialized hardware that increases the speed of graphics manipulation.

accomodation—Change in the focal length of the eye's lens.

actor—A CAD (computer-aided design) representation of a player performing actions for the user, as in the Mandala system. (See "agent," "character," "vactor.")

aesthetics—The philosophy dealing with the human sense of pleasure and artistic merit.

agent—A CAD (computer-aided design) representation of a human form capable of guiding navigators through a virtual reality. (See "actor," "character.")

aliasing—An undesirable jagged edge on many three-dimensional renderings on bitmapped displays. Creates jaggies along the sides of objects and flickering of objects smaller than a pixel (See "anti-aliasing.")

allocentric—That which is other than egocentric, such as a bird's-eye view, or adopting another person's viewpoint.

altered states—The psychology of changes in perception and other states of consciousness that result from changes in external and internal stimulation.

alternate world disorder—Range of discomfort from mild headaches and disorientation to nausea as a result of participating in virtual reality ("barfogenic zone"). (See also "simulator sickness.")

ambient light—General nondirectional illumination.

Archie—A utility that can be used to search for files on FTP (file transfer protocol) sites.

articulation—Objects composed of several parts that are separably moveable.

artificial intelligence—The attempt to mimic and automate human cognitive skills through rules and knowledge representation techniques (for example, understanding visual images, recognizing speech and written text, solving problems, making medical diagnoses, and so forth).

artificial life—Digital agents that evolve, reproduce, grow, and change in similar ways to biological life-forms.

artificial reality—A term introduced by arts and computer visualization scholar Myron Krueger in the mid-1970s to describe his computer-generated responsive environments. He has emphasized the nonintrusive ("second-person virtual reality") systems that track people with pattern recognition techniques and display them and their surroundings on projection systems (see "cave"). Artificial reality involves a computer display system that perceives and captures "a participant's action in terms of the body's relationship to a graphic world and generates responses (usually imagery) that maintain the illusion that his actions are taking place within that world." (See also "virtual reality" and "cyberspace.")

aspect ratio—Ratio of width to height of the field of view.

augmented reality—Involves the use of transparent displays worn as glasses on which data can be projected. This allows someone to repair a radar, for example, and have the needed data displayed in the glasses while walking around the radar.

avatar—A person's likeness, image, or "puppet" in the virtual reality.

back clipping plane—A distance beyond which objects are not shown on the display.

backface removal—The elimination of those polygons that are facing away from the viewer.

backward raytracing—Tracing the path of light from the eye to the object (currently how most raytracing is done).

bandwidth—A measurement of how much data can be transmitted through a line during a given period of time.

binaural—Stereo sound.

biosensors—Special glasses or bracelets containing electrodes to monitor muscle electrical activity.

bodysuit—A complete human covering with virtual reality sensors and effectors. (See "datasuit.")

BOOM—Binocular omni-orientational monitor. A three-dimensional display device suspended from a weighted boom that can swivel freely about so the viewer doesn't have to wear a head mounted display; instead, it steps up to the viewer like a pair of binoculars. The boom's position communicates the user's point of view to the computer.

browser—Overviews such as indexes, lists, or animated maps that enable one to navigate through the physical, temporal, and conceptual elements of a virtual reality.

CAVE—A virtual reality using projection devices on the walls and ceiling to give the illusion of immersion.

character—A being with a virtual body in virtual reality. (See "agent," "vactor.")

chat—Involves sending messages back and forth to someone in real time, usually to a "chat-room" on the Internet.

concept map—A browser containing terms, definitions, and/or icons arranged in semantic proximity.

convergence—The angle between the two eyes at a fixation point. This changes for objects at varying depths in the real world and on three-dimensional displays.

convolvotron—A system for controlling binaural sound production in a virtual reality.

consensual reality—The world, or a simulation of a world, as viewed and comprehended by a society.

cyberia—An Autodesk project and the first virtual reality project by a CAD (computer-aided design) company. (See "cyberspace.")

cybernaut—A voyager in virtual reality.

cybernetic simulation—Dynamic model of a world filled with objects that exhibit lesser or greater degrees of intelligence.

cyberpunk—A dystopian vision of the future, replete with technological dazzle, anomie, and jacked-in cybernauts. A modern literary style.

cyberscope—A viewer that can be attached to a monitor to enable stereoscopic viewing of software-controlled images.

cyberspace—1) A place filled with virtual "stuff" populated by people with virtual bodies. A special kind of virtual space that promotes experiences involving the whole body; 2) A term coined by William Gibson in his book *Neuromancer* to describe a shared virtual universe or "matrix" operating within the sum total of all the world's computer networks. (See also "artificial reality" and "virtual reality.")

cyberspace playhouse—Social center or place where people can go to play roles in simulations.

dataglove—A glove wired with sensors and connected to a computer system for gesture recognition. It is used for tactile feedback and enables navigation through a virtual environment and interaction with three-dimensional objects within it.

dataspace—A visualized representation of complex information.

datasuit—Same as a "dataglove," but designed for the entire body. Only one datasuit has been built, and that with limited capabilities.

deck—A physical space containing an array of instruments that enable a player to act within, and feel a part of, a virtual space.

depth cuing—Involves the use of shading, texture, color, interposition (or many other visual characteristics) to provide a cue for the z-coordinates or distance of an object.

de-rez—Techniques to make pixels less visible in a display.

detail texture—A texture superimposed on another to increase the apparent resolution of the original texture image. Used when the eyepoint is so close to the textured object that the base texture is being magnified. A detail texture, typically a noise image, is blended into the image at a higher resolution adding a gritty realism to the appearance of the object.

direct manipulation—A term coined to reflect the use of computer icons or text as if they were real objects.

disorientation—Confusion about distances and directions for navigation.

droid—A puppet that embodies a human intellect (as in an android).

DSI—Defense Simulation Internet: A component of the Internet that supports DIS (distributed interactive simulations) and SIMNET, and permits scheduled guaranteed bandwidth.

dynamic lighting—Changes in lighting effects on objects as they and the observer move.

dynamics—The way objects interact and move; the rules that govern all actions and behaviors within the environment.

effectors—Output techniques that communicate a user's movements or commands to the computer and to the virtual reality.

egocenter—The sense of self and personal viewpoint that determines one's location in a virtual reality.

Electronic Cafe International (CAFE is an acronym for Communications Access For Everyone)—This concept was born when the Los Angeles Museum of Contemporary Art commissioned Sherrie and Kit to create a project for the 1984 Olympic Festival. A telecom link between five diverse ethnic Los Angeles communities and the museum was maintained for the seven weeks of the festival. It allowed users to trade video and still images, collaborate in writing and drawing on a common virtual canvas, transmit musical pieces, retrieve information, and communicate in dynamic, yet nonaggressive ways. With more advanced equipment and alliances, the ECI is now able to provide a virtual collaborative and real space for anyone to interact with the global village.

e-mail—Electronic mail, often sent over the Internet or a commercial carrier.

endoscopic—Part of a family of new surgical procedures that avoid cutting open major portions of the patient in favor of making small holes through which tools and sensors are inserted and the surgery performed. In a virtual reality or "telepresence" application, the surgeon manipulates the tools by observing the surgery site on a monitor via optical fibers and a tiny video camera.

environment—A computer-generated model that can be experienced from the "inside" as if it were a place.

exoskeletal devices—In order to provide force feedback, designers have added these rigid external supports to gloves and arm motion systems.

eyeball in the hand—A metaphor for visualized tracking where the tracker is held in the hand and is connected to motion of the projection point of the display.

EyeGen—A HMD (head mounted display) made by Virtual Research that combines visual and auditory displays.

Eyephone—A HMD (head mounted display) made by VPL Research that combines visual and auditory displays.

eye tracking—Involves devices that measure the direction of one's gaze. Most HMDs (head mounted displays) do not currently support eye tracking directly.

field of view (FOV)—The angle in degrees of the visual field. Most HMDs (head mounted displays) offer 60 to 90 degrees FOV. Since our two eyes have overlapping 140 degree FOV, binocular or total FOV is roughly 180 degrees horizontal by 120 degrees vertical in most people. A feeling of immersion seems to arise with FOV greater than 60 degrees. (See also "geometric field of view.")

Finger—A command that enables one to inquire about another Internet user.

flame—A hostile electronic message, usually sent to someone who has posted an inappropriate message on-line.

force feedback—The computer guides a machine to offer just the degree of resistance to motion or pressure that a situation would offer in real life; representations of the inertia or resistance objects have when they are moved or touched.

fractal—Any function that contains elements of self-similarity. Often used for fast texture modeling for mountains, trees, clouds, and so forth.

frustum of vision—Three-dimensional field of view in which all modeled objects are visible.

FTP—File transfer protocol; a means of sending and receiving documents and programs over the Internet.

gateway—An electronic pipeline between different computer networks.

geometric field of view (FOVg)—The angle in degrees of the computed visual scene. Most HMDs (head mounted displays) offer 60 to 90 degrees FOV (field of vision), but the scene can be computed to fit into anything from 0 to 360 degrees FOV for any particular projection point. If FOVg is larger than the FOV, then objects will appear pincushioned and distorted; if FOVg is smaller than the FOV, then objects will appear barreled and distorted.

gesture—Hand motion that can be interpreted as a sign, signal, or symbol.

GIF—Graphic interchange format. This picture format is common to on-line graphics.

goggles—Often used to refer to a HMD (head mounted display) or other displays.

Gopher—A software tool that uses menus to navigate the Internet.

gouraud—Shading polygons smoothly with bilinear interpolation.

haptic interfaces—Interfaces that use all the physical sensors that provide us with a sense of touch at the skin level and force feedback information from our muscles and joints.

head-coupled—Displays or robotic actions that are activated by head motion through a head tracking device.

head related transfer function—A mathematical transformation of sound spectrum that modifies the amplitude and phase of acoustic signals to take into account the shape effects of the listener's head.

head tracking—Involves monitoring the position of the head through various devices.

heads up display (HUD)—A display device that lets users see graphics superimposed on their view of the world. (Created for aviators to see symbols and dials while looking out the window.)

hidden surface—Parts of a graphics object occluded by intervening objects.

HMD (head mounted display)—A set of goggles or a helmet with tiny monitors in front of each eye that generate images, seen by the wearer as being three-dimensional. VPL Research refers to their HMDs as eyephones.

holodeck—Virtual reality simulation system used primarily for entertainment by the crew of the starship Enterprise in the *Star Trek: The Next Generation* television series.

HOOD—Swinging wraparound display. Used instead of a HMD (head mounted display); hung from pulleys.

HTML—Hypertext mark-up language. Used to design interlinking "pages" on the World Wide Web.

hypermedia—The combination of digital text, video, and sound with navigation techniques such as buttons, links, and hotspots into one system.

hyperspace—The space of hypertext or hypermedia documents.

hypertext—A means of linking information based on key words.

immersion—The cognitive conviction or feeling of presence—of "being there"—surrounded by space and capable of interacting with all available objects in a virtual reality.

impressionists—A nineteenth-century group of artists whose paintings were directed at capturing color and mood, rather than exact perspective outlines.

interactive fiction—Dramatic creations that encourage user and viewer participation through computer technology.

interface—A set of devices, software, and techniques that connect computers with people to make it easier to perform useful activities.

Internet—A worldwide digital network.

IRC—Internet relay chat.

jack (or "jack in")—To connect to the matrix of virtual space. (See William Gibson's *Necromancer*.)

joystick—Graphic interface device (invented by aviators).

keyframe animation—A process involving interpolating images between stored frames. Also known as "sequence." (See "tweening.")

kinaesthetic dissonance—Mismatch between feedback or its absence from touch or motion during virtual reality experiences.

kinesthesia—The sensation of position or movement.

lag—Delay between an action and its visual, acoustic, or other sensory feedback, often because of inherent delays in the tracking devices, or in the computation of the scene.

laparoscopy (laparoscopic surgery)—Less invasive forms of surgery that operate through small optics and instruments, lending themselves to robotic manipulation and virtual reality training.

LBE (location-based entertainment)—A virtual reality game that involves a scenario based on another time and place.

LCD (liquid crystal display)—Display devices that use bipolar films sandwiched between thin panes of glass. They are lightweight and transmissive or reflective, ideal for a HMD (head-mounted display).

LOD (level of detail)—A model of a particular resolution among a series of models of the same object. Multiple LODs are used to increase graphics performance by drawing simpler geometry when the object occupies fewer pixels on the screen. LOD selection can also be driven by graphics load, area-of-interest, or gaze direction.

magic wand—A three-dimensional interface device used for pointing and interaction; an elongated three-dimensional mouse.

mailing list—A topical discussion held through e-mail on the Internet.

metaball—A kind of "equipotential surface" around a point. You specify a point, a radius, and an "intensity" for each ball; when balls come close, their shapes blend to form a smooth equipotential surface. They seem to be very useful for modeling shapes like animals and humans. They can be rendered by most raytracing packages (also "blobs" or "soft spheres" or "fuzzyspheres").

metaphysics—The philosophical study of basic concepts of existence such as aesthetics, ontology, epistemology, and the meaning and purpose of life.

microsurgery—A form of surgery that lends itself to robotics and virtual reality. (See also "laparoscopy.")

MIDI—A digital sound standard for music.

mirror worlds—Bird's-eye views of a virtual reality in which the viewer also exists and can be seen.

monitor—Display, head mounted display, goggles, liquid crystal display. All computer screens are monitors.

MOO—A MUD (Multiuser dungeon) that is object-oriented. (See also "MUD.")

MOOD—Monoscopic omni-orientational display. (See also "HOOD," "HMD," "goggles," "LCD.")

motion parallax—Objects at different distances and fixation points move different amounts when the viewpoint is dollied along the x-axis (left-right).

motion platform—A controlled system that provides real motion to simulate the displayed motion in a virtual reality.

MRI—Magnetic resonance imaging; a way of making internal organs and structures visible by analyzing radio frequency emissions of atoms in a strong magnetic field. Can be made three-dimensional with rendering of large amounts of data.

MUD—A Multiuser dungeon; a place on the Internet where people can meet and browse (see "MOO").

multiperson space—1) Multiplayer space involving two or more human players; 2) A type of interactive simulation that gives every user a sense that he or she, personally, has a body in virtual space.

multiplayer space—Cyberspace that emerges from a simulation generated simultaneously by two or more decks. Players can be made up of one human and the rest artificial intelligence.

nanomanipulation—Ability to visualize and affect objects in the nanometer range (extremely small).

navigation—Moving through virtual space without losing one's way.

netiquette—Network etiquette.

NetNews—Topical discussion groups found on the Internet.

neural interface—A version of the ultimate interface that connects a virtual reality directly to a human brain or nervous system.

newsgroup—A topical discussion group found on USENET.

newsreader—A software program that allows users to post and retrieve messages on USENET.

objects—Graphical entities that can be dynamically created or loaded from model files. Many functions act upon them:

Tasks—each object performs a specific function per frame; *Hierarchies*—objects can be "linked" together; *Sensors*—objects can be connected to sensors; *Modify*—color, texture, scale, and so forth; *Collision Detection*—between objects and polygons; *Vertices*—these can be dynamically created along with the definition of a vector normal for Gouraud-shading.

occipital cortex—The back of the brain receiving retinotopic projections of visual displays.

occlusion—Hiding objects from sight by the interposition of other objects.

ontology—The metaphysics of existence.

pan—The angular displacement of a view along any axis or direction in a three-dimensional world; or a move through translation in a two-dimensional world.

parietal cortex—The area of the brain adjacent to and above the occipital cortex, thought to process spatial location and direction.

paths—Objects or viewpoints can follow predefined paths that can be dynamically created and interpolated.

perspective—Rules that determine the relative size of objects on a flat page to give the impression of three-dimensional distance.

phong shading—A method for calculating the brightness of a surface pixel by linearly interpolating points on a polygon and using the cosine of the viewing angle. Produces realistic shading.

photorealism—An attempt to create realistic images with much detail and texture.

pitch—The angular displacement of a view along the lateral axis (front-back).

pixel—The smallest element of a display that can be adjusted in intensity.

polygons—An ordered set of vertices connected by sides. These can be dynamically created and texture-mapped using various sources of image data. Various hardware platforms support different texturing methods and quantities. Rendering is performed in either wireframe, smooth-shaded, or textured modes.

pop—When an object's visible appearance suddenly changes or an object appears out of nowhere. Usually an undesired artifact of poor LOD (level of detail).

portals—Polygons that, once passed through, automatically load a new world or execute a user-defined function.

PPP—Point-to-point protocol; used for dial-up connections to the Internet.

presence—A defining characteristic of a good virtual reality system; a feeling of being there, immersed in the environment, able to interact with other objects there.

projected reality—A virtual reality system that uses projection screens rather than HMDs (head mounted displays) or personal display monitors. (See "real projection.")

puppet—An "avatar" or other virtual reality object that can be manipulated.

raytracing—A rendering system that traces the path of light from objects to light sources. (See "backward raytracing.")

real projection—A virtual reality projection system (a pun on rear projection).

real-time—Appearing to be without lag or flicker.

render—Convert a graphics object into pixels.

resolution—Usually the number of lines or pixels in a display—for cxample, a VGA display has 640 by 480 pixels.

roll—The angular displacement of a view along the longitudinal axis (left-right).

scan conversion—The change of video signals from one form (for example, RGB) to another (for example, NTSC, PAL).

scintillation—The "sparkling" of textures or small objects. Usually undesirable and caused by aliasing.

second person virtual reality—The use of a computational medium to portray a representation of you that is not necessarily realistic, but still identifiable ("puppet", "avatar," "vactor"). In the Mandala system, for example, a video camera allows you to see yourself as another object over which you have control by your own bodily movement.

sensor—A mechanism or function that acts to change objects in response to multiple devices connected to lights, objects, viewpoints, and so forth, in the real world.

sensor lagtime—Delays in the feedback or representation of your actions caused by computation in the tracker or sensor.

sensory substitution—The conversion of sensory information from one sense to another (for example, the use of auditory echoes and cues to "see" the shape of your surroundings).

sequence—Also called "keyframe animation," this involves the interpolation of images between stored frames. (See "tweening.")

shared worlds—Virtual environments that are shared by multiple participants at the same location or across long-distance networks.

shutter glasses—LCD (liquid crystal display) screens or physically rotating shutters used to see stereoscopically when linked to the frame rate of a monitor.

SIMNET—For SIMulator NETworking, the advanced technology development of large scale, fully interactive, widely distributed simulations created by ARPA with significant Army participation and executed by scientists and engineers from BBN and Perceptronics. Begun in 1983, the first networked simulators were operational in the summer of 1986. This program proved the feasibility of real-time, shared synthetic environments, and has resulted in numerous follow-on programs in the Department of Defense as well as in the commercial/entertainment sector (for example, CyberMind and Virtual World). Using networked graphics and displays built into physical mock-ups, it has been called a vehicle-based virtual reality or synthetic environment. (See also "DIS," "DSI.")

simulator sickness—The disturbances produced by simulators, ranging in degree from a feeling of unpleasantness, disorientation, and headaches, to nausea and vomiting. Many factors may be involved, including sensory distortions such as abnormal movement of arms and heads (because of the weight of equipment), long lags in feedback, and missing visual cues from convergence and accommodation. Simulator sickness rarely occurs with displays less than 60 degrees visual angle.

SLIP—Serial line Internet protocol; used for dial-up connections to the Internet.

SMTP—Simple mail transfer protocol; specifies how electronic mail is transferred over the Internet.

spamming—Refers to posting multiple copies of the same message. A violation of netiquette.

spatial navigation—Accurate self-localization and orientation in virtual spaces is not as easy as real-world navigation. Devising techniques for embedding navigational assists in complex dataspaces remains an important research goal.

spatial representation system—The cortical and other neural structures and functions that maintain spatial orientation and recognition.

spatial superposition—Refers to the fact that in augmented reality displays, accurate spatial registration of real and virtual images remains difficult.

striate cortex—Visual cortex. (See "occipital cortex," "parietal cortex.")

supercockpit—An Air Force project led by Tom Furness that advanced the engineering and human factors of HMDs (head mounted displays) and virtual reality. It used digital displays of instruments and terrain.

Sword of Damocles—Nickname for the first helmet mounted display at the University of Utah.

synthetic environments—Virtual reality displays used for simulation.

Sysop—System operator of a computer bulletin board system.

tactile displays—Devices such as force-feedback gloves, buzzers, and exoskeletons that provide tactile, kinaesthetic, and joint sensations. (See also "exoskeletal devices.")

TCP/IP—Transmission control protocol/Internet protocol; a suite of computer protocols that govern how computers exchange information over the Internet.

tele-existence—Remote virtual reality.

telemanipulation—Robotic control of distant objects.

telepresence—Virtual reality with displays of real, remote scenes.

telerobotic—Robotic control of distant objects. (See "telemanipulation," "teleoperation").

telesurgery—Surgery using teleoperation. (See also "laparoscopy.")

Telnet—A means of connecting one's computer to another non-local computer via the Internet.

terrain—Geographical information and models that can be either randomly generated or based on actual data. Dynamic terrain is an important goal for current SIMNET applications.

texture mapping—A bitmap added to an object to give added realism. (See "detail texture.")

texture swimming—Unnatural motion of static textures on the surfaces of objects as they are rotated. Caused by quick and dirty texture interpolation in screen coordinates. Correctable by subdividing polygons or by doing perspective correction.

tracker—A device that emits numeric coordinates for its changing position in space. (See also "enactive tracking.")

transparency—Refers to how invisible and unobtrusive a virtual reality system is.

transterritorial—Beyond physical space, as in cyberspace.

trompe l'oeil—Perspective paintings that deceive viewers into believing they are real (for example, a painting of the sky and clouds on the inside of a dome).

tweening—The interpolation of images between stored frames.

universe—The "container" of all entities in a virtual reality. Entities can be temporarily added or removed from consideration by the simulation manager. The sequence of events in the simulation loop can be user-defined.

URL—Uniform resource locator; the standard addressing method that identifies pages on the World Wide Web.

USENET—A series of topical discussion groups found on the Internet.

vactor—A virtual actor, either autonomous or telerobotic, in a virtual reality theater.

Veronica—Very easy rodent-oriented netwide index to computerized archives; a search utility for the Internet.

viewpoints—Points from which raytracing and geometry creation occur; the geometric eye-point of the simulation. You can have multiple viewpoints that can be attached to multiple sensors.

virtual environments—Realistic simulations of interactive scenes.

virtual patient—Telerobotic or digitized animations of humans with accurate disease models.

virtual prototyping—The use of virtual reality for design and evaluation of new artifacts.

virtual reality—A term coined by Jaron Lanier to describe an immersive, interactive simulation of realistic or imaginary environments.

visualization—Use of computer graphics to make visible numeric or other quantifiable relationships.

voxel—A cubic volume pixel for quantizing three-dimensional space.

WAIS—Wide area information server.

waldo—A remotely controlled mechanical puppet.

WAN—Wide area network; a computer network that encompasses a large geographic area.

windows—On some hardware platforms, you can have multiple windows and viewpoints into the same virtual world.

wire frame outlines—Displays of the outlines of polygons, not filled in.

world—An entire virtual reality environment or universe.

world in the hand—A metaphor for visualized tracking where the tracker is held in the hand and is connected to the motion of the object located at that position in the display.

World Wide Web—A global collection of linked "pages" that utilizes hypertext to navigate from one site to another.

> *The original version of this "Cyber Glossary" was written by Joe Psotka and Sharon A. Davison. It was revised by Marc Bernatchez, and then edited and adapted by George Otis, Jr. for use at the Compasspoint/Sentinel Seminar, Atlanta, Georgia, November 1996, where Tal Brooke and George Otis were keynote speakers.*

For further information:

Benedikt, M., ed., *Cyberspace: First Steps* (Cambridge, MA: The M.I.T. Press, 1991).

Earnshaw, R. A., M.A. Gigante, and H. Jones. *Virtual Reality Systems* (New York: Academic Press, 1993).

Ellis, S. R., ed., *Pictorial Communication in Virtual and Real Environments* (London: Taylor and Francis, 1991).

Heim, M. *The Metaphysics of Virtual Reality* (New York: Oxford University Press, 1993).

Kalawsky, R. *The Science of Virtual Reality and Virtual Environments* (New York: Addison-Wesley, 1993).

Latham, R. *The Dictionary of Computer Graphics Technology and Applications* (New York: Springer-Verlag, 1991).

Laurel, B. *Computers as Theater* (New York: Addison-Wesley, 1991).

Pimentel and Teixeira. *Through the Looking Glass* (Intel, 1992).

Rheingold, H. *Virtual Reality* (New York: Simon & Schuster, 1991).

BIBLIOGRAPHY

Aukstakalnis and Blatner, *Silicon Mirage: The Art and Science of Virtual Reality.* Peach Pit Press, 1992.

Bender, Gretchen and Timothy Rucker, eds. *Culture on the Brink: Ideologies of Technology.* Seattle: Bay Press, 1994.

Bloom, Harold. *The American Religion: The Emergence of the Post-Christian Nation.* New York: Simon and Schuster, 1992.

Brook, James and Iain A. Boal, eds. *Resisting the Virtual Life: The Culture and Politics of Information.* San Francisco: City Light Books, 1995.

Bukatman, Scott. *Terminal Identity: The Virtual Subject in Postmodern Science Fiction.* Durham: Duke University Press, 1993.

De Kerckhove, Derrick. *The Skin of Culture: Investigating the New Electronic Reality.* Toronto: Somerville House Publishing, 1995.

De Rougemont, Denis. *The Devil's Share.* New York: Meridian Books, 1944.

Ehrenfeld, David. *The Arrogance of Humanism.* New York: Oxford University Press, 1978.

Ellul, Jacques. *The Technological Bluff.* Grand Rapids: Eerdmans, 1990.

Ellul, Jacques. *The Technological Society.* New York: Vintage Books, 1964.

Gergen, Kenneth J. *The Saturated Self: Dilemmas of Identity in Contemporary Life.* New York: Basic Books, 1992.

Jones, Peter. *The Gnostic Empire Strikes Back.* Philipsburg: Puritan and Reformed Publishing, 1992.

Juenger, Freidrich Georg. *The Failure of Technology.* Chicago: Henry Regnery, 1949.

Kroker, Arthur and Michael Weinstein. *Data Trash: The Theory of the Virtual Class.* New York: St. Martin's Press, 1994.

Lochhead, David. *Theology in a Digital World.* Canada: The United Church Publishing House, 1988.

Lukacs, John. *The End of the Twentieth Century and the End of the Modern Age.* New York: Ticknor & Fields, 1993.

Mander, Jerry. *Four Arguments for the Elimination of Television.* New York: William Morrow, 1978.

McLuhan, Marshall. *Understanding Media: The Extensions of Man.* New York: McGraw-Hill, 1964.

Mitchell, William J. *City of Bits: Space, Place, and the Infobahn.* Cambridge: The M.I.T. Press, 1995.

Moravec, Hans. *Mind Children: The Future of Robot and Human Intelligence.* Cambridge: Harvard University Press, 1988.

Moser, Mary Anne and Douglas MacLeod, eds. *Immersed in Technology: Art and Virtual Environments.* Cambridge: The M.I.T. Press, 1996.

Muggerage, Malcolm. *Christ and the Media.* Grand Rapids: Eerdmans, 1977.

Raschke, Carl. *The Interruption of Eternity: Modern Gnosticism and the Origins of the New Religious Consciousness.* Chicago: Nelson-Hall, 1980.

Rheingold, Howard. *The Virtual Community: Homesteading on the Electronic Frontier.* Reading, MA: Addison Wesley Publishing Company, 1993.

Rushkoff, Douglas. *Cyberia: Life in the Trenches of Hyperspace.* New York: HarperCollins, 1994.

Schwartau, Winn. *Information Warfare: Chaos on the Electronic Superhighway.* New York: Thunder's Mouth Press, 1994.

Stoll, Clifford. *Silicon Snake Oil: Second Thoughts on the Information Highway.* New York: Doubleday, 1995.

Toffler, Alvin. *Future Shock.* New York: Random House, 1970.

Veith, Gene Edward. *Postmodern Times: A Christian Guide to Contemporary Thought and Culture.* Wheaton: Crossway Books, 1994.

Walsh, Brian J. and J. Richard Middleton. *The Transforming Vision: Shaping a Christian World View.* Downers Grove: InterVarsity Press, 1984.

Weiner, Norbert. *Cybernetics.* Cambridge: The M.I.T. Press, 1948.

Weiner, Norbert. *God and Golem, Inc.* Cambridge: The M.I.T. Press, 1964.

Wurman, Richard Saul. *Information Anxiety.* New York: Doubleday, 1989.

Zerzan, John and Alice Carnes, eds. *Questioning Technology: Tool, Toy or Tyrant?* Philadelphia: New Society Publishers, 1991.

When the World Will Be As One

— THE NEXT PHASE —

Beyond the New Age Movement

by Tal Brooke

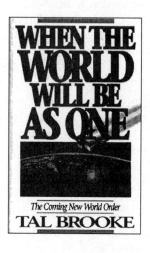

In recent years the New Age movement has been touted by many as the spiritual rebirth of modern man. But this popular movement is just one phase of a broad agenda which is only now coming fully into view. The pieces have been shifting into place for a quantum leap more radical than the one that replaced the Dark Ages with the Age of Reason. A momentous global event is upon us—the birth of a New World Order.

SPIRITUAL COUNTERFEITS PROJECT

Tal Brooke is president of Spiritual Counterfeits Project (SCP), a nationwide ministry. SCP's core staff is from top-ranked universities and have each traveled various spiritual paths before becoming Christians.

SCP's major publication is the *SCP Journal*, which has won three first-place EPA awards. This in-depth publication explores the latest deceptive spiritual trends such as near-death experiences, deep ecology, UFOs, and the Jesus Seminar, and exposes their inside workings from a biblical perspective. SCP also publishes the *SCP Newsletter* four times a year with the latest news and developments on the spiritual frontlines.

The SCP Journal and *SCP Newsletter* are sent to those who contribute at least $25 annually ($35 outside the USA). The newsletter is available separately for a $10 annual donation (to offset publication, printing, and postage costs).

SCP, Inc.

Box 4308, Berkely, CA 94704
Business Office: (510) 540-0300
ACCESS Line: (510) 540-5767
Web Site: http://www.scp-inc.org

Enclosed is a gift of $25 or more—please send me the *SCP Journal* and *SCP Newsletter*.

Name _____

Phone _____

Address _____

City _____ State _____ Zip Code _____